TELLING OF THE ANTHRACITE
A PENNSYLVANIA POSTHISTORY

PHILIP MOSLEY

an imprint of Sunbury Press, Inc.
Mechanicsburg, PA USA

OXFORD SOUTHERN

an imprint of Sunbury Press, Inc.
Mechanicsburg, PA USA

Copyright © 2023 by Philip Mosley.
Cover Copyright © 2023 by Sunbury Press, Inc.

Sunbury Press supports copyright. Copyright fuels creativity, encourages diverse voices, promotes free speech, and creates a vibrant culture. Thank you for buying an authorized edition of this book and for complying with copyright laws. Except for the quotation of short passages for the purpose of criticism and review, no part of this publication may be reproduced, scanned, or distributed in any form without permission. You are supporting writers and allowing Sunbury Press to continue to publish books for every reader. For information contact Sunbury Press, Inc., Subsidiary Rights Dept., PO Box 548, Boiling Springs, PA 17007 USA or legal@sunburypress.com.

For information about special discounts for bulk purchases, please contact Sunbury Press Orders Dept. at (855) 338-8359 or orders@sunburypress.com.

To request one of our authors for speaking engagements or book signings, please contact Sunbury Press Publicity Dept. at publicity@sunburypress.com.

FIRST OXFORD SOUTHERN EDITION: January 2023

Set in Adobe Garamond | Interior design by Crystal Devine | Cover by Lawrence Knorr | Edited by Lawrence Knorr.

Publisher's Cataloging-in-Publication Data
Names: Mosley, Philip, author.
Title: Telling of the Anthracite : A Pennsylvania Posthistory / Philip Mosley.
Description: First trade paperback edition. | Mechanicsburg, PA : Oxford Southern, 2023.
Summary: This is the first book about how we tell the Pennsylvania anthracite story in the postindustrial age, and it places this discourse in the broader context of environmental and socioeconomic change. It is a work of regional history that is scholarly in tone yet written in a style accessible to the general reader. It explores the various ways in which anthracite history has been represented and remembered since 1960.
Identifiers: ISBN : 978-1-62006-951-6 (softcover) | ISBN : 979-8-88819-031-9 (ePub).
Subjects: HISTORY / United States / 20th Century | HISTORY / United States / 21st Century | HISTORY / United States / State & Local / Middle Atlantic (DC, DE, MD, NJ, NY, PA).

Product of the United States of America
0 1 1 2 3 5 8 13 21 34 55

Continue the Enlightenment!

Cover photo: Joseph E.B. Elliott/HAER, *St. Nicholas Breaker, from the yard office,* b&w photograph, c. 2000. (Image: courtesy of the artist.)

CONTENTS

Acknowledgments	v
Preface	vii
Chapter One: Historicizing Anthracite	1

Industrial history; Environmental history; Social history; Local history; How we tell of the anthracite; Descriptive categories

Chapter Two: Representing Disaster	25

Establishing a historical perspective; Disaster and memory; Representing Knox; Representing Centralia; Knox and Centralia on film: documentary, fiction; Other posthistorical disasters

Chapter Three: Modes of Recall	57

Material culture: aesthetics of the anthracite landscape, abandoned sites, repurposed sites, purpose-built sites, signs, souvenir merchandise, historical archaeology; Interpersonal activity: oral history, associations, festivals and gatherings, Internet sites

Chapter Four: Representational Forms	122

Literature: historiography, fiction, drama, poetry; Performance: theater, music; Visual arts: photography, painting/drawing/printmaking, mixed media, sculpture

Chapter Five: Mine with a Movie Camera: Anthracite on Film	189

The silent era; The sound era: heyday of the industrial film, fiction; Posthistorical film: fiction, television documentary of the 1960s, postmodern documentary

Conclusion: A Heritage to Save	214
Bibliography	221
Filmography	230

Discography	232
Gazetteer of Anthracite Region Place Names	233
About the Author	235

ACKNOWLEDGMENTS

Several friends and colleagues kindly read my draft manuscript and gave me valuable feedback: Bob Wolensky, Bill Conlogue, Richard Fitzsimmons, and Michael Knies. A special mention for Cindy Carmickle, whose photographic skills and genial company enhanced our field trips across anthracite country.

Many thanks to those artists of various arts who generously furnished me with illustrative material and information on their work: Zenos Frudakis, Joe Elliott, Ray Klimek, David Brocca, Denis Yanashot, Heather Evans, Joe Sapienza II, John Welsh, David Grabias, Sue Hand, Herb Simon, Bob McCormick, Jim Goode, and Ryan Hnat.

I am also grateful to those with whom I had valuable conversations and who responded to my queries: Charlie Petrillo, Scott Herring, David DeKok, Jeanne Shaffer, Valentine Mountjoy, Jay Smar, Tom Flannery, Darlene Miller-Lanning, Michael Thomas, David Klevinsky, Annie Sanders, Jennie Levine Knies, Melissa Meade, Mary Ann Moran Savakinus, Sarah Piccini, Maureen McGuigan, Pat Hinchey, Bob Shlesinger, Zachary Petroski, John Bodnar, Paul Shackel, Bode Morin, Chester Kulesa, John Fielding, Mike Korb, Nat Bohlin, Joe McCallus, Steve Varonka, Paul Frisch, Rick Sedlisky, Jeff Ludwig-Dicus, Joe D'Arienzo, Martha Capwell Fox, Suzanne Morgan, and Maria Capolarella-Montante.

Some of the work on this book was supported by a stipendiary fund for Distinguished Professors of Penn State University. Thanks to Amy

Gruzesky, Brent Wilson, and Jeremy Palko at Penn State Scranton for word and image processing support.

Many thanks to Lawrence Knorr and his team at Sunbury Press. And thanks to Shu-ching Mosley, as always.

Parts of the section on Knox and Centralia on Film in Chapter Two, on Theater in Chapter Four, and on early anthracite films in Chapter Five appeared respectively in *Mining History Journal 20* (2013), *Anthracite! An Anthology of Pennsylvania Coal Region Plays* (2006), and *Proceedings of the Fifth Annual Conference on the History of Northeastern Pennsylvania* (1993).

PREFACE

This book is not a conventional academic work, for I am not a professional historian—my fields are the study of literature and cinema as well as the practice of literary translation. Thus, I follow here neither established historiographic methodologies nor any historical ortho-/hetero-doxies. I am purely an amateur local history enthusiast who came to this project in retirement following a forty-year career in another sector of the humanities. My book represents a tribute to the region where I have made my home for over thirty years and to its people whose lives were long dominated by a single industry, one that brought great prosperity to a few but greater poverty and hardship to many others. I hope this book may also serve as an introduction to the study of anthracite historiography and as a source of information for those curious to learn about how anthracite history has been told over the last six decades. With sources of information in mind, I hasten to acknowledge an unusual publication: *Scranton Area Heritage Mining Guide* by John R. Park. Author of several guides to the mining heritage of various parts of the USA, Park prepared this booklet as a complimentary publication "for the exclusive personal use of members of the Mining Heritage Association who attend[ed] the 2005 Scranton meeting." A useful historical and geographical reference tool, it was edited by prominent regional industrial historian Lance E. Metz.

Furthermore, I write out of deep respect for the work of anthracite miners, the communities in which they lived, and the pride they took in their identity. Yet I cannot regret the decline and near disappearance of the industry. If humankind, as the main architect of its future on Planet Earth, is to have a fair chance of survival, then it must accept responsibility for its injurious actions and move away as fully and swiftly as possible from fossil fuel production toward renewable, greener, and more environmentally friendly sources of energy. In June 2021, the G7 partnership of the most economically powerful nations committed itself to completely phasing out coal production, a vital step in tackling global warming and mitigating the effects of climate change. Following the August 2021 publication of a report by the Intergovernmental Panel on Climate Change (IPCC, a United Nations working group), UN Secretary-General Antonio Guterres stated that no new coal plants should be built after 2021, that OECD countries should phase out existing coal by 2030, and that all others should do so by 2040. Even a right-wing politician such as Boris Johnson, former Prime Minister of Great Britain, declared that we must "consign coal to history and shift to clean energy sources." At the 26th UN Climate Change Conference of the Partners (COP26) in Scotland in the fall of 2021, over forty countries committed to phasing out coal, though the US, China, India, and Australia regrettably declined to sign up. Despite its lingering commercial and political boosters, we need to acknowledge that coal extraction has run its useful course, that its negative consequences far outweigh its positive ones, and that the future of energy production lies elsewhere. If this means the end of the coal industry, including the latter-day anthracite sector, then so be it; by transitioning to a post-carbon economy, we will come a little closer to saving Planet Earth.

However, we cannot allow this radical shift in energy production to happen again at the expense of the hardworking people who live in the anthracite region and whose roots go back many generations. We cannot betray them again through the indifference, irresponsibility, and oppressiveness of more powerful forces in society. In due course, it will be incumbent upon governmental authorities and business interests alike to develop worthwhile new occupations in the region to replace those, main or ancillary, that will inevitably disappear with the ultimate demise of coal. We cannot afford socially, economically, politically, or morally to repeat the mistakes of the past. It should be apparent that I intend to express myself freely, being no apologist for the following: the coal industry, private or public institutions, organizations or movements, political parties, or governmental agencies at any level.

Industrial landscapes and their architecture have intrigued me from an early age. As a small child in Grimsby, England, once that nation's principal fishing port, I recall my awe on visits with my father to the town's vast docks and the factories stretching for miles up the broad estuary of the River Humber. Moreover, my paternal grandparents lived in the county of Yorkshire, in the city of Sheffield, the "Pittsburgh" of England; the image of its massive steel mills—"dark, satanic" perhaps, per William Blake's famous line, but solid, vibrant, and active around the clock in those days—imprinted itself on my infant brain. Later, as an undergraduate at the university in Leeds, a short distance north of Sheffield, I was equally impressed by the looming structures of the Yorkshire coal mines. Following one journey by train between those two biggest cities in the county, the formations of the mining landscape moved me to pen some lines of adolescent verse: "Further north we see slag heaps / covered in snow / like Spanish plateaus / surmounted by whitewashed castles"; again, "white lights on pit heaps / unbending slag banks / rising behind square stone houses / at precious field ends."

Much later, I grew interested in coal miners and their struggles while teaching in Glasgow, Scotland, at the time of the British Miners' Strike in 1984-85, a stout resistance chiefly to widespread pit closures, one that the Conservative government of Margaret Thatcher eventually crushed. During the strike, I became involved in the local Miners' Families Support Group, which raised money to buy food and household supplies for families on or near the breadline.

On arriving in northeastern Pennsylvania (NEPA) in 1988 to take up an academic position, I grasped the opportunity to explore a rich seam, if you will, of regional history. I soon discovered that the area had once been the largest anthracite producer in the world and that the city of Scranton, to whose Penn State campus I had been appointed, had been one of its centers. My interest was all the greater for coal having

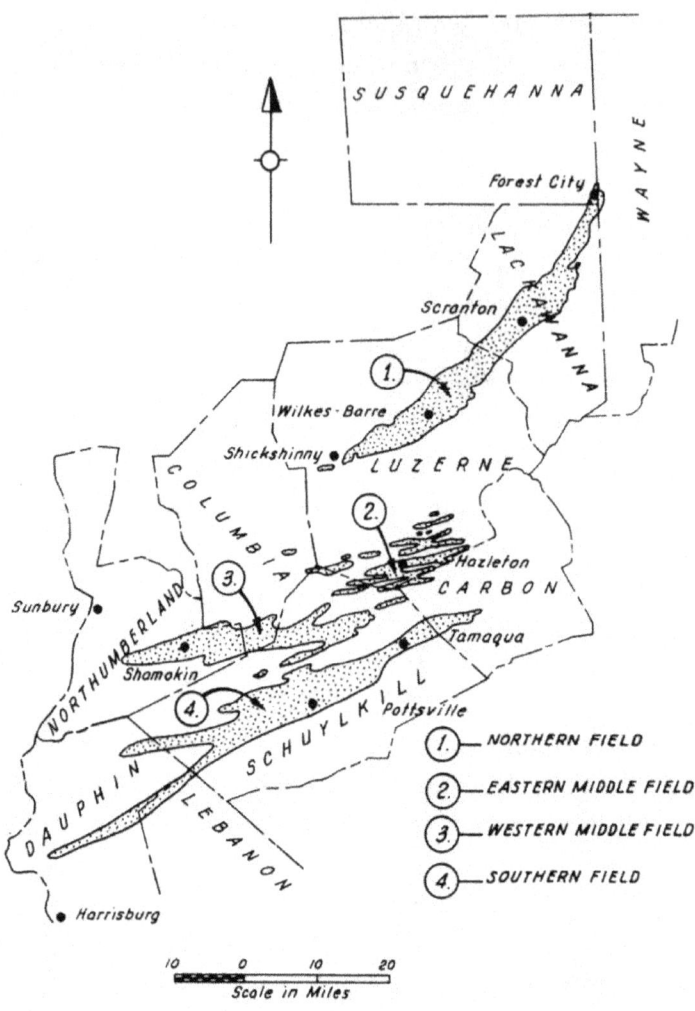

NEPA mine region map (US Bureau of Mines). (Image: courtesy of Mining History Association.)

been equally important to that part of western Scotland that I had left behind. It did not take me long to understand that anthracite coal had defined NEPA economically, socially, and culturally. To a certain extent, its legacy still affects life in the area and influences how we choose to envisage a better future for the generations to come. If we accept the famous words of philosopher George Santayana—"Those who fail to learn from history are doomed to repeat it"—then we should feel obliged to preserve the history of the anthracite region by remembering not only the pride, strength, and loyalty of its people but also the devastating human, economic, and environmental costs to it. I believe this history deserves to be taught in every regional high school and college, and it dismays me to see that invariably it is not the case.

The anthracite industry of northeastern Pennsylvania spread its activities over a relatively small ten-county area in a discontinuous coal field subdivided into northern (centered on Scranton/Wilkes-Barre), eastern middle (Hazleton area), western middle (Shenandoah/Shamokin area), and southern (centered on Pottsville). This area covers 484 square miles, is 125 miles long, and is a mere 35 miles wide. At its peak in 1917, the anthracite industry produced 100 million tons of coal annually and employed 160,000 workers, many in highly dangerous conditions. Thereafter, faced with competition from cheaper domestic heating fuel in the forms of oil, manufactured gas, bituminous (soft) coal, and its coke derivative, the industry steadily lost its ground through the next two decades. Furthermore, as Robert Wolensky and William Hastie argue in a co-authored book on anthracite labor wars, intra-industrial problems also contributed to this collapse: fraught labor relations, lack of technological reinvestment, geologically determined operational constraints, and corruption-prone tenancy and subcontracting systems. Despite a brief resurgence during World War Two, the industry continued its downward slide throughout the 1950s and 1960s. The corresponding deindustrialization of the region ushered in an era of chronic depression and irrevocable decline. The Knox mine disaster of 1959 delivered a near-fatal blow, an accident caused by illegal mining beneath the Susquehanna River in Jenkins Township between Wilkes-Barre and Pittston. This catastrophe was the catalyst for the immediate end of industrial-scale deep mining in the northern field and throughout the region within the next two decades. Another blow to the dying industry came soon thereafter, in 1965, with the amendment of the Pennsylvania Clean Streams Law to require treatment of drainage from the mines. Faced with this legal exigency, most major coal companies stopped pumping out their mines within a year or two and ceased their colliery operations. Abandoned mine drainage (AMD) then became an ongoing problem, one of huge volumes of acidic wastewater constantly finding its way into the region's rivers, streams, and lakes to poison and discolor them. Beside this crisis of environmental spoilage and toxicity, the corresponding problems of unemployment, social dislocation, and economic hardship grew ever more severe.

Though various initiatives have been launched periodically to offset postindustrial decline and to return the region to some measure of socioeconomic and environmental stability, the conscious and subconscious effects of the loss of "King Coal" are still being felt in numerous ways. Visible signs of this once ubiquitous industry remain few apart from scattered strip-mining operations and family-run "coal holes" (successors to Depression-era bootleg mines) that continue, along with culm processing, to yield around eight million tons of anthracite annually. Most production is in the middle and southern fields, where a handful of independent deep mines may still be found. Traveling through the region, we may also see an occasional reminder in the form of a culm bank formed by mine waste or an abandoned and rusting colliery structure. The gigantic coal breakers that once dominated the regional landscape have all been demolished, while many of the culm banks have been removed or reclaimed. The names of individual places associated with mining remain on the map, but the tight-knit mining communities that constituted the social fabric of the region have largely disappeared, their traditional way of life now little more than a fading memory. Nonetheless, other traces of "coal cracker" culture—manifested in language use, communal values, and certain persistent patterns of social behavior—remain powerfully present in the life of the region and may be said still to define its identity broadly as the home of "The People of the Black Diamond."

Some pointers to the structure of this book may be helpful to readers. In Chapter One, "Historicizing Anthracite," I consider the subject in the context of environmental, social, and local histories; discuss my approach to the subject; and define several key terms that I use in doing so, notably *posthistory, modes of recall,* and *representational forms*. Readers who may be less interested in the theoretical underpinnings of my approach may perhaps wish to move presently to Chapter Two, "Representing Disaster," the first of my specific analyses. In it, I focus on the Knox mine disaster (1959) and the Centralia mine fire (1962-), whose occurrences were a twin hammer blow to an already failing industry and whose dates provide an unofficial start of the transition to a posthistorical era of anthracite. Furthering some observations on memory and place in the first chapter, Chapter Two discusses collective memory and forgetting in the context of Knox and Centralia; it concludes by referring to other posthistorical disasters and the field of disaster studies. In Chapter Three, "Modes of Recall," I consider physical sites, signs, souvenir merchandise, historical archaeology, oral history, and interpersonal activity (festivals, associations, online groups). In Chapter Four, "Representational Forms," I examine the presentation of anthracite history and culture in literature (historiography, fiction, drama, poetry) and the arts (theater, music, photography, painting, mixed media, sculpture). In Chapter Five, "Mine with a Movie Camera," I explore the entire history of documentary and narrative fiction films on anthracite mining other than those on Knox/Centralia, which I cover as part of my discussion in Chapter Two. In Chapter Five, unlike in earlier ones where my purpose differs, I offer some more detailed textual analysis. In the Conclusion, I draw together the various strands of my study and emphasize the role of education in preserving anthracite heritage for future generations.

CHAPTER ONE

HISTORICIZING ANTHRACITE

> Little by little, the town names began to take on a frank industrial tone . . . and I realized I was entering the strange, half-forgotten world of Pennsylvania's Anthracite Region (Bill Bryson, *A Walk in the Woods*)

It matters that we remember and tell the history of anthracite in northeastern Pennsylvania because it can teach us much about the region's environment, industry, and society. It is also local history, one to which the region's inhabitants may relate more readily and directly than to histories writ larger about places, people, and events that bear only vaguely and impersonally on their own experiences of life.

INDUSTRIAL HISTORY

Though northeastern Pennsylvania has a rich history, coal has been the principal reason the region has figured in conventional histories of the United States. Industrial history is the most easily accessible and best-rehearsed part of the anthracite story; it is one of how vast deposits of almost pure carbon were discovered, mined, and put to use in powering iron forges, factories, railroads, and steamships, and as a fuel for domestic and commercial heating. Since this industrial story turns most effectively on names, dates, and scientific facts, it fits well into conventional educational frameworks and has long been a dominant narrative geared to the history of regional development, power, and influence. It has been told invariably in a "top-down" manner and, within a broader context of the meteoric rise of the USA to global power status by the late nineteenth century, often in a triumphalist one. Unsurprisingly, it is a narrative underpinned by the names of prominent individuals ranging from discoverers and inventors to industrialists and retail entrepreneurs. Individuals such as venture capitalists George and Seldon Scranton, railroad bosses Asa Packer and Franklin B. Gowen, dime-store pioneers F.M. Kirby and F.W. Woolworth, and established local family dynasties such as Coxe, Pardee, and Kidder held the reins of socioeconomic power. They were hard-coal region equivalents of individuals like Andrew Carnegie and Henry Clay Frick in the soft-coal, coke, and steel world of central and western Pennsylvania.

Ronald L. Filippelli states that "the greatest single factor favoring Pennsylvania's development as an industrial giant was its vast storehouse of natural resources" (3): coal, limestone, timber, iron ore, oil, and gas. 120 billion tons of soft and hard coal lay waiting to be unearthed. Beginning in earnest in the nineteenth century, anthracite mining in northeastern Pennsylvania soon came to play a central role in the national narrative, one disproportionate to the size of the region, for it was in this sharply delimited area that anthracite became a key element in forging the American Industrial Revolution of which Pennsylvania as a whole became the national driving force. Over the course of two centuries, many milestones in anthracite history have been erected. One example will suffice: industrial entrepreneurs Josiah White and Erskine Hazard's hiring in 1840 of Welsh ironmaster David Thomas in Catasauqua, in the Lehigh Valley adjacent to the southern coal region, led to the first commercially viable use of anthracite in the nation. While the production of steel was fed subsequently by the soft coal and coke industries in central and western Pennsylvania, hard coal from the northeastern corner of the state was critical to the development of numerous other manufacturing industries, of iron and associated metallurgies in particular, while its use in generating steam power enabled factories, railroads, mercantile and military shipping fleets to grow extensively in number and size.

Moreover, between 1850 and 1910, with the development of the breaker as a mechanized facility to sort, clean, and size coal, especially for domestic use, anthracite became a major household fuel, mainly in the mid-Atlantic and northeastern states. During that same period and especially after the Civil War, a heavy capitalization of the anthracite industry, bolstered by an 1869 state law allowing large-scale mergers, led to a near monopolistic combination of several major railroads and coal companies. The advent of the railroads, which had replaced canals as the major transportation mode for coal, ushered in an era of the greatest expansion and power of the anthracite industry.

This industrial saga remains a vital story, but it is not the only one that should concern us, and we owe to a turn in the study of history in the 1970s the revelation of other anthracite stories, such as that of a huge immigrant labor force without whose toil the mines could not have functioned and prospered. The history of those largely nameless workers is also that of the larger and smaller communities they formed and the distinctive culture they created in every single nook and cranny of hard coal land.

ENVIRONMENTAL HISTORY

Intrinsically linked to anthracite's industrial history is its consequence on the natural environment. We cannot mince our words: anthracite mining has been physically devastating to northeastern Pennsylvania, and any environmental history of the region must take it into account. This legacy can teach us much about the harm done to the environment during the long heyday of the coal industry and in its shorter yet equally damaging aftermath. Affecting both the physical resources of the region and its residents' quality of life, this legacy has become an increasingly pertinent aspect of the anthracite story.

We have arrived at a point in the history of Planet Earth when it becomes nigh impossible to justify the continued development of non-renewable natural energy sources such as coal, oil, and gas. We may usefully and must now urgently consider this matter in the light of environmental history. One approach is via the epochal and now well-established concept of the Anthropocene, a term coined by Paul Crutzen to describe the seismic impact of human activity in changing the natural world. Over time, we have transformed predominantly agrarian societies into industrialized ones. Crutzen initially dated this momentous shift from 1784 when the appearance of a refined version of James Watt's steam engine in that year symbolized the birth of the Anthropocene in place of a climatically stable 12,000 years of the Holocene. The Industrial Revolution and the consequent carbonification of the atmosphere from the burning of coal was a major turning point. Crutzen and other Anthropocene theorists have since broadened their concept to refer to the entire history of human reshaping of the natural world, one marked especially by extractive industries that take all from the earth but replenish virtually nothing. The idea of the Anthropocene forces us to acknowledge an ecological emergency, to weigh the environmental havoc we have wreaked, and to consider how, henceforth, we may best restore and protect the planet. Some scholars prefer the term Capitalocene deeming it more precise in describing an age wherein the principles and practices of free-market capitalism have determined the pace, intensity, and effect of environmental exploitation—the mining of coal being a prime example. A capitalist ethos oversaw the channeling of financial profits away from the region by the coal companies and their eventual desertion of unprofitable coal fields. Those expedient practices played a large part in the economic collapse of the region and the corresponding social dislocation of many who had worked in or depended upon the anthracite industry for a steady though hard-won and often precarious living.

Anthracite is between 86 to 98% pure carbon and has correspondingly high BTUs (British Thermal Units). What remains today of the industry thus seeks to promote its product as (relatively) clean, economical, and efficiently produced. A coal conveyor belt crossing above the highway between Shenandoah and Mahanoy City bears the slogan "Coal Keeps The Lights On," a pointed message reminding the public of the value of coal mining to the production of electricity in co-generation (combined heat and power) plants. Anthracite is still used for domestic and institutional heating, sugar beet refining, and public water filtration. Furthermore, the industry has revived a portion of its traditional sales to steel producers as foreign companies look for a cost-effective alternative to coke as a carbon additive in the steelmaking process. It has also sought

Co-gen booster sign over PA Highway 54, Schuylkill County. (Photo: Cynthia A. Carmickle, 2021.)

to diversify its activities, notably in the recent promotion of a rare-earth metal processing initiative, in the continued re-mining of coal waste from culm banks for co-generating plants, and in the use within the horticultural industry of ash and cinders to aerate nursery and greenhouse soil. The industry stresses that it prepays the cost of reclaiming stripped land in "full cost" government bonds and places a portion of the price of each ton of coal sold into a federal mine reclamation fund.

By contrast, environmentalists argue that no full regeneration of spoiled land is possible, given the severe ecological damage to flora, fauna, watercourses, and the ground itself. Air and noise pollution levels continue, as they have always done, to affect the local population adversely with an ongoing incidence of respiratory and other related ailments. As both science and history reveal incontrovertibly, the extracting and burning of coal in any form can only perpetuate serious environmental harm in the forms of atmospheric emissions, cumulative waste matter, acidic mine and culm drainage, flooding, subsidence, open shaft hazards, undetonated explosives, denuded landscapes, and so forth. In his "State of the Planet" speech on December 2, 2020, UN Secretary-General Guterres insisted on science being clear that disaster looms unless we cut global fossil fuel production drastically and "forge a safer, more sustainable and equitable path." He added that "the coal business is going up in smoke [because] more than half the coal plants operating today cost more to run than building new renewables from scratch."

Nonetheless, in recent years the US coal industry overall has received a boost in support, if an overly optimistic one, from influential Republican politicians, including former president Donald Trump down to ex-Hazleton mayor and former 11th District US congressman Lou Barletta. We have seen slogans such as "Lou Digs Coal" (less so since his failed 2018 US Senate run) and "Trump Digs Coal" displayed on signs at many regional mining sites. Many regional residents who still depend on coal mining for their livelihood are understandably concerned that the election in November 2020 of a Democratic federal administration under President Joe Biden has hastened the prospect of a moribund industry well before the promised creation of new green energy jobs will be able sufficiently to counter that loss. A native of Scranton, Biden has found it challenging to reconcile his anthracite region credentials and support of the working class with his administration's commitment to develop and intensify the "War On Coal"—a phrase coined by the coal industry and its supporters to describe the policy introduced by Biden's Democratic presidential predecessor Barack Obama and subsequently rejected by Trump.

Present-day anthracite mining consists primarily of stripping operations that advanced engineering technology has permitted to go as deep as 400 feet below ground. The Commonwealth of Pennsylvania classifies all of this activity as re-mining; consequently, almost no new permits for anthracite mines have been issued for many years. A focus on reclamation has led inter alia to the daylighting of old galleries and tunnels, some of which date from the nineteenth century, and, in turn, has revealed newly harvestable coal pillars and intermediate blocks that once served as key supports of the traditional mine structure. Most anthracite is now exported, and while strip-mining avoids the mass exporting of un- or minimally processed raw materials that are the hallmark of neo-Extractivism (as practiced widely, for instance, in Latin America), we must acknowledge that all coal mining is extractivist and that stripping has scarred the regional landscape in ways beyond the surface depredations of colliery complexes and their related spoil heaps. As Canadian

Political booster sign, Jeansville. (Photo: Cynthia A. Carmickle, 2019.)

industrial landscape photographer Edward Burtynsky said of his visit to Frackville: "I realized that as far as my eye could see everything had been transformed, there was nothing natural left" (158).

Reclamation efforts are central to the gradual recovery of the region. They received an early boost in 1968 with the passing of the state Land and Water Conservation and Reclamation Act, a national first. The state Department of Environmental Resources (DER) came into being in the same year (1970) as the federal Environmental Protection Agency (EPA). A comprehensive state government initiative followed, known as "Operation Scarlift," which continued through the 1970s until funds evaporated. The federal Surface Mining Control and Reclamation Act of 1977 recharged these efforts. Authorized by that act, the DER-administered Title IV Abandoned Mine Lands Program began in 1982 with federal funding. These reclamation projects have since been allied to economic recovery efforts, such as the establishment in 2015 of the federal Abandoned Mine Land Economic Revitalization program (AMLER). The state Department of Environmental Protection (DEP) was established in 1995 out of the former DER, and in that year, the Eastern Pennsylvania Coalition for Abandoned Mine Reclamation (EPCAMR, with a bituminous region equivalent WPCAMR) was formed as a partnership of watershed associations and reclamation agents. It has since done exceptionally valuable work, while a volunteer group known as Underground Miners seeks to expand awareness of environmental issues via online documentation and physical exploration of old mine sites. Yet, into the third decade of the twenty-first century, much remains to be done. In April 2020, for instance, a group of politicians and environmental workers gathered at the site of the former Harry E Colliery in Swoyersville to advocate for the clearance of its culm bank, a long-projected step following the demolition of its breaker in 1995, but one repeatedly stalled for reasons financial or otherwise.

It is deeply ironic that much of what passes nowadays for new occupational opportunities in the region—such as in warehousing facilities, food processing plants, gas stations, and convenience stores—draws heavily on a fresh influx of immigrant labor that is now mainly of Asian, Latino, Middle Eastern, and Sub-Saharan African origins. Furthering the irony, many of these warehouses (or "distribution centers") in northeastern Pennsylvania have been built on former sites of anthracite mining. These parcels of land lie within a state-controlled network of tax-free business investment zones known collectively as the Keystone Opportunity Zone (KOZ). Around the city of Hazleton, for instance, we witness the presence of a low-income and highly transient labor force deriving largely from the Dominican Republic and routed primarily via New York City and northern New Jersey. The irony of old mine sites housing a new service industry extends indirectly to the presence in this postindustrial environment of "sanitary landfills" (a euphemism for garbage dumps) whose looming piles in various locations resemble no less than a new type of culm bank. A prominent regional historian expressed to me a view that "we are repeating the immigrant experience which made the coal industry possible; an economy of rote work, low wages, and likely a service economy with an even shorter life span than coal."

Within northeastern Pennsylvania, though not in former coalmining counties (apart from small semi-bituminous and semi-anthracite belts in the southeastern corner of Tioga and southern Sullivan counties, respectively), we have also begun to see recurring today the kind of environmental damage and landscape degradation formerly caused by the coal industry in the drilling via hydraulic fracturing (fracking) of the Marcellus shale field for the production of natural gas. Existing or potential problems such as contaminated groundwater, cumulative wastewater, leaking methane gas, spilling of hazardous chemicals added to the fracking water, and destabilization of the earth's crust have dogged this sector since it took off regionally in 2008. If, as Santayana warned, we fail to learn our lessons from history, then the natural gas industry will have mirrored uncannily the pioneering but short-lived national role of Pennsylvania in the extraction of oil, an industry of boom and bust in the northwestern part of the state in the late nineteenth century. It will have mirrored even more painfully and lengthily the effects of a century and a half of relentless anthracite mining leading the aforementioned regional historian to ask: "Did we learn nothing from the coal industry?"

SOCIAL HISTORY

Anthracite social history has come to the fore as we have moved away from anthracite history as principally a scientific, technological, and economic subject toward a greater understanding of the people of the region without whom the industry could not have existed and whose lives had been invariably overlooked in received historical accounts of the region. Such accounts had focused more on history "from above," on the doings of governments, coal companies, and influential and powerful political and business figures whose views and actions were deemed largely to have determined the course of regional history.

An anthracite social history that seeks to recuperate the lives of the working-class majority foregrounds components of identity—ethnic, linguistic, and gender, among them—as key factors. An understanding of how these factors contributed to the emergence of an overarching collective identity offers a framework for tracing the broader social formation and eventual transformation of the anthracite region. Its natives have long associated their social identities with the prevalence of anthracite mining, as terms like "coal cracker" and "People of the Black Diamond" attest. The latter became the totemic name celebrated by the Anthracite 250th Anniversary festival held across the region in 2018. The festival's president Scott D. Herring emphasizes that the name represents a unique culture not found in any other coal-producing area on earth and that its people have identified themselves with the traditional presence of the coal industry even into an age when it no longer dominates the regional scene. Born of hard graft and hardship, we perceive "Black Diamond" people as a proud, determined, and stubborn breed that has passed down through generations a set of shared values based on principles of industriousness, self-reliance balanced by reciprocity, and communal solidarity. Over a period spanning more than a century, much early ethnic and religious separateness among immigrant communities gradually gave way to a sense of regional togetherness arising from the shared experience of work, from union and church membership, intermarriage, and social life in its multifarious aspects. This identity is so inextricably bound up with the production of coal that natives may refer to the region simply as "the Hard Coal" or "the Anthracite," the latter a synecdoche that underlies my choice of phrase for part of this book's title.

With twenty-six languages being spoken in the region at one time, ethnic identity was a barrier at first to the growth of a common bond. Language difficulties for non-English speakers, as well as different religious affiliations, culinary preferences, and distinctive social customs, combined to keep immigrant communities apart and frequently in conflict with one another. Over time, this diverse span grew less obstructive, and a coal region identity slowly coalesced around what its population recognized as common interests and what united rather than divided it. Moreover, as the children of first-generation immigrants grew up and were educated as young American citizens, they began to depend for their self-identification less on their immigrant otherness than on their shared status as native-born Americans. They saw themselves not only as Pennsylvanians but expressly as from the coal country of the northeastern part of the state. As the generations passed, a gradual loosening

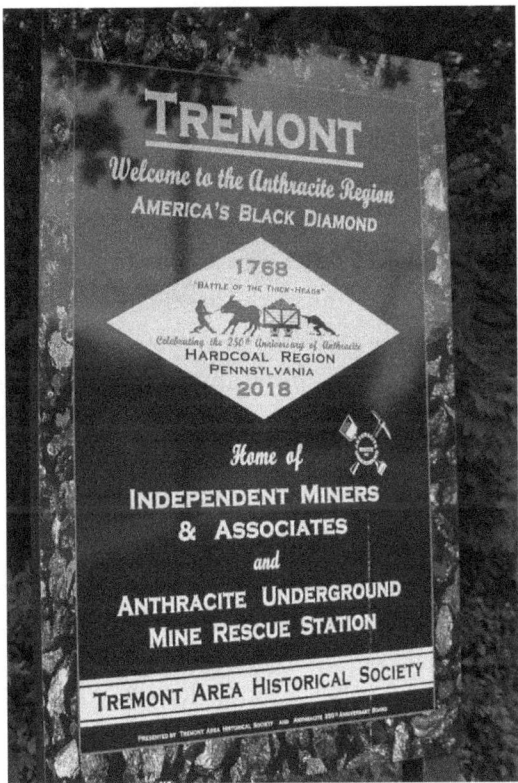

Anthracite 250th Anniversary sign, Tremont. (Photo: Cynthia A. Carmickle, 2019.)

of ethnic ties inevitably took place, though the relatively self-contained and broadly unchanging social and topographical make-up of the region has ensured that these ties survive mainly in the form of cultural associations and social clubs. The expansion of genealogical research via online capabilities has proven to be a valuable development in gaining new information and knowledge of the forms and patterns of regional ethnicity, and it has allowed this strand of social history to flourish as never before.

Feeding into the mix was a distinctive regional idiom developed from words, phrases, and pronunciations drawing on multiple ethnic backgrounds, first from English and German, then from the English-speaking Irish and Welsh, and later from Italian and Polish, with traces of other European languages fed into the mix. Whether in the soft, lilting Irish or the harder-edged Slavic inflection, a manner of speaking identified a person as coming "from da hard coal" where people understood one another's speech perfectly, and outsiders were conspicuous by their different or "proper" use of the language. Glossaries of "Coal Speak" have appeared in an effort to document, preserve, and celebrate this colloquial usage—for instance, in *The Anthracite Idiom* by Tom Klopfer—and local particulars and variations have been noted by compilers working in different parts of the region. However, as with all local dialects and accents in an age of mass media and information technology, much of this rich and expressive idiom, especially its wide-ranging vocabulary and curious figures of speech, though less so its more ingrained habits of pronunciation, has begun to disappear as older generations generally fixed in place have given way to more mobile younger ones whose language use is more standardized, functional, and influenced by the pervasive norms of popular culture.

Anthracite social history has also revealed a gender component in the life of the region. By a combination of law and superstition, women did not work in or around the mines except on rare occasions in male disguise. Instead, as well as forming the bedrock of domestic life, women supported their families by dominating the labor force in textile factories, notably producing silk and lace; cigars too. These occupations were introduced to the region specifically to counter the loss of jobs in the mining industry. Women helped to offset those heavy losses by working in "runaway" garment factories. These operations sprung up in northeastern Pennsylvania in the 1930s as companies sought to lower wage rates, loosen restrictions, and gain the protection of organized crime by moving their operations away from strongly unionized big-city garment districts, especially that of New York City. In several books, the Wolensky family of regional scholars, for instance, has explored this history and the struggle to organize these workers. Karol K. Weaver has examined another previously unheralded and critical area of women's work: as neighborhood medical caregivers in communities where public and professional health services were either absent or inadequate.

Yet, in the postindustrial era, a cohesive anthracite identity is much more difficult to recognize than it was in former days. The decline of mining meant the corresponding decline of a communality that had drawn together a once disparate mass of people. As one prominent anthracite cultural leader remarked: "No replacement industry, so no replacement identity." The consequent fragmentation of the workforce allied to a growing outmigration from the region, especially among younger people pursuing better career opportunities elsewhere, has contributed to a fading collective identity. Furthermore, a greater cultural heterogeneity—augmented by unlimited, borderless, and ubiquitous communication technologies, especially the Internet and social media—has replaced the narrow world, reinforced by its physical ruggedness, which characterized northeastern Pennsylvania in the anthracite era.

Nonetheless, those readily accessible information technologies have enabled anthracite region identity to survive largely through the work of memory, perhaps the largest key in unlocking an authentic people's history. Memory is arguably the only active means of accessing much of this history. Traditional oral history has long fulfilled this function, and the region offers some excellent examples, such as the Northeastern Pennsylvania Oral and Life History Project (NPOLHP) established by anthracite historian Robert Wolensky, but it remains a labor-intensive task dependent upon skilled interviewers, willing subjects, and a great deal of paperwork, tape recording, and physical archiving. Much work of this kind remains to be done, and time is running out, as with each passing year, fewer individuals remain to recollect the details of anthracite-era life. Wolensky also warns of the loss of priceless historical materials, as more paper documentation is getting discarded at a time when we are seeking to form a fuller historical perspective on anthracite. Stefan Berger and Christian Wicke remind us that we are still learning about the effects of deindustrialization on collective memory and identity: "Especially since the turn of the millennium, there has been a noticeable call for a closer look 'beyond the ruins' of industrial decline, and to bring forward the memory of the working classes and their misery caused by deindustrialization." (11)

As I will reiterate in my Conclusion, any effort to encourage regional people to engage with and own their heritage remains challenging. For many older members of society, especially those who grew up in and lived through the anthracite era, their memories understandably produce mixed feelings about dwelling on a past marked greatly by poverty, deprivation, injustice, discrimination, and physical hardship. Oral histories of workers often reveal this ambiguous response. In *Beyond the Breaker*, a 2019 documentary film on the loss of the Huber breaker in Ashley, Wolensky alludes to the often-difficult task of persuading coal region people of the value of their heritage when one fairly typical response is "Why do you care about that dirty, gritty history of anthracite? Thank God the mines aren't here anymore." Though some ex-mineworkers become involved in promoting and operating anthracite tourism, Berger and Wicke offer the reservation that for everyone "who became a heritage activist, there was at least another worker who was glad to see the industry go because of unpleasant memories associated with his or her place of labor" (16).

LOCAL HISTORY

Once considered a marginal branch of the "true" study of history, of interest mainly to amateurs and antiquarians, local history has grown in stature as its practice has reflected new historiographic ideas and methods. The work of scholars such as Carol Kammen and Joseph Amato has helped to discredit the myth of narrow provincialism that in the past tended to devalue the subject. We have become more cognizant of the degree to which the local and regional may illuminate the national and international. "Think locally, act globally" is a well-known maxim. The effects on the margins of what originates and happens in the center (and vice versa) are likewise being re-evaluated. By the same token, Amato suggests that "local and regional historians . . . must inquire into the practice of power" (184). In this spirit, the local invites us to explore history "from below" by giving a hitherto concealed or suppressed voice to the thoughts and deeds of ordinary people. Local forms of commemoration, both individual and communal, value the recording of personal experience and, in many respects, are more relevant and meaningful to the average individual than is history conceived on a grander, more public scale.

Local history is rooted in specific places; in broadening its spectrum, writes Stephanie Pasternak, it has focused "more on deconstructing how a place is remembered than on the history of a place itself" (13). Applied to the anthracite region, a similar metanarrative lies at the heart of this book. A developing science of place concurs with a revitalized approach to local history in which we pay greater attention to how we register our physical environment and respond cognitively and affectively to the places and spaces where we lead our daily lives. An influential early approach is *The Poetics of Space* by French philosopher Gaston Bachelard, who draws on phenomenology and psychoanalysis to examine our relationship to our architectural surroundings. Another field of inquiry is psychogeography, whose precepts influence a range of cultural productions in literature, painting, photography, and film. Deriving their ethos and methods from an unconventional concept of urban exploration developed in Europe by Lettrists and Situationists from the 1940s to the 1960s, the new psychogeographers map our interacting physical, intellectual, emotional, and aesthetic responses to space and place.

We are thus finding new ways to understand and articulate how we constantly perceive, organize, and monitor the myriad coordinates of our surroundings. We do it deliberately or accidentally, consciously or subconsciously, almost as if by a process of psychophysical osmosis. In *The Experience of Place*, Tony Hiss explores how this process works: "Both the pinpoint focus of ordinary perception, which lets us shut ourselves off from our surroundings, and the broad-band focus of simultaneous perception, which keeps us linked to our surroundings, are inherited skills built into each of us" (3-4). The body of knowledge we build from this ceaseless process allows us to form and consolidate our sense of belonging to a familiar environment composed of natural and manmade features. Memory is also central to this process, for our ability to identify with places always hinges on negotiating actively between our awareness of them as they are and our remembrance of them as they were at any number of earlier junctures and significant moments. Our memory permits us to construct a sense of continuity between past and present as well as to distinguish clearly between them, and our identification with places reinforces that sense of continuity. As the philosopher of history Michael Stanford states, "A knowledge of history brings a sense of historicity, a feeling that we are part of a fellowship that runs through the ages" (52). The anthracite region bears witness to this strong sense of spatial and temporal continuity as a basic means whereby we create and maintain our individual and collective identities and whereby we understand and act upon the dynamic exchanges between them.

HOW WE TELL OF THE ANTHRACITE

My approach is meta-historiographic: to investigate how anthracite history has been recounted and interpreted since the demise of mining as a major industry in northeastern Pennsylvania. Since the industry had already begun an irreversible decline by the late 1940s, it is impossible to fix a specific date for that demise. I choose 1960 as the starting point of my study given its approximation to both the Knox mine disaster (1959) and the start of the Centralia mine fire (1962), two traumatic events that served to hasten the collapse of deep mining in the region. I make one exception to this starting date: Chapter Five discusses examples from the entire thirteen-decade history of motion-picture film to trace how a representational form has evolved throughout that time in depicting anthracite coal. I call my guiding narrative a *posthistory* of anthracite, one charting a discourse constructed from the moment of that symbolic "end" of the industry. Its necessarily arbitrary starting point eschews a mere chronology of factual details and emphasizes instead a view of gradual transition into the postindustrial era. It seeks to reveal a posthistory that is active on multiple levels and takes many forms. This is to approach such discourse as "the general domain of all statements" on the subject, in Michel Foucault's familiar phrase. Since, for Foucault, discourse and power are inseparable, the very idea of an anthracite posthistory begs the questions of *whose* history is being told, *how*, *by whom*, and *to which ends*. It also engages with the fundamental relationship between history and memory, both individual and collective, and opens up the anthracite story to some highly contentious issues of personal and social identities, politics, the economy, and the environment.

Another reason for choosing 1960 is to recognize the early onset of a theoretical turn that reconceptualized the historical field. History "from below," in E.P. Thompson's celebrated term, or what Guy Beiner chooses to call "vernacular historiography," gained momentum in the wake of the 1968 student revolution in France that intensified calls to democratize society and to account accordingly for the histories of underrepresented members and sectors of society. In the 1970s, a further challenge came in the form of "New Historicism," which views the field of history operable as literary narrative; as discourse on the past but separate from it; as performance, an ever tentative and problematic staging of the past; as a radical "people's history" that speaks its truth to power. Such history appeals to and relies strongly on the role and function of social memory. As Jacques Le Goff writes, "this quest for collective memory less in texts than in the spoken word, images, gestures, rituals and festivals, constitutes a major change in historical vision." Conterminous with this reshaped mission is the startling rise since the 1960s of a commemorative culture corresponding to the demand for and growth of a heritage industry. Le Goff suggests that the public's obsession with memory springs from "a fear of losing its memory in a kind of collective amnesia—a fear that is . . . shamelessly exploited by nostalgia-merchants; memory has thus become a best-seller in a consumer society" (95). This pervasive culture further risks becoming imprisoning rather than liberating. Pierre Nora, a pioneer of the study of multifarious "realms of memory," finds cause to lament "a bedlam of commemorations, a mushrooming of museums, and a revitalization of tradition in all its forms. No era has ever been as much a prisoner of its memory, as subject to its empire and its law" (xii). Paul Connerton, who has examined how societies both remember *and* forget, chooses the term *hypermnesia* to describe what he sees as "an excess of cultural memory" in a society avid for memorial activity of various kinds. Yet, the dominant driver of our materialistic society is directed toward subordinating the past to an immediately gratifying present and endless fantasies of future repetition promising even greater satisfactions. Connerton perceives a paradox: "Our world is hypermnesic in many of its cultural manifestations and post-mnemonic in the structures of the political economy" (146). We have more ways than ever to remember anthracite history, but how much do we wish to forget?

A further reason for choosing 1960 is that it anticipates establishing a heritage industry in the anthracite region linked to this commemorative appetite. Two national events were propitious in its development. One was the passing in 1966 of the National Historic Preservation Act and the establishment of the National Register of Historic Places, which helped to change perceptions of the value of historic locations and structures. The second was the six-year celebration of the Bicentennial of the American Revolution, a remembrance that culminated in 1976. This event built upon a palpable national mood of nostalgia largely absent in previous decades and encouraged greater popular participation in experiences related to American history. Bearing in mind Nora's lament, that rising tide of enthusiasm for memorializing may have ebbed considerably in more recent years, as the relative lack of interest in the 2011 anniversary of the start of the Civil War may have indicated.

A regional heritage industry, such as that of the anthracite, arises from cooperative conjunction—strategically planned but occasionally serendipitous—of governmental bodies, business interests, planners, (re)developers, communal associations, and a raft of enthusiastic individuals. All become agents in a historicizing process that legitimizes, facilitates, and promotes the creation of tourist attractions, cultural artifacts, educational tools, and programs. All answer variously to the growing needs of a society whose members seek personally fulfilling leisure experiences yielding differing degrees of cultural value. A popularized history further requires a network of advertising, educational, and informational services publicizing these cultural opportunities. In the anthracite region, a vision of cultural renewal continues to match an economic one to counter industry loss and its attendant unemployment problems. Due to that loss, this revitalization project involves moving away from a production-based to a service-based economy within which anthracite history may be represented to the general public in various innovative ways. Intellectuals, artists, and academics committed to a vision of a recuperated past are typically the primary agents of this project. Seeing the prospective socioeconomic benefits of a strong regional heritage, government agencies and business interests ideally take the lead in implementing the project. For instance, regarding repurposing disused mine sites, recruiting knowledgeable and experienced ex-mineworkers as guides is particularly valuable. The general public, both local and from further afield, may be invited to take advantage of these new opportunities to participate in the experience of regional history. Once these opportunities exist, they form part of an expanding leisure economy within an affluent society endowed with a high degree of disposable income and time, one in which a relentless demand for new recreational activities and forms of entertainment generates an expanding tourist industry organized around multiple types and patterns of cultural consumption.

However, the development of an anthracite heritage culture as part of a burgeoning tourist industry may be conceptually problematic since the primary goal of this initiative is to help revitalize the region by means of a *commodified* history to be offered to visitors and residents alike. The dominant anthracite-related historical attraction of the region remains the saga of the Molly Maguires, a late-nineteenth-century band of renegade miners whose story notoriously rests on a great deal of myth, superstition, and scarcity of documented evidence. A controversial Molly Maguire Historical Park in Mahanoy City was openly conceived more as a means of injecting valuable tourist dollars into the economy of that depressed coal town than as a somber gesture of public commemoration. A "Molly Maguires Weekend" in Schuylkill County annually from 1996 to 2002 was, as the director of the county visitors' bureau at that time acknowledged, "about history, about tourism, about economics, people spending their money in Schuylkill County." The town of Jim Thorpe (formerly Mauch Chunk) has eagerly exploited its Mollies connection as the main cog in a tourist wheel turned otherwise by the town's picturesque natural setting and plentiful Victorian buildings. In examining this phenomenon, Philip Jenkins points to anomalies both in the town's eagerness to capitalize on the romantic and mysterious aspects of the Mollies as victims and in the preferred celebration of the Mollies as passive victims of the law rather than as active resisters of coal company oppression. In reopening the county jail where several Mollies were executed as The Old Jail Museum in 1995, the town chose to emphasize their fate rather than their anti-establishment struggles waged in less salubrious locations across Carbon and Schuylkill counties. Jenkins reminds us that Jim Thorpe anyway was primarily the turf of the mine owners and their managerial cadres, concluding his analysis with a crowning irony: "If there is a real Molly Maguire landscape, it is to be found in the decaying patch towns that [visitors] drive to on the way to the sumptuous glories of old Mauch Chunk."

At the dawn of the 1960s, proposals for the development of anthracite region tourism began to appear. A notable example is a 1961 article whose authors, Penn State geography professors George F. Deasy and Phyllis R. Griess, argued that the mining landscape—the region's "man-made Bad Lands"—while far from being beautiful was nonetheless unique and awe-inspiring. They proposed several possible attractions "fascinating to the stranger" willing to risk his footing: high walls, deep holes, and giant earthmoving equipment in former strip mines; one- and two-man "hole in the ground" mines with an attendant opportunity to get acquainted with their operators; breakers and abandoned mine shafts; culm banks as fossil hunting grounds; "quaint gables of old-fashioned row-houses," and ethnic peculiarities of area communities such as Orthodox church domes, foreign names on shop signs, and "exotic" foods to be found in markets. In hindsight, their elaborate proposal may seem overly ambitious and, in some respects, so far-fetched and romanticized as to be almost risible and certainly invalid by today's health and safety standards. Yet, it anticipates an emerging historicized regional heritage since by focusing on tourism as a remedy for unemployment, the authors base their argument on socioeconomic and purely cultural grounds. By invoking the possibilities of a blighted landscape transformed for the tourist gaze, their proposal looked forward to an aesthetics of ruin that has become a feature of many postindustrial environments, if not, ironically, in the anthracite region where very little physical evidence remains of the once all-important industry.

Deasy and Griess may have presented an ultimately fanciful vision of tourists tripping lightly over piles and pits of coal, but they understood what was at stake for the region and the heavy price to be paid in the absence of radical change. Noting that tourism was already Pennsylvania's fastest-growing economic sector, they saw the logic of the region becoming a viable part of it. They recognized too that if tourism, through a vital expansion of trade and services, were to offer a palliative if not a cure for the chronic problem of unemployment, then any "realization of [the region's] full . . . potential" would "require the cooperative efforts of both private and public sectors of the economy, each in its proper field" (1). Moreover, such efforts would have to involve substantial public and private investments—in highways, accommodations, and restaurants, for instance—in order to raise inferior and inadequate facilities to a standard that would draw visitors to the region. In pressing too for the introduction of widespread advertising and promotional campaigns as well as for the cultivation of fresh attitudes and enthusiasm on the part of the regional population, they foresaw that "the image of the region . . . in the public eye must be changed," (7) a call that has proven ever since to be a difficult one to answer with confidence and certainty.

In researching their article, the authors noted the scarcity of regional tourist activity related to coal mining. They observed that the only attractions, all small scale, were the Brooks Model Mine and the "Pioneer," an old coal company gravity car, both located in Scranton's Nay Aug Park, and a gift shop in Frackville selling souvenirs, especially items of jewelry carved from anthracite. The Pioneer Tunnel mine and train tours in Ashland opened in 1962, but it was not until 1971 that the promotion and marketing of anthracite history became a significant regional initiative with the founding of the Anthracite Heritage Complex by the Pennsylvania Historical and Museum Commission (PHMC). This complex eventually grew to comprise three sites: Eckley Miners' Village, the Anthracite Heritage Museum (AHM), and the Museum of Anthracite Mining (MAM). On being separated from mining operations at the former Council Ridge colliery, Eckley, a patch town in the eastern middle field, was sold by the Huss Coal Company in 1969 to a consortium of Hazleton-area businessmen committed to creating a heritage site. This group deeded the village to the Commonwealth of Pennsylvania in 1971, and the PHMC developed the site as a "living history" experience. The museum opened in 1975, and the visitor center exhibit was completed and formally opened in 1980. Interpretive tours of restored village buildings were underway by 1983.

The construction of the Anthracite Heritage Museum in Scranton was completed in 1975, and the museum opened its first exhibit in 1976. The 6.2-acre site of the Museum of Anthracite Mining in Ashland was donated to the state by the Reading Anthracite Company in two parts between 1967 and 1970. The construction of this museum building began in 1975, and its display of mining tools and equipment was open by 1980, a year in which the entire tripartite heritage complex was operational. An institutionalized base for the evolution of a posthistorical discourse on anthracite had thus been formed. Though no longer officially designated as parts of a complex, Eckley and the AHM, which includes the downtown Scranton Iron Furnaces site, today continue much as before, though operating as separate entities, while the lesser visited MAM was closed from 2005 to 2007, since when the Borough of Ashland has leased the building from the PHMC for office space. The museum exhibit hall, whose contents remain the property of the state, is open to the public during regular borough office hours; visitors entering the lobby pay their admission fees to a municipal employee.

The anthracite posthistorical discourse has thus unfolded around a set of principal developments: the opening of museums and guided tours; the formation of groups and associations; the establishment of festivals, ceremonies, and other commemorative events; the construction of historical markers, monuments, and related memorial sites; and the building of a large body of literature and other cultural productions. They all function beneath the symbolic umbrella of the regional heritage industry outlined above.

DESCRIPTIVE CATEGORIES

Two descriptive categories that I call *modes of recall* and *representational forms* underpin this book and serve as my framework in exploring the discourse of anthracite posthistory. With regional memory and identity particularly in mind, my category of modes of recall comprises *material culture* in the form of sites, signs, souvenirs, and historical archaeology; *interpersonal activity* in the form of oral history, associations, festivals, gatherings, and Internet sites. Prompted by cultural theorist Stuart Hall's work in the 1990s, my idea of representational forms refers to a cultural production of texts in literature and the arts (music, photography, film, mixed media, painting, sculpture) that describes, depicts, evokes, and challenges various aspects of anthracite history. Textual production of this kind—not least the historian's work—is always the issue of an informed, creative mind; it, therefore, represents a subjective view of that history and delivers a strong intellectual and artistic message. The category of literature, for instance, includes the writing of history, especially if we follow the New Historicism of Hayden White and others in viewing it as open to the full range of the literary imagination. Given my choice of "representation" as a classifying term, we should also remember that postmodern relativism has largely undermined (an apt verb perhaps in this context) representation as a stable concept since we can no longer rely on "truth" necessarily residing in the transparent or consistent relation of a subject to its representation in any cultural form. Such epistemological challenges have grown more troublingly Orwellian since the spread of information technology, in particular, has facilitated unprecedented levels of visual and verbal ambiguity, alteration, and distortion to the extent that some refer now to as a "post-truth" age. In unscrupulous hands, political or otherwise, these malleable choices of meaning are both unethical and dangerous. Yet equally, this questioning has sanctioned the dismantling of absolutist master narratives that claim to be privileged vehicles and arbiters of historical truth. In pursuit of anthracite posthistory, we may be reminded from either position that in any discourse, the relations of language and image to the shifting play of ideology and power are always complicated and heavily invested in matters of interpretation and meaning.

Employing these two categories allows me to guide the reader by organizing the different areas of anthracite posthistory accordingly. These categories, however, are not always mutually exclusive. If we accept Hall's fundamental assertion that any meaning created by a language, be it verbal or visual, represents reality, then commemorative items—for instance, a historical marker—are also representations. Equally, if we accept, for instance, that a novel set in the anthracite region in the 1930s is a literary representation, then we may also consider it a commemoration of that particular time and place. We may proceed by understanding that these modes and representations overlap and interrelate at various points in time and space. A miners' memorial statue in a city street has a public commemorative function but also has an aesthetic value as an example of the representational form of sculpture. Again, while the practice of oral history has a commemorative function, when transcribed into written language, it becomes an example of literature as a representational form. As a subjective performance of memory, it meets the dual criteria of being a commemorative act *and* creative production of text. In this performance, as in any representation of the past, the relationship between speaker and listener (or reader), following Hall again, is "always double-sided, always interactive . . . The 'taking of meaning' is as much a signifying practice as the 'putting into meaning' . . . . It is, as they say, *dialogic*" (10). This dialogism, respecting the integrity of plural positions and acknowledging that history is understood and written by diverse and multiple agents, is at the heart of a balanced construction of an anthracite posthistory.

CHAPTER TWO

REPRESENTING DISASTER

The Knox mine disaster of January 22, 1959, resulted in widespread underground flooding, the loss of twelve miners, and the imminent end of deep coal mining in the northern anthracite field. Seven thousand five hundred jobs were lost directly or indirectly. The disaster happened when the Susquehanna River broke into the Knox Coal Company's River Slope mine in Port Griffith, Jenkins Township, south of Pittston, following illegal mining practices. The Centralia mine fire began on May 27, 1962, and still burns today, eradicating in the interval the small Columbia County town of which there remains a leveled, vacant, and almost entirely depopulated area. Recovery in a material sense has sadly not been an option for Port Griffith or Centralia, but we may still "recover" the history of these two disasters to try to set the record straight. This form of recovery hinges on those modes of recall and those representational forms through which we may understand and seek to preserve these tragic histories complicated throughout by a web of legal, financial, political, and ethical issues.

Though only four years separate the Knox disaster from the onset of the Centralia fire, we should recognize some temporal and spatial distinctions between their respective histories. Sixty-plus years on, Knox remains a painful event in the collective memory of local communities. Officially, however, it reached closure within a year or so of its occurrence, though its legal ramifications persisted through the mid-1960s. By contrast, Centralia did not reach official closure until the 1990s following a painfully extended period of urban demolition and residential

Location of Centralia in relation to major eastern cities. (Map credit: Thomas Koch.)

Centralia locator map, from David Dekok, Unseen Danger, 1986. (Image: courtesy of the author.)

relocation projects carried out by state and federal authorities. For the community, we cannot speak of full closure even now, six decades on, since a handful of residents have won the right to remain in their formerly condemned homes by virtue of a 2013 civil judgment. Knox was a sudden disaster, whereas Centralia, like the coronavirus pandemic, was a catastrophe unfolding over time. Despite their twin status as symbolic "end of anthracite" disasters, Knox and Centralia have run their historical courses at their own pace and have followed substantially different pathways of remembrance.

Memory has a powerful spatial dimension embedded in landscapes and other coordinates of the physical world. These two disasters present differing spatial scenarios. At Knox, despite massive pumping efforts as

Emptied space, Centralia: Pennsylvania's Lost Town, film, 2017. (Image: courtesy of Joe Sapienza II.)

Knox Disaster marker, Port Griffith. (Photo: Cynthia A. Carmickle, 2019.)

part of the rescue mission, the mine was written off, while its surface structures had disappeared by the mid-1960s. To all intents and purposes, Knox no longer existed. All that remains in an otherwise amorphous area is a set of dignified commemorative monuments. In the village of Port Griffith, a black granite memorial to the twelve lost miners was erected in 1983, and a PHMC marker followed in 1999. Both stand in front of the former St. Joseph's Roman Catholic Church, now belonging to the Baloga family, who lost one of their own in the disaster. In 2003, at the spot where the fatal breach occurred, at no more than two hundred yards from the church, a marble marker was set flat in the ground. In 2004, another marker was installed at the entrance to the Eagle Air Shaft, whence thirty-three miners miraculously escaped. These monuments were funded by community and union donations, while the PHMC marker depended on a local matching of state funds. More recently, a rails-to-trails project has improved public access to the site. Nonetheless, visitors are few in contrast to the many who have descended on the unofficially commemorated site of Centralia, where markers exist only in the forms of ruin and spray-painted graffiti.

In stark contrast to Centralia, the memory of Knox has been committed to respectful observation by local individuals, colleges, museums, and historical societies. On January 22, 1960, the first-anniversary date, a Sacred Mass was held at the behest of citizens and victims' families, initially at St. Joseph's and since 2009 at St. John the Evangelist's Roman Catholic Church in the adjacent city of Pittston. Since 1983, on the same date, a gathering in front of the Port Griffith monument is followed by a walk to the mine site. The Knox Mine Disaster Memorial Committee, a representative body of dedicated volunteers, organizes these events. A clear and formalized pattern of remembrance is established on and around the disaster site.

This pattern does not hold for Centralia. Despite near total abandonment and dereliction, the borough survives in two public buildings—the inactive municipal office and adjacent fire house—and several homes dotted around a grid of otherwise vacant streets that connect with the highways passing through the town. Centralia has yet to gain status as a heritage site, lacking any formal or institutional historical memorials even though the fire is less visible and the area less hazardous than in earlier years. Instead, a cultural palimpsest in the form of "Centralia" overlies a strangely emptied space. Whereas the Knox site does not invite "dark" (or "disaster") tourism on account of its complete reabsorption into the surrounding land mass and its restrained monuments, Centralia has neither that topographical anonymity nor that set of memorials and so remains subject to the free play of disaster tourism, much of which consists predictably of voyeuristic, fetishistic, self-serving activity mostly of dubious merit.

In 1991, *National Lampoon* magazine published a piece on Centralia titled "Don't Go There," which almost inevitably produced a contrary reaction to its tongue-in-cheek recommendation. Perhaps the most influential cultural text in turning Centralia into a "dark" tourist destination was a popular travel book. Occupying only a brief section in one chapter of *A Walk in the Woods*, Bill Bryson's bestselling 1997 memoir of experiences hiking the Appalachian Trail, the author took a sidebar excursion to Centralia, which he called "the strangest, saddest town I believe I have ever seen" (231). Imagining a future flood of visitors and at the same time questioning his curiosity, Bryson reflected on how odd it seemed "that I, or any other severely foolish person, could drive in and have a look round a place as patently dangerous and unstable as Centralia, and yet there was nothing to stop anyone from venturing anywhere" (237). The success of his book generated more interest in the Centralia story than at any time since a dramatic rescue from a sink hole in 1981 excited the news media, though the coverage has since switched to a largely online mode. A slew of subjective and often bizarre commentaries began to emerge on the Internet and contributed, as Bryson had foreseen, to a regular invasion of the town by rather too many ghoulish observers to the liking of its slowly dwindling populace.

Such exercises in "ruin porn" depend on the space of Centralia at least remaining recognizable and yielding signs of the fire itself or of the destruction it has wrought. These signs included a three-quarter-mile stretch of Pennsylvania 61 known as the "Graffiti Highway," which had buckled and cracked from the fire; the basic grid of city blocks whose lots show foundational evidence of former buildings; and the continuing presence of bore pipes and surface fissures releasing billows of smoke and steam from underground. An unregulated meeting place for random and undirected foot and vehicular traffic, the highway, which geoscientist Ben McGee, likened in a 2013 Travel Channel segment to "an apocalyptic mural," became part of history in April 2020 when various factors, including crowding risks during the coronavirus pandemic, chronic problems of vandalism, and longstanding liability issues resulted in the highway being buried permanently under truckloads of dirt by its owners Pitreal Corporation, a subsidiary of Pagnotti Enterprises, one of the larger remaining anthracite producers. Disaster tourism may have a quietly dignified side, as at the Knox site; in Centralia, an annual reunion of former residents, who may barely be called tourists, is held on Memorial Day. This bittersweet commemoration of "home" is far removed from the many gratuitous and communally uninvested gatherings that have taken place regularly in the disheartening remains of the town.

In addition to the Internet, where we may find, among much else, a dedicated web site (www.centraliapa.org), the popularity of horror movies and video games has contributed greatly to Centralia's public profile. A noxious atmosphere wedded to an eerie sense of desolation provides ready fodder for paranormal and other eccentric, often lurid interpretations of the site. Whether we judge such promiscuous and idiosyncratic readings as prurient and inappropriate or somehow imaginative and deferential, all have ethical implications. If the kind of vulgar commercialism evident at such sites, an activity that Marita Sturken describes so disturbingly in her 2007 book *Tourists of History* as a self-protective and self-comforting response to a national trauma, has not happened yet in Centralia, then it

"Dark" tourists on the "Graffiti Highway," Centralia. (Photo: Cynthia A. Carmickle, 2019.)

may be only because the place is remote and no local infrastructure exists any longer to support such proliferating consumerist desire.

ESTABLISHING A HISTORICAL PERSPECTIVE

That the representation and commemoration of the two disasters did not begin substantially until the beginning of the 1980s prompts us to weigh the twin questions of how we form a historical perspective as well as how we probe the dynamics of social memory and its corollary, social forgetting. While our first step may be to acknowledge the objective status of official records and factual news reports of disasters as "the first rough drafts of history," in the celebrated 1943 words of *Washington Post* journalist Alan Barth, we should not ignore the discursive distances between eye-witness reports, official records, journalism, and historiography. Equally, though the first three modes hew closely to events as they happen, while the fourth removes itself from them, they enter nonetheless into a symbiotic relationship wherein their respective accounts of historical events interrelate and their consonant or dissonant ideological positions—implicitly even in the case of official documents—manifest themselves accordingly. In this respect, the historical representation of the Knox and Centralia disasters began immediately afterward in the documenting by authorities and mass media of mainly official responses: literal descriptions of the occurrence, rescue and repair efforts, obituaries, inquests, public meetings, legal actions, and so forth. Those formalities represent the first steps in a gradual process of committing the disasters to record and beginning to understand, evaluate, and judge them. While we may argue that these steps contribute little more than the establishment of a formal historical record—"just the facts, ma'am"—we know that mass media, which at the time of Knox and the start of the Centralia fire consisted of the press, radio, television, and that long-lost form the movie newsreel, are not mere repositories of public information. The standardized use of interviews, bystander accounts, and editorial commentaries shows their status as interested organs with a will and often an incentive to interpret and present their content in an opinionated or partial manner.

As for official and journalistic records of Knox and Centralia, the first two decades reveal significant differences. Dramatic scenes of the place where the river broke into and inundated the mine put Knox immediately on the national stage. Nonetheless, several state and federal investigations were all wrapped up before the end of 1959, unsurprisingly, given that the authorities needed to act promptly and decisively in the wake of the disaster's occurrence earlier that year. In 1960, a Pennsylvania Grand Jury was convened to try several individuals on charges of conspiracy and labor law violations. Other trials within the Commonwealth of Pennsylvania, including lawsuits brought by victims' families, took place through the mid-1960s, but little further attention was paid to the disaster until the intervention of historians in the early 1980s. By contrast, only sporadic national media attention followed the outbreak of the Centralia fire, though local media consistently covered its impact on and potential threat to the community. David DeKok, a journalist on the Shamokin *News-Item* assigned to the story in 1976 and who later wrote two books on the fire, states that the first national press coverage of the crisis since 1969 occurred in 1977 when the *Wall Street Journal* and *CBS News* picked up his story about citizens' concern over poisonous gases escaping from below ground. As for the operation of collective memory, DeKok adds that "the Centralia mine fire was almost forgotten in 1976, even by the people of Centralia. [. . .] Most . . . residents believed the problem solved" (80-81). Governmental complacency and inaction over the fire had lulled the citizens into a false sense of security. This changed dramatically in February 1981. Centralia became international news when twelve-year-old Todd Domboski narrowly survived falling 150 feet into a scorching sink hole that opened up in his back yard. For the best part of two years thereafter, the international media engaged in a feeding frenzy over this "unseen danger" (the title of DeKok's first book on the subject) of the fire burning beneath the town. As soon as Centralia was deemed no longer newsworthy, the media departed as quickly as they had arrived and left the townspeople and the authorities to deal with a bleak and uncertain future.

DISASTER AND MEMORY

The active historiography of Knox and Centralia began in 1981-82 with the making of one regionally produced documentary film on each disaster. I will return to these and other films later in this chapter and to other anthracite films in Chapter Five. Before considering the many subsequent historical representations—or "acts of evocation" in Geoffrey Cubitt's preference for a less detail- and more function-oriented term—we may fairly ask why two decades of near silence had passed before those representations began to emerge. Firstly, a deeper analysis of the meaning of the disasters had yet to appear. Secondly, a measured perspective on the disasters and anthracite history generally began to form when a sufficient critical mass of historical information had accumulated to allow for comprehensive and reliable interpretations of the subject. As Cubitt writes, "acts of evocation presuppose . . . the existence of at least a degree of common understanding about the way a particular past is—or might be—constituted" (204). Yet, writes Paul Connerton, "we need to distinguish social memory from a more specific practice that is best termed the activity of historical reconstruction" (1989, 13). Such reconstructive activity is more the work of the professional historian than the general public, which contributes to this reconstruction through acts of memory happening in informal, spontaneous, and (in the best sense) disorganized ways. Either of these agents, historical expert or recollecting individual, may remain independent of one another in their interpretation of the past. Ideally, though, their approaches and attitudes may interact, as in the moment of the oral historical exchange (reminding us of Hall's idea of dialogic representation). Thus, again Connerton, "the practice of historical reconstruction can in important ways receive a guiding impetus from, and can in turn give significant shape to, the memory of social groups" (14).

We tell our histories and give voice to our memories through language. Where spoken or written words are absent, silence is an understandable response to a collective trauma such as Knox or Centralia. In the wake of such widely shared psychological pain, public silence may be a preferred, perhaps even a necessary, option for a specific population group until the initial phase of shock gives way to the healing phases of remembering and storytelling. This is all very well, and received ideas in social psychology of the post-traumatic process confirm it, but it may not be the last word. If we approach this topic from another angle, then positing the disasters as inevitably causing an inability or refusal to speak of them is as problematic as the term "collective amnesia," one that has been used to describe this kind of stunned mass silence, one following a traumatic event such as a war, a loss, or a prolonged period of hardship and oppression. These last two apply to Knox and Centralia, indeed to the entire anthracite region in decline. The idea of social forgetting as less an obstacle and more a necessary counterpart to social remembering better describes the complex responses to trauma on the part of an entire population group. It is important to see the differences and tensions between a purportedly collective silence and a multiplicity of private recollections, a study of which would be productive in understanding further the posthistory of the anthracite region. This kind of study could closely examine, writes Guy Beiner, "what happens behind the scenes when communities try, or profess to try, to forget discomfiting historical episodes, but actually retain muted recollections" (27).

By introducing the term "collective memory," Maurice Halbwachs, furthering the work of his teacher Émile Durkheim, understood it to mean a fundamental and fluid, if not always fluent, interaction between individual and group mentalities. This exchange frees up both the uninterrupted circulation of memories and the option to repress or suppress them, willed or not, within private and informal spaces among families, neighbors, friends, and workplace colleagues, as well as within formalized social, ethnic, and religious groups. Private rather than public memories, for Pierre Nora, are "mute historical experiences passed on through family and acquaintances, memories involving individual experiences and communal customs and associated with local, regional, religious, professional, or folk traditions, as well as memories of individual apprenticeship and proximity" (633).

Given the complex nature of memory and its differing use-value to individuals and communities alike, we may reasonably view the delay in historical representation as the result of a prolonged hesitation within the anthracite region over *how* to remember the two disasters in a timely and appropriate manner. The operation of memory always produces impulses both to remember some things and deliberately to forget others. In the case of disasters, a deep-seated *need* to forget may prevail. That the social vessel has increasingly unmoored itself from its stable ethnoreligious and communal anchors to drift in a sea of hypermobility, arch individualism, indifference, and disposability renders an understanding of this hesitation more difficult. Nor is it easy to isolate the memory of those gradual, less dramatic changes in the recent regional past, since they occur in a relatively slow continuum that unsettles our reliance on the fixed coordinates of time, place, and person. Our constantly shifting perspective on the sands of time means that history is always being remade by an active process of remembering and forgetting—no matter how, why, or by whom. Memory is about facing the present as much as the past, about how we transmit it from one generation to the next, and about how it gets recontextualized with the passing of time. As Marc Bloch puts it, "the knowledge of the past is something progressive which is constantly transforming and perfecting itself" (58). We may apply this tenet, if differently in each case, to the histories of Knox and Centralia. The history of Knox has been codified and settled, though physically the mine is no more; that of Centralia continues to unfold as long as town and fire still exist, however falteringly, as physical entities.

On eventually being committed to oral or written record, anthracite region memories reveal deeply ambivalent attitudes to a departed industry and its former places of work. Such attitudes, though occurring to a lesser degree as memories grow dimmer, are typical of a region doubting its renewed identity and facing the difficulty of being what Cathrine Degnen, in describing the coal and steel regions of South Yorkshire in England, calls "a place which is known for what it no longer does and . . . [one] grappling with the in-betweenness of post-industrial rupture." In an analysis that would, in principle, apply equally to the anthracite region, Degnen asserts the importance of understanding various "experiential landmarks that people use to help negotiate the shifting social worlds beneath their feet which move backwards and forwards between what is and what was."

In continuing with daily lives that had always been fraught with danger and insecurity, the survivors of Knox and Centralia and their fellow citizens, older and younger, have sought to leave the memory of disaster behind, but that does not mean the erasure either of their pain or of their proud memory of a tightly woven working-class way of life. The two disasters dramatically pinpointed an ongoing reaction to the fate of a region already experiencing huge job losses and having to readjust—under extreme stress, with an imperfect degree of comprehension, and generally with quiet resignation—to the slow death of its traditional way of life. This transformation both preceded and preconditioned an emerging cultural discourse on the regional industrial past. A historiographic turn to memory has added value and weight to this discourse by inviting unofficial as well as official narratives to be constructed from previously untapped personal and archival sources. The narratives unlocked by memory help to reshape collective identities and redefine the hopes and aspirations of particular social groups. In Robert Wolensky's view, "remembering . . . takes pivotal events out of the past and places them in the present, where people can reconsider and re-interpret their causes and consequences" (2005, 250).

The range of representation has expanded greatly in the posthistorical era. In considering the remembrance of Knox and Centralia, we have noted the role played by modes of recall such as monuments, formal or informal gatherings, oral histories, and entire physical sites. In these histories in the making, we observe several other cultural forms coming into play, especially those in literature and the arts. Academic conferences and museum exhibitions also play a significant role in furthering knowledge of these histories by granting them institutional attention. For instance, in 1995, the eighth annual regional history conference at Luzerne County Community College (LCCC) in Nanticoke devoted itself to the Knox disaster, while in 1999, an exhibition at the Anthracite Heritage Museum in Scranton coincided with the publication of a book on Knox by three members of the Wolensky family. An outcome of these events is an annual Knox commemoration at the AHM held on or close to the date of the disaster, a program that continues to this day. That this program came into being sixteen years after one began informally in

Port Griffith shows that institutionalized heritage initiatives, subject to many more stages of planning and bureaucracy, often lag behind those launched by small groups of enthusiasts and volunteers. The historicization of Knox and Centralia over the last forty years has greatly illuminated these terrible disasters and has further stimulated questions of *how* we may henceforth continue to remember them.

REPRESENTING KNOX

The work of professional historians occupies its own niche as a subsection of literature as a representational form. The most detailed work on Knox is that of Robert, Kenneth, and Nicole Wolensky, who have co-authored two books on the subject: *The Knox Mine Disaster: January 22, 1959. The Final Years of the Northern Anthracite Industry and the Effort to Rebuild a Regional Economy* (1999) and *Voices of the Knox Mine Disaster: Stories, Remembrances, and Reflections on the Anthracite Industry's Last Major Catastrophe, January 22, 1959* (2005). While the first book offers a conventional historical analysis of the disaster and its aftermath, including a final chapter on efforts to rebuild the region, the second is based on interviews from 1988 to 2003 for the Wyoming Valley [later Northeastern Pennsylvania] Oral History Project, which Robert Wolensky had established in 1982. By seeking to reveal *how* the disaster is remembered, the second book shows how a mode of recall (oral history recordings) may also function as part of a representational form (transcribed oral history within a historiographic work). Concentrating on the human side of the disaster, it contains various first-person accounts and views—in the first instance, either oral or written—by survivors, victims' relatives, and other individuals with recollections of the event.

In their penultimate chapter, the authors focus on poetry as another subsection of literature and on music as another major representational form. They draw chronologically on a range of poems created between 1959 and 2004 that bring out an emotional response to the catastrophe. The poems, most of which were published in the Wilkes-Barre newspapers, are by men, women, and in one case, a child. Though written by amateur poets, they display remarkable qualities of language, tone, and mood that testify to the depth and strength of feeling behind their composition. As for music, acoustic folksong released in limited quantities by semi-professional artists with strong emotional investments in the history, geography, and society of the region has been the principal musical means of representing the disaster (see also the section on music in Chapter Four). The Wolenskys reprint six songs: "Port Griffith, Pennsylvania" by brothers Frank and Tom Murman, released as a 45 rpm record on the Mask label shortly after the disaster occurred in 1959; "The Knox Mine Disaster" recorded by The Irish Balladeers on their 1968 album *The Molly Maguires*; "Stigma" and "The Ballad of Myron Thomas" (aka the eponymous song) on the 1992 album *Last Day of the Northern Field* by the Donegal Weavers; "The Knox Coal Mine Disaster" recorded by Lex Romane on his 2004 album *Diggin' Dusty Diamonds*; and the unreleased "When the Walls Came Tumbling Down: The Knox Mine Disaster" by Adrian Mark ("Dr. B") Bianconi. The book's final chapter transcribes interviews with individuals who have been involved in commemorating Knox in various ways and concludes with a short essay by Robert Wolensky on the need to understand and appreciate anthracite history. This essay offers valuable early insight into the reasons for Knox remembrance and the various forms it takes.

REPRESENTING CENTRALIA

Countless mine fires—large and small, most extinguished and often with difficulty, several still burning—have long wreaked havoc on the anthracite region. In the northern field, for instance, the Laurel Run fire has been burning since 1915; the Cedar Avenue fire in Scranton burned from 1965 to 1970; the Carbondale fire began in the 1940s and burned until the mid-1970s. These are notorious fires and have received their share of attention, but among true stories of manmade disasters in the United States, few have run as long or caught the public imagination as much as the Centralia fire in the western middle field. In its heyday as a mining community, Centralia had well over 2000 residents, with at least another 500 living in adjacent neighborhoods. By 1962, the year the fire broke out, this number was down to around 1100, as the town began to feel its lifeblood—the coal industry—draining away. Centralia became infamous after the 1981 Domboski sinkhole incident that marked the beginning of the end for the town. In 1983, amid great civic upset and a series of highly charged public meetings, residents voted in favor of a $42 million government buy-out program that ushered in a period of steady relocation beyond Centralia of residents and the consequent demolition of vacated properties. In 1992, the Commonwealth of Pennsylvania claimed eminent domain over all remaining properties in the borough, thus effectively condemning them, and in 2002 the US Post Office revoked Centralia's zip code. By 2005, the population was down to twelve, and in 2009 those remaining—squatters in homes they no longer owned—faced formal eviction notices from the state. Some chose to fight this order as a civil rights case, and in 2013 a court ruled in their favor. Barely anyone remains today in what once was a vibrant and thriving town.

Befitting a disaster longer in duration, more consistently reported, and more susceptible to flights of fancy, representations of Centralia are far more numerous than those of Knox. Since the appearance of DeKok's *Unseen Danger* in 1986 (revised as *Fire Underground*, 2009), several other substantial historical studies have appeared; notably, *The Real Disaster Is Above Ground* (1990) by Stephen J. Kroll-Smith and Stephen Robert Couch and *The Day the Earth Caved In* (2007) by Joan Quigley. In addition to Bryson's curious digression on Centralia in his popular book on the Appalachian Trail, photojournalist Renée Jacobs published *Slow Burn* (1986), a collection of black-and-white images. Jacobs's photographs directly inspired bestselling novelist and Pennsylvania native Dean Koontz's eponymous novella in his collection *Strange Highways* (1995), in which his alcoholic protagonist returns to his hometown (loosely based on Centralia) where he experiences an opportunity to travel back in time. Centralia is also a key location in *Vampire Zero* (2008), one of Pittsburgh native David Wellington's vampire hunter Laura Caxton novels. This twilit zone also appeals to Andrew Shecktor in *Centralia PA: Devil's Fire* (2014), wherein a plot involving marauding demons and heroic resisters figuratively traces the lasting struggle between coal mining companies and their workers. Though the allegory may seem farfetched, Shecktor's novel shows how popular fiction may draw both on the specific saga of Centralia and broader political themes in anthracite history. Natalie S. Harnett's *The Hollow Ground* (2014), inspired by fires in Centralia and Carbondale, tells the story of an accursed family stuck in a desolate town from the viewpoint of a twelve-year-old girl. Even a Christian thriller writer, Mike Dellosso, weighed in with *Centralia* (2015), a lightly faith-based thriller somewhat in the mold of Robert Ludlum's Jason Bourne novels. Such speculative fictional excursions are consistent with the strangeness, darkness, and sense of fractured time associated in popular culture with the doomed town and its seemingly endless fire.

Over three years, the archaeologist/cultural anthropologist/paranormalist John G. Sabol produced no less than four books on Centralia that operate on the edge of science and superstition, and in the spaces between truth and fiction: *Centralia PA: The Fiction That Fuels the Fire* (2013); *The Absence Above, A Presence Below: Re-envisioning Centralia, Pennsylvania* (2013); *Centralia: A Vision of Ruin* (2014); *The Afterlife of Centralia: Presences in a Landscape of Destruction* (2015). Sabol has written several other books on anthracite posthistory, one example of which is *Anthracite Heritage: A Still "Unmined" Landscape* (2014). In that book, Sabol reasserts his trademark view that regional emphasis has been wrongly placed on "eradicating" rather than on recovering those physical presences that bear rich memories of the coal era. This preferred process of recovery relies on a method of "ghost excavation" that draws on archaeology, ethnography, and performance studies to unearth a valuable "afterlife" of "cultural hauntings." He brings a personal immersion in the popular subculture of the paranormal to this process; his books tend to be critical of conventional heritage initiatives and academic approaches to anthracite history. Unsurprisingly too, he views the alternative and iconoclastic approaches to postindustrial history by urban explorers and "dark" tourists as contiguous to his own. To those inclined to discount his work because of his interest in occultism and the fact that he self-publishes all his work, I would argue that he deserves his share of attention. Far-out theories and practices notwithstanding, Sabol has a deep feeling for the spirit of the devastated anthracite landscape in which he was reared.

KNOX AND CENTRALIA ON FILM

DOCUMENTARY

By combining sound and image with immediacy, the art of film is a powerful representational form. Documentary film, in principle, reaches a wider audience for history and does so more effectively than other specialized forms, such as monographs, museum and gallery exhibitions, or site-bound memorials. Technically and conceptually advanced from earlier styles, postmodern documentary opens up historical subjects by using a range of creative methods and techniques that includes archival images (still and moving), animation, captions and intertitles, dramatic reconstructions, narration (voiceover, talking head, dialogue), musical scores, and sound effects. All of these, married to skillful editing, may be mobilized in constructing an entertaining and persuasive historical film. Ken Burns's series of historical films for television is perhaps the most popular American example of this style in action.

Documentary filmmakers were the first artists to represent the Knox disaster, albeit twenty-two years after it had happened. *The Knox Mine Disaster: A Photographic History of Hard Coal Mining in Northeastern Pennsylvania* (1981) also lays claim to be the first historical analysis of

Joe Stella cartoon, *The Knox Mine Disaster*, film, 2019. (Image: courtesy of David Brocca/Ben Mackey.)

any kind on Knox. Produced by CBS-affiliated local area television station WYOU and based on exclusive news footage of the disaster shot (for its predecessor WDAU-TV) by cameraman Jack Scannella, it features a voiceover by its writer Thomas Powell whose early television career saw him covering the disaster as an on-air reporter. Focusing on the sheer power of the image, the film offers a basic take on the subject consisting of continuous archival footage of the disaster scene and the subsequent investigative hearings. Other notable scenes show the immediate care given to survivors at the Pittston Hospital, as well as clips from on-site interviews with Pennsylvania Governor David T. Lawrence and United Mine Workers of America (UMWA) President Thomas Kennedy. *Knox: A Disaster*, made by local public television station WVIA and directed by Ray Pernot, was released three years later, in 1984. Considerably longer than the WYOU film, its approach to the subject is more sophisticated. Much of the credit for this progressive treatment is due to its writer and narrator, WVIA's Erika Funke, who devised a detailed, nuanced, and eloquently delivered script that begins by setting a historical context for the anthracite industry and continues through the event to the hearings and beyond. Archival footage is intercut with sequences in color of interviews with two survivors, Joseph Stella and George "Bucky" Mazur. The account of their struggle to escape from the flooded mine introduces a strong element of suspense rendered more poignant by the powerful testimony of their still vivid memories. These interviews are counterpointed by footage of WDAU's Powell and his WBRE (NBC-affiliate) local counterpart Franklin D. Coslett interviewing survivors in their hospital beds shortly after the rescue.

Twenty-five years later, in 2019, a new documentary appeared: *Knox Mine Disaster: The End of Anthracite*, directed by David Brocca. In its broad approach to the subject and polished demonstration of contemporary documentary style, it benefits from almost forty years of accumulated knowledge and interpretation of the disaster. The opening caption, "A coal mine has a million ways to kill a guy," quoting the last surviving Knox employee William Hastie, who commentates elsewhere in the film, sets the tone, says Brocca, for "an exposé . . . but an amazing story about survival and adversity." Having set up a Facebook page to help identify surviving miners, Brocca interviewed more than twenty individuals from 2008 to focus on stories he "felt a responsibility" to bring out. In keeping with the film's investigative angle, he focuses closely on the legal aftermath of the disaster in three segments: "The Inquiry," containing footage of gripping testimony; "The Racketeers," exploring the context of links between regional organized crime and the wider world of the mob; and "The Silent Partner," concerning August J. Lippi, convicted double agent of both the district union, of which he was president, and the Knox coal company, of which he was found to have been a co-owner. To depict the events of the disaster afresh, Brocca obtained Jack Scannella's original 16 mm news footage owned by CBS, restored and digitized it, scanned all the newspaper articles held by the Office of Surface Mining, and selected still images owned by the Associated Press many of which had been shot by local photographer Steve Lukasik. As an imaginative visual accompaniment to the interviews, Brocca brought in comic book artist Ben Mackey to recreate scenes via charcoal illustrations based on old photographs. The film's narrator is Lex Romane, best known as a writer and performer of anthracite coal songs. Brocca neatly bookends his film by returning to a firsthand source: Powell's initial WDAU news report of the event.

Replacing in the American imaginary the frontier ghost town represented in countless Westerns, the postindustrial version epitomized by Centralia offers up images of a spectacular death by fire, demolition, and evacuation—a narrative, in turn, generating broader ones of fear for physical safety and loss of communal life. Established media companies occasionally revisit the story; in 2012, for instance, BBC-TV produced a four-minute report by Matthew Danzico, including interviews with author David DeKok and several remaining residents. More common now is that any individuals with a video camera may film and exhibit their own takes on the story. A glance at YouTube reveals a plethora of amateur videos adding to the multiple blogs and off-beat websites that Centralia has spawned. Though worthy of note as representations of Centralia, many of these videos are unreliable, superficial, sensational, or plainly weird. Despite their variable quality, they confirm a persistent interest in a story now better known to the general public than at any time since the 1981 cave-in briefly pushed Centralia into the national headlines. Several exceptions offset the prevailing amateurism and flippancy of these texts. For instance, *Verge Science*, a subsidiary of the online compendium *The Verge*, which has almost one million subscribers and has won Webby awards, produced an episode on heat-seeking microbes in Centralia. *Centralia to Remember* (2010), a tripartite YouTube presentation by New York geology professor Yuri Gorokhovich, is a pedagogical film that bears comparison with some full-length professional documentaries on the subject, such as "Centralia, PA—Death of a Small Town" (2009-10), a segment of one installment of the *Life After People* series on the History Channel. This series, the channel's most popular ever program up to that time, presents a set of international case studies that speculates on the fate of an Earth left without mankind. The Centralia segment is subtitled "25 Years after People," thus presuming, conveniently but incorrectly, a total vacation of the town to have coincided fully with the demolition and relocation programs of the mid-1980s.

Along with Gorokhovich's film, five other documentaries deserve close attention, three of which interrelate by virtue of their makers having personal ties to the region and state: *Centralia Fire* (1982), directed by Tony Mussari, Stan Leven, and Bob Achs; *The Town That Was* (2007), directed by Chris Perkel and Georgie Roland; and *Centralia: Pennsylvania's Lost Town* (2017), directed by Joe Sapienza, II. To these, we may add *Baptism by Fire* (1983), made independently for PBS by the Press and the Public Project; and *Centralia* (1999), directed by David Grabias. In these films, we may observe the development of a postmodern documentary style and the history of the disaster itself since they attest to discursive shifts in the posthistorical telling of Centralia. By combining various techniques, interpretive strategies, and performative elements, the films engage with complex questions of truth, historical representation, and ideological positioning. They share an effort to portray both the six-decade history of the fire and the human saga surrounding it, especially from the viewpoint of the victims. In this way, these films articulate the often-bitter contesting of a gradually emptying space as residents struggle to deal with being trapped not only in a physically dangerous environment but also in a tangled web of governmental bureaucracy and repeated official failures to control and extinguish the fire. In the process, many of these residents—emotionally, physically, and economically pushed to the limit of forbearance yet ever loyal to and proud of their identity as Centralians—believe their individual and collective rights to have been ignored or denied by decisions made at state and federal levels and deemed by those authorities to have been made for the greater good of all.

Released in 1982, *Centralia Fire* aired nationally on September 13, 1983, as an installment of the PBS *Matters of Life and Death* series. Already in the process of being made in 1981, it deals only briefly with the Domboski incident and the subsequent national media frenzy. Its narrator, actor Martin Sheen, states that "this event catapulted Centralia into national prominence" and led to the evacuation of twenty-seven families near the cave-in. By directing our attention instead toward inaction or impotence at various official levels, the film works primarily as a social action document for the use and benefit of citizens in their dealings with the government. The filmmakers gave no third party any opportunities to profit from the film. It includes no music and avoids captioning citizens' names in interviews to protect individual identities and accentuate the communal voice. The only concession to celebrity is the choice of Sheen following his presence in the region at the time for the filming of Jason Miller's 1972 Pulitzer Prize, Scranton-based play *That Championship Season*, also released in 1982. As in other films on similar subjects produced since the 1970s (e.g., by the Appalshop collective in Kentucky), *Centralia Fire* reminds us that the coal industry overran and then deserted vast areas of the coal mining states and that the social, economic, and environmental consequences of that history have critically determined the lives and welfare of those left behind. Perhaps the most striking aspect of the film, one attributable largely to its local origin, is the extent to which it stresses the continuity of communal life brought about by a history of social, religious, and industrial ties. Centralia appears as a typical American small town despite its extraordinary ordeal.

One citizen sets the tone with almost the first voiceover of the film: "I didn't know that the community was being slowly destroyed." Over a series of establishing shots, the narrator contrasts the formerly positive image of the town and its shared values with the "environmental nightmare which burns relentlessly sixty-five feet below the surface." Where once were unity and security are now division and fear. Among the most poignant statements of the meaning of home and being forced to leave comes from the Buckleys, one of the first families to be evacuated. After sixteen years in a home about to be bulldozed, the family has moved a mere twenty miles north, hardly any distance in most people's minds, but one of major proportions for persons so deeply attached to their community. As Mrs. Buckley points out, "it's just a house here; it was a home in Centralia." It remains in tune with the filmmakers' sympathetic stance that they nonetheless choose to end the film with a spirited, if unrealistic, assertion of hope. In the words of Mr. Buckley: "I shall return. I will be back in Centralia someday, living."

Baptism by Fire offers a very different take on the story. The film forms the main segment of an installment of the *Inside Story* series, sharing program space with a shorter "Back Page" segment on a Massachusetts housing project. According with the reflexive theme of the series, the film focuses on press attention to and media expectations of the Centralia story, elements that are integrated seamlessly into the overall structure of the program. It opens with interviews of two prominent residents, Catherine Jurgill and Father Samuel Garula, who state their objections to the coverage. A montage of five news reports follows: from ABC, CBS, NBC, and two regional television stations, broadcast from February through July 1981. A tidy segué leads to Hodding Carter as studio anchor and main narrator. As the segment's title rolls, Carter proposes the film's thesis: "Sometimes the press can be too much of a good thing . . . As much as the coal burning below, the press invasions have given these people a baptism by fire in the ways of American journalism, and they have something to say about it." Later, in his summary, Carter refers to Centralia as a "chronic disaster area" on a par with New York's infamous Love Canal, adding that the residents "distrust the government, which they feel is dragging [its] feet . . . and they've come to distrust the press, which they find is more interested in stories than solutions." The film's critique of journalistic practice embraces national, regional, and local television and press. For instance, it examines ABC's *Nightline* story from October 1981, in which three residents interviewed in a no-go area understandably felt sick afterward. The presenter, Ted Koppel, chose to wrap the scene with an alarming exhortation: "Get away from that gas, will you?" Catherine Jurgill, one of the interviewees, expressed her displeasure with the *Nightline* episode, but executive producer William Lord defended the interview set-up as appropriate and the wrap line as proper. As he put it, "one of the magic things of television as well as one of the unfortunate things" is that the telephoto effect of the camera lens in relation to foreground and background foreshortens the distance. Contrary to the image—and Koppel's line—the interviewees were standing twelve feet away from the escaping fumes. Nonetheless, despite Lord's justification, the scene shows the interviewees manipulated by the television crew and production team's technical and content decisions. Jurgill became a media favorite due to her supposedly risky pregnancy. This culminated in a normal birth, however, much to the disappointment of reporters from organs as disparate as the *National Enquirer* and the *Washington Post* on the trail of "deformed baby" stories, an obsession that understandably left Jurgill "perplexed" and "dismayed."

Exploiting the competitive element inherent in a free market of news providers and invoking the shibboleth of serious investigative journalism, *Baptism by Fire* attempts—with a perspective offered by passing time and a relatively leisurely programming slot—to venture beyond its competitors in the depth of its coverage. Its critique exposes a tendency by news organizations in both word and image to maximize sensational or popular elements in the story and to minimize the sense of community and the lasting effects of the fire upon it. Yet, like any mainstream documentary, it gets caught in a vicious cycle. No matter how much it tries to adopt a detached and critical stance regarding the practices of the mass media, it remains subject to the expedient principles governing news and current affairs departments. Despite the film's sensitivity to the need for openness and fairness in news reporting, PBS was obliged to compete for an audience conditioned to expect an appealing and convincing viewing experience. *Baptism by Fire* is an intelligent analysis, but it remains embedded within an "infotainment" vision that typifies much contemporary programming, even more so today than when it was made forty years ago. National news teams left Centralia as quickly as they had come, while even local media outlets were limited in the extent to which they felt they could reasonably continue to cover the story. As Father Garula astutely observes at the end of the film, the problem does not go away, but we lack the social and cultural structures to respond adequately to a long-term crisis of this kind.

Between 1983 and 2007, the only documentary to tackle the story afresh was *Centralia*, released in 1999. When writer, producer, and director David Grabias shot it in 1995 on Ilford black-and-white film stock, about forty citizens remained, of whom only two were teenagers, while some buildings still stood, though a series of tracking shots reveals a fast-diminishing space. An Irish immigrant context with a particular connection to County Tipperary bookends the film with shots of St. Ignatius's Church and the legend recounted by Tom Larkin, accompanied by Celtic music, of its priest having placed a curse on the town. This spooky tale predictably resurfaces in the many eccentric online speculations on the cause of the Centralia fire. Grabias unusually includes a comparative social aspect by exploring a division between western middle and southern coalfield communities, a separation intensified by the mountain between them. Though the film eventually focused on Centralia (in Columbia County)—perhaps in response to the town's growing notoriety—Grabias began by exploring coal region culture across adjacent Schuylkill County and originally titled his film *Above the Mountain*. Among the Schuylkill scenes retained by Grabias are polka dancing in McAdoo, churchwomen making perogies in Shenandoah, bingo at a school in Pottsville, and Molly Maguire descendants interviewed in Girardville. The Centralia-oriented final cut stresses the financial shortfall that caused the government twice to miss opportunities to act decisively in putting out the fire and to resort instead to backfilling as a stopgap measure. Locals largely trusted such official measures until the mid-1970s, when they had begun to suspect the authorities of double talk. By the time of the 1983 town referendum, two-thirds were in favor of relocating and had accepted that Centralia was doomed. We meet a lady selling souvenirs from her isolated house: "There's one thing they can't take from us—the memories." At least to the government, it had become unquestionable that a $42 million relocation program was preferable to an estimated one-billion-dollar price tag on extinguishing the fire once and for all.

Compared to when Grabias filmed less than a decade earlier, little is left of Centralia in *The Town That Was*, a film that took five years to make on a $35,000 budget. It recalls the thrust of *Centralia Fire* by emphasizing a sense of continuity and solidarity on the one hand and one of loss and futility on the other. It casts as a narrator one of the town's remaining residents, 33-year-old John Lokitis, Jr., who lives in his grandfather's two-story row house. He explains that the county allowed him to deed the property, albeit in an unofficial document, since the federal government legally owns his home. A surprisingly youthful self-appointed custodian of the town and its proud tradition, Lokitis commutes two hours to work in the state capital Harrisburg. He seems determined to keep the town alive by painting the public bench, flying the flag, and putting up Christmas lights in the empty streets. In many ways, he is the film's main subject. Co-director Roland says that meeting Lokitis was the decisive factor in making the film: "We couldn't help but wonder why someone so young would choose to live in the remnants of a dying town with no one his age . . . We went into the film to tell a story about a human being, to tell his story against the backdrop of the fire." By presenting Lokitis as "not simply an eccentric who refuses to accept the death of his hometown, but rather a case study in the pathology of an entire region mired in decline," the directors present him as a sympathetic, yet ambivalent figure caught between his belief in the survival of Centralia and his memories of the past. This leads him, for instance, to keep his grandparents' house almost as it was during their lifetime, as well as to discount the danger to himself and his home posed by the presence of the fire about one hundred feet from his backyard. The wistful tone of the film—enhanced by Paul Henning's original score, limpid lighting, and moody shot compositions—offers a subtle counterpoint to Lokitis's characteristic passion and energy in the cause of the town, though the filmmakers smartly allow their camera to dwell at times on a sadness already etched in the young man's face. As a footnote, Lokitis was ordered to vacate in 2009, his home was demolished before the year was out, and he moved to a new one several miles away.

Despite its low production value—it was shot on DV and edited on Adobe Premiere Pro for $500—*Centralia to Remember* stands up well to its professional media equivalents made with television, festivals, and DVDs in mind. Describing the town's past and present, college professor Gorokhovich made the thirty-two-minute film for the benefit of students in his environmental geology class. The film is edited with a flair for the dramatic potential of its subject and carries an inventive soundtrack, including "Paradise Lost" by Australian vocalist-composer Lisa Gerrard and Irish composer Patrick Cassidy, as well as several classical piano compositions performed by Svetlana Gorokhovich. Moreover, *Centralia to Remember* opens on a high cultural note by quoting from Anton Chekhov's play *Uncle Vanya*, one of Astrov's speeches bemoaning environmental ruin through man's careless and greedy exploitation of natural resources. "This story," Gorokhovich continues, referring to Centralia, "is yet another page in the book of human aspirations ruined by human negligence and incompetence." Befitting its primarily didactic purpose, the film combines a historical overview with a measure of technical detail required by its original student audience. The expert witnesses, however, keep most of this information at the level of the general viewer's understanding. One of them, Steve Jones, chief of the Mine Hazards Division of the Pennsylvania DER, makes the telling point that the cost of isolating and extinguishing the fire at that point would have been prohibitive given the limits of the $25 million annual allocation to the state's entire abandoned mine reclamation program. The film's dialectical edge comes from interviews with residents who recapitulate old divisions within the community. John Comarnisky, a teacher then still living in the town, suggests that most citizens willingly relocated less out of fear for their health and safety than out of an expectation of healthy profit from their compulsory home sales. And when Comarnisky alludes to the lucrative prospect of some three million tons of coal remaining in a twenty-five-foot vein beneath a watercourse and thus safe from the fire, we are reminded of a long-held suspicion of the official motives for having cleared the town. Jones, however, refutes this assertion, insisting that the government acquired surface properties alone and held no mineral rights. Comarnisky, like Lokitis before him, firmly believes that Centralia could revive if people were allowed to buy back the land, an intriguing but unlikely scenario in the present circumstances. Asked if a lesson is to be learned from the tragedy, 88-year-old Lamar Mervine, the last mayor of Centralia, is succinct: "If there's a mine fire today, put it out tomorrow."

In making *Centralia: Pennsylvania's Lost Town*, Joe Sapienza follows his predecessors by approaching the subject from a position broadly sympathetic to the trials and tribulations of the local community. The film emphasizes the role played by local activists, especially a body known as the Concerned Citizens Action Group, formed to challenge a relocation of residents that had begun as early as 1969. Correspondingly, the film implies a criticism of government for its poor judgment of the situation, for not providing enough money at a time when the fire could have been extinguished, and for failing to determine the true extent of the fire's reach within the town lines. The epigraphic shot that opens the film sets this tone. It quotes US President Ronald Reagan: "The nine most terrifying words in the English language—I'm from the government, and I'm here to help." By 1983, twenty-one years after the fire had broken out, state and federal governments had already given up on extinguishing it since the estimated cost of putting out the fire had risen to $660 million. According to talking head Jack Carling, the state's Disaster Programs Director assigned to the Centralia case (and a northeastern Pennsylvanian himself), Reagan's Interior Secretary, James G. Watt, had effectively written off Centralia with the aforementioned $42 million grant from the Abandoned Mine Land Trust Fund to help the state underwrite the relocation process. Meanwhile, residents had been offered a maximum relocation payment of $15,000 plus incidentals and moving costs.

Sapienza's film mirrors Gorokhovich's by reintroducing the conspiracy theory that government was aware of potential coal company interest in a massive vein of anthracite untouched by the fire. We learn that the north side of the town is safe from the fire for geologic and geographic reasons. It would seem to follow that if the borough of Centralia eventually ceases to exist, then the state acquires the rich coal deposits there.

The implication is that a depopulated area could be reopened to coal mining and that this possibility may have played a part in official thinking about how best to deal with the fire. An anti-relocation group led by former resident Helen Womer had long suspected a tacit arrangement regarding the residual coal that might ultimately be advantageous both to the Commonwealth of Pennsylvania and interested coal companies. However, as Jones had earlier told Gorokhovich, this proffered scenario was unrealistic since the government held no mineral rights that it could feasibly sell to any mining operator. In this context, we meet John Comarnisky again, whom Sapienza ran into by chance while filming in the town. The tactic of introducing a younger Centralian's perspective recalls a similar role played by John Lokitis in *The Town That Was*. Comarnisky re-emerges as an engaging talking head with strong and unchanged opinions on the fate of his hometown and the potential exploitation of the untouched northside coal reserves.

FICTION

To date, there have been no fiction films based on the Knox disaster, but as the Centralia story entered the popular imagination, several filmmakers and producers recognized its potential as a formative element in constructing narrative fiction destined for commercial release. *Made in USA* (1987), directed by Ken Friedman, introduces two young unemployed men—played by Adrian Pasdor and the late Chris Penn—eager to leave the grim reality of their deserted and boarded-up hometown for the possibilities of a cross-country adventure. The film's opening image, Centralia's faded town sign, is soon followed by the two men passing one of the signs indicating a closed-off highway—in reality, that notorious section of PA 61—cracked by heat from the fire. These quasi-documentary shots form part of an extended opening sequence shot in Centralia and other regional coal towns. Thereafter, in the critical consensus, the film becomes a nondescript road movie, its attempted messages of postindustrial trauma soon lost amid high jinks with hot cars and even hotter girls. A horror comedy, *Nothing but Trouble* (1991), written and directed by Dan Ackroyd, was released to uniformly poor reviews and box-office failure despite the presence of Aykroyd, Chevy Chase, John Candy, and Demi Moore. Another road movie, it follows four friends who, on a trip from Manhattan to Atlantic City, detour from the New Jersey Turnpike only to get stuck in Valkenvania, a burnt-out city directly inspired by Centralia, and composed of dilapidated houses, vent pipes for boreholes, and a population of roving rednecks.

The increasing popularity of video games led to the creation of *Silent Hill*, a long-running Japanese horror survival series set in a small American town, abandoned and fog-shrouded in one of its several multiversal dimensions. In 2006, the game, which had garnered a devoted following, inspired the most interesting of these Centralia-inspired movie fictions, *Silent Hill*, directed by Christophe Gans. It begins with Rose Da Silva (Radha Mitchell) taking her adopted daughter Sharon (Jodelle Ferland) to the town of Silent Hill, the name of which Sharon has been crying out while sleepwalking. Having taken the now familiar closed-off highway, their car crashes, and, on coming around, Rose discovers that Sharon is missing. Continuing on foot, Rose passes a decaying town sign and gets sprinkled with falling ash. By adding the highway and falling ash to the video game's clouds of fog, the movie's writer, Roger Avary, acknowledged the influence of Centralia since his father, a mining engineer, used to tell him stories about the town. Avary had been fascinated since childhood by the idea of a town decimated by an uncontrollable underground fire, so he decided to use Centralia as the basis for *Silent Hill*. Mixed reviews called the movie visually striking but hampered by a rambling and confusing plot. One reviewer, Don Lewis, called it the "best-looking bad film" he had ever seen. Whatever its merits—or those of its 2012 sequel, *Silent Hill: Revelation*—it remains the best example of how the Centralia story has been appropriated occasionally and fragmentarily by the commercial film sector.

OTHER POSTHISTORICAL DISASTERS

The momentous consequences of disasters for entire communities, their elements of human and technological drama, and their sheer newsworthiness have rendered them—along with major episodes of labor strife such as the Great Strike of 1902—the most visible milestones in the chronology of anthracite history. In the posthistorical period, Knox and Centralia were followed by the 1963 mine disaster at Sheppton and the 1977 Porter Tunnel disaster near Tower City when nine men were lost following a flood in the Kocher mine. To these four catastrophes, we may add the untoward consequence of drilling the 400-foot-deep, 3.5-foot-wide Old Forge Borehole in 1961 to relieve the build-up of water from the post-Knox flooded mine system that threatened to inundate basements in an area covering the boroughs of Duryea, Old Forge, and Pittston. Acid mine drainage from the borehole seeping into the Lackawanna River became the biggest source of Susquehanna River-borne pollution to reach the Chesapeake Bay. Though the amount has lessened over the years from a high of nearly 150 million, between forty and sixty million gallons of contaminated water are still discharged daily from this drain. Plans have long been drawn up for a treatment plant to be built a short way downriver, but it has yet to materialize. Only a few miles away,

George Harvan, *Mine Rescue Team, Porter Tunnel*, b&w photograph, 1977. (Image: courtesy of National Canal Museum, a program of the Delaware & Lehigh National Heritage Corridor, Easton, Pennsylvania.)

the Butler Mine Tunnel in Pittston, built in the 1930s to facilitate drainage of a five-square-mile underground complex, became another notorious disaster site from 1979 after it was discovered that billions of gallons of toxic industrial waste, notably oily liquids, had been poured illegally into an old ventilator shaft going down to the tunnel and thence into the Susquehanna River. The federal government designated the tunnel a Superfund site; in 2021, the Environmental Protection Agency finally took it off the list of such sites.

To the casual observer, the Old Forge and Butler sites may be small, insignificant, and unprepossessing features of a lengthy waterway in endless flow, yet both are historical disaster sites out of all proportion to their size, and both tell grimly of anthracite posthistory in the form of their effluent, the yellow-orange iron oxide precipitate ("Yellow Boy") that stains the rocks of the river bed a garish rusty shade. Despite the dramatic visual and environmental effects of its disgorged contents, the Old Forge Borehole lies off a side street in an unremarkable location. The Butler Tunnel discharge point, perhaps seen best from the west side of the Susquehanna River, appears equally inconspicuous as a relatively minor feature in the overall aquatic scene, but it lies in a picturesque riverscape close to Pittston Junction, the confluence of the Susquehanna and the Lackawanna, the smaller river joining the larger on the eastern side. From a distant vantage point, particularly in sunshine, the eastern shoreline in places gives the illusion of an inviting sandy beach; the reality, though, is of discoloration and defacement. For miles, we see glaring proof of toxic emissions from the old deep mine network, the unmistakable evidence of a long-term accumulation of acidic pollution from the Northern Anthracite Mine Pool, a blight moreover that shows no sign of coming to an end.

This contaminated scenario is by no means confined to the northern field. We find another prominent example in the eastern middle field: the five-mile-long Jeddo Tunnel near Drums, built in the 1890s. In the posthistorical era, it has run the Old Forge Borehole close in its record of toxic drainage into the Susquehanna River via the Nescopeck and Little Nescopeck Creeks watershed, of which 55.38 miles are AMD affected. Numerous other incidents of subsidence, underground mine fires, and abandoned mine drainage have occurred across all four anthracite fields and have received lesser or greater degrees of publicity. The Schuylkill Action Network, for instance, an alliance of over 100 partners active since 2003, currently reports eleven AMD mitigation projects in the Schuylkill River headwaters stretching across Schuylkill County and into Carbon County at the eastern end of the Panther Valley.

Also, less well-known or less officially documented have been the shorter- or longer-term effects of such disastrous occurrences on individual victims and regional communities at large. Though the historical record associates these traumatic experiences with specific dates and places, their fuller history in the sense of a constructed narrative continues to develop and change over time. Correspondingly, individual and group perceptions of these events, as well as interpretations of their meaning, remain fluid and often contestable on an arc of tension between public and personal spheres, between memory and forgetting, between then and now.

The academic study of hazard and disaster has existed since the 1920s, mostly anchored in the natural and social sciences and various forms of engineering. Much research in the field has concentrated on applying scientific and technical knowledge to managing risk, response, and recovery. Social science research in been extensive. More recently, an emerging branch known as critical disaster studies seeks to challenge some established viewpoints and methods. In their introduction to the subject, Jacob Remes and Andy Horowitz set out "three core principles," namely that "disasters are interpretive fictions, disasters are political, and disasters take place over time" (2). By following this set of principles, critical disaster theorists do not ignore the reality of human suffering and loss, or damage to the environment, which would be both absurd and irresponsible; rather, they suggest ways of understanding and responding to disasters that go beyond the immediate and the pragmatic. We may hope that this interdisciplinary broadening of the field will allow for further valuable work on the numerous disasters that have become synonymous with the turbulent history of the anthracite region.

CHAPTER THREE

MODES OF RECALL

MATERIAL CULTURE

We may define material culture as the physical evidence of man-made objects. For the anthracite historian, material culture offers a rich source of evidence in the form of industrial, commercial, and domestic artifacts. Originating in the disciplines of archaeology, anthropology, and art history, the study of material culture, according to an early description by Thomas J. Schlereth, examines through artifacts "the belief systems—the values, ideas, attitudes, and assumptions—of a particular community or society, usually across time" (313). Over the past several decades, the field has grown increasingly interdisciplinary and now plays a substantial part in studying history. The meaning of historical objects invokes a strong sense of nostalgia whereby we perceive a satisfying link between past and present, a search for continuity across time and through successive generations. Jules David Prown reminds us that "objects created in the past are the only historical occurrences that continue to exist in the present" (3) and are, therefore, "excellent and special indexes of culture, concretions of the realities of belief of other people in other times and places, ready and able to be reexperienced and interpreted today" (16). Traditionally, however, museum collections, as the main repositories of historical artifacts, have been selective in favor of unique items of monetary and rarity value or of association with famous persons, places, and events. Mass-produced items have often been overlooked or underestimated, though this is less the case today, especially within collections specializing in the history of industrial and working-class communities, such as the Anthracite Heritage Museum. These collections have opened up prominent space for ordinary domestic and commercial items that stimulate, in turn, the construction of personal and social narratives wherein we engage our faculty of memory. In applying the evidence of material culture to the story of anthracite, we should remember, as with any historical phenomenon, that the process moves logically through several necessary stages. Industrial archaeologists call the first stage a *recording* of the raw data of an object for purposes of basic identification and classification. The second stage of *deductive analysis*, write Briann Greenfield and Patrick Malone, "leads to insights on form, function, materials, and manufacturing techniques." The third stage, of greatest interest to the social historian, is of *interpretation* of the object's meaning within broader domestic, communal, and industrial contexts and its significance to underlying patterns of personal or public history.

As for the various branches of material culture open to these investigative stages, Prown proposes a broad categorical list of artifacts "that progresses from the more decorative (or aesthetic) to the more utilitarian" (2). His six categories consist of art, diversions, adornment, modifications of the landscape, applied arts, and devices. For my purposes, I discuss the category of "art" in Chapter Four since I identify it primarily as an umbrella opened over several representational forms. Since material culture embraces the built environment, my discussion of sites below addresses Prown's "landscape modification" category, including interior and exterior aspects of anthracite-related structures. Even the design of a museum is relevant insofar as its architectural features, internal layout, and logistical methods are influential factors in shaping our experience of that site and its contents. Prown's category of "devices" is central to our understanding of anthracite history, as it includes industrial machinery, tools, implements, scientific and musical instruments, and vehicles. Though such devices, smaller ones, in particular, may also be found in the collectors' marketplace, they are typically standard items in the collections of museums and historical societies. For instance, the Museum of Anthracite Mining in Ashland focuses its display on devices, the vast majority of which date from the industrial era, since posthistorical production of mining-related artifacts has grown sparser due to shrinking demand.

My focus is on four areas of material culture bearing particularly on anthracite posthistory: sites, signs, souvenir merchandise, and historical archaeology. The second and third of these areas function principally in an associative manner. While signs also conform to Prown's "art" category due to their aesthetic dimension, they belong mainly in a discussion of modes of recall for their primary indexical function and, therefore, by their direct relation to the physical location of specific sites. The area of souvenir (by definition a "token of remembrance") merchandise, which in any age feeds a commercialized taste for nostalgia and commemoration, is one that may "speak" historically by way of its looser connotative value. This area includes clothing and jewelry (Prown's "adornment" category), posters, postcards, stickers, other printed items, reproduction artworks ("art"), ornaments, and receptacles ("applied arts").

The physical evidence of the anthracite industry in objects and landscapes is a powerful marker of its history. Most objects of historical value find their way into museums or private collections. Sites, whether accessible or not to the general public, remain visible as a distinctive element in the region's landscape. In telling of the anthracite, the experience of visiting sites connected with the industry in one way, or another offers an incontrovertible visual testament and, in some cases, an emotionally charged experience, as for some visitors, it may trigger poignant memories of a vanished and once familiar way of life. We may categorize anthracite region sites as active, abandoned, repurposed, or purpose-built. Some sites—for instance, monuments and memorial areas indicative of both modes of recall and representational forms—may fall into either repurposed or purpose-built categories. Active coal mining sites incorporating modern processing plants and ancillary structures, waste mounds, and stripping pits concern us less from a historical viewpoint, though any active site offers its own story to be told as a part of a complete anthracite history. By being aware of the present, we may better understand the past and vice versa. As long as anthracite continues to be mined in the region, a continuity exists between active and abandoned sites. Culm banks, for instance, which are sites literally of towering significance to the telling of this history, are still formed and utilized by companies, as coal waste must accumulate somewhere before it can be disposed of or transported onward to other processing facilities such as co-generation plants.

AESTHETICS OF THE ANTHRACITE LANDSCAPE

It may be difficult for some to appreciate a shattered anthracite landscape for its formal qualities, but a long tradition of representing industrial landscapes, architecture, and artifacts exists in the work of artists, be they writers, sculptors, painters, photographers, or filmmakers. I look more closely at their work in Chapters Four and Five. To understand the principles of this appreciation and the historic conjunction of art and industry, we may look back to the later eighteenth century. Aesthetics of the *sublime*, defined originally in a treatise by the Roman author Longinus, found fresh expression in the work notably of Edmund Burke, whose main claim to fame is *Reflections on the Revolution in France* (1790). The sublime re-emerged at the dawn of romanticism to challenge neoclassical definitions of form and beauty established in the age of the Enlightenment. Burke proposed as sublime the beauty in nature epitomized by vast and powerful aspects of the natural world, such as mountains, cliffs, ravines, volcanoes, cataracts, and waterfalls. These phenomena have in common an ability to inspire in the beholder a sense of wonder and exhilaration combined at once with fear, terror even. In the true sense of a much-misused word, they were awesome to the point of overwhelming body and mind.

To grasp the connection with anthracite history, we should understand that the developing sublime in England and then elsewhere in Europe corresponded to the birth of the Industrial Revolution. An alternative concept of the sublime thus existed alongside and in contrast to nature, one in which huge man-made structures were perceived to have many of the same attributes and effects on their viewers as their natural counterparts. In the United States, the sublime referred initially to natural wonders such as the Grand Canyon or Niagara Falls and especially to mountainous scenes in the West whose size and grandeur were keenly captured in the work of landscape painters. Subsequently, as David E. Nye has shown, the Industrial Revolution of the nineteenth century and its continued development in the twentieth century spawned an American technological sublime in structures such as bridges, dams, skyscrapers, train stations, tunnels, and airports, and in which the *industrial sublime*—represented by grain elevators, blast furnaces, factories, collieries, and so forth—played a major part.

At the height of the anthracite industry, colliery structures imposed their forms upon the northeastern Pennsylvania landscape. Those structures included powerhouses, smokestacks, sorting and washing sheds, tipples, headframes, and various other facilities necessary for coal mine operations. Among these structures, none was more imposing than the coal breaker, which, along with the equally massive culm bank, loomed large in the anthracite landscape—triumphantly and authoritatively to some, oppressively and menacingly to others. No matter that the breaker was a dirty, noisy, dangerous place to work, nor that it symbolized the power and will of the company that owned it, its indispensability to the processing of hard coal made it a unique feature of the landscape and a central symbol of the industrial identity of the region. Yet, despite its functional role, it could also be appreciated for its architectural and mechanical forms; above all, for its sublime mass and power.

ABANDONED SITES

Across the coal region, we may still see remains of the former anthracite industry, though less so as years pass and demolition or removal run their course. Our sightings may range from a few pieces of rusting machinery, a pile of brickwork, or a cluster of buildings to something as unavoidable as a culm bank or, as in the notorious case of Centralia, the entire site of a town. Concrete City, in the Hanover section of Nanticoke, is less known than Centralia but with its own small measure of notoriety. As described by its historian, the late Robert A. Janosov, it was an innovative housing scheme for its time, solely using poured concrete as a construction material. Built by the coal division of the Delaware, Lackawanna, and

Concrete City, Nanticoke. (Photo: Cynthia A. Carmickle, 2019.)

Western Railroad Company (DL&W) in 1911 to house mine workers at its Truesdale Colliery, the project was abandoned in 1924 after its ownership had passed to the Glen Alden Coal Company. Despite the structural problem of dampness that doomed the project as a habitable space, its sheer durability guaranteed its physical survival, and in recent years it has attracted its share of "dark" tourists whose visits have resulted mainly in a plethora of colorful graffiti adorning a peaceful, yet somehow disquieting site hidden from street view (where stands a historical marker) by a patch of wooded ground.

Until the 1980s, it was still possible to visit many semi-intact coal-related sites across the region. During the protracted decline of the industry, abandoned collieries proliferated, their structures often standing derelict for years, awaiting eventual demolition and removal. Though these structures stood on private property, they were dispersed over large areas of land that were generally deserted and well-nigh impossible to patrol. It was not difficult for the general public to access them on foot or in motorized vehicles. Having grown up in the Wilkes-Barre area in the 1970s and 1980s, Michael G. Rushton describes the area as "our playground: the old coal buildings, the culm dumps, and the old railroad lines and trestles" adding that it was "like exploring a lost world," one offering an irresistible thrill despite his acknowledgment that "we probably should not have been around any of it, to say the least" (11). Conscious of the risks he took in photographing anthracite relics, he refers pointedly at the beginning of his book on them to the "Stay Out, Stay Alive" state program designed to discourage casual visitors to former mining sites. As they roamed these places, Rushton and his friends, like countless others in the area, immersed themselves in anthracite history, often unconsciously. Older residents of the region have tended anyway to view such sites as fundamental to their former experience of daily life. When coal was king, those sites, whether or not one liked them, were taken for granted in the struggle for communal and economic survival. Only in their desolation have they become historical curiosities. Simple and gratuitous recreational pleasures, taken regardless of trespass during the anthracite era, persist in today's popularity of dirt bike and ATV riding on culm banks and old mining grounds. Such unauthorized outings have even been legitimized and redirected toward regional tourism, as I describe below in the section on repurposed sites.

Exploring subsurface mining sites is another matter altogether. It remains an experience that is largely off-limits to the general public, as it is extremely dangerous and requires specialized knowledge of complicated subterranean geography and geophysics. One anthracite region group dedicated to this pursuit is the Underground Miners, who, among other more restricted projects, periodically offer guided tours of old mine shafts and tunnels. By the 1990s, most surface sites had disappeared, and a process of repurposing (for instance, the rehabilitation of culm banks and renovation of buildings) had gotten underway. In addition, underground mine sites in Ashland, Lansford, and Scranton have been adapted to the demands of public history and reopened for organized tourism. Besides the remnants of coal, the region still has many other abandoned manufacturing sites, notably factories, of which some escape wholesale demolition to be converted into residential or commercial properties.

Ironically, at a time when most anthracite relics have disappeared, the informal and unauthorized exploration of abandoned industrial sites has become a widespread and documented subcultural movement since the mid-1990s, a phenomenon intensified by the rapid growth of the Internet and its boundless interactive capabilities. Scholars have interpreted this adventurous practice, mainly the province of a younger generation emboldened by a spirit of transgressive daredevilry, as representing a dynamic and radical alternative to a static and conservative heritage culture typified by museums, art exhibitions, memorial sites, and commercialized tours. These unconventional tourists belong to an exclusive group of leisure seekers; their intrepid expeditions are prompted and facilitated via the reach of information technology. Underlining the subjective and indeterminate nature of the tourist gaze, their resistance to prescribed accounts of history results in what John Urry calls a "performativity of reminiscence" in which "sites are not uniformly read and passively accepted by visitors" (101-02).

In telling of the anthracite, abandoned sites invariably lack interpretive aids. Markers, monuments, or exhibits rarely offer descriptions or explanations of a site and its history. However, this does not mean they cannot contribute to the anthracite narrative. Rather, it suggests that individual beholders may let their imaginations roam freely within their private stock of historical knowledge and personal associations. This contrasts with most repurposed and purpose-built sites where history presents itself as a relatively fixed and systematic telling of stories via the intermediaries of written language and visual image, and in the case of organized tours via the spoken word of the guide. In these settings, the spoken word often also takes the form of audio recordings transmitted through loudspeakers or headphones. However imaginative or challenging, this kind of authoritative history telling unfolds very differently from noncurated experiences, for even if soft-pedaled, it has a didactic as much as a purely informational function. Hence the importance placed on the educational aspect of interpreted history by heritage initiatives, organizations, and institutions, from the smallest memorial sites to the largest museum spaces. The telling of history at any conventional site thus engages with and may even be contested by the highly subjective viewpoint of an individual visitor. To that extent, any engagement with history, any conscious reflection on the past, whether public or private, may be seen as an interpretive act. Our understanding and judgment of wide-ranging and often complex historical evidence depend as much on our sense of identity, ideological profile, and emotional state as our measured assessment of the hard evidence. The science of hermeneutics teaches us that history has an ontological element: the interpretive act is not only about the facts of the past as they are variously represented but also about our present existence. We bring our whole selves to our historical responses.

To some, the disappearance of material evidence in the anthracite region is no cause for regret; to others, though, its survival is a strong reminder of the industry's dominance; to others, yet, albeit a minority, the remainder is worth appreciating. Dilapidation and disintegration may give rise to new aesthetic experiences. Twists and tangles of rusting metal; crumbling and rotting of wood, brick, and stone; broken glass—such may take on intriguingly abstract or surreal forms. Visual artists working in multi-media forms have explored this aesthetic in creative ways. Valuable memories may be stimulated by the sight of processed materials or manufactured objects discarded and scattered in a semblance of order (e.g., culm banks) or in complete disorder. It is not too fanciful to consider abandoned anthracite sites in this way, as studies of how memory works and how places affect us have broadened our understanding of the strange appeal of such sites and their particular meanings to those individuals who experience them. The skeptical view may be of useless rubble and hideous scars on the earth, but that would discredit the responses of diverse interpretive communities, each of which, writes David Nye, may claim "the right to establish its own aesthetic standards" (xvii).

These sites may have lost their original functionality and, with it, their symbolic industrial value, but their obsolescence and ruination, their roughened and broken forms have allowed them to survive as spaces for formal appreciation tied to an overriding sense of loss. Returning to the debate begun in the eighteenth century, these relics have morphed from the industrial sublime into the *industrial picturesque*, whereby we understand "picturesque" not as "quaint" or "pretty" but as visually and affectively striking *because* they have become ruins, mere vehicles of memory. As such, they can arouse deep nostalgia for a vanished industry and its way of life. Open to the elements and recolonization by nature—animal and vegetable—they carry a similar historical weight and atmospheric power as does, for instance, a ruined medieval abbey set amid the scenic European countryside.

Unfortunately, few coal region sites remain either in a state of repair or even disrepair, for the field of *industrial archaeology* directs us toward the value of preserving them and placing them in a historical context. A term coined in the 1950s by American scholar Michael Rix, industrial archaeology, in the words of one of its pioneers, British scholar Angus (R.A.) Buchanan "is concerned with an examination of the process of industrialization through a systematic study of its surviving monuments and artefacts." (21) The field expanded rapidly in the late-1960s and 1970s as interest grew in identifying, documenting, and interpreting industrial relics. The art of photography has proven especially important in securing an archaeological record of those relics, constructing their sociohistorical meanings, and encouraging appreciation of their formal qualities. Fortunately, we have removed many anthracite artifacts—as small as a miner's lamp or as large as a coal car—to museums of varying size and scope. In this respect, a good comparison in McDade Park in Scranton is between the state-run Anthracite Heritage Museum with its ample exhibition space and the adjacent county-run Lackawanna Coal Mine tour, which includes a single-room museum space within its complex.

It is a different matter when the size or bulk of buildings and other structures prevent them from being removed from their original sites and relocated to exhibition spaces. Unless they can be repurposed in situ, they are at risk otherwise of becoming derelict and likely demolished. Regarding such relics, preservation has proven to be a most pressing and controversial activity in the anthracite region. The most lamentable example of regional loss is the classic anthracite breaker. By the 2010s, only two breakers still stood: the St. Nicholas, between Shenandoah and Mahanoy City, and the Huber, in Ashley. Once the largest coal breaker in the world, "St. Nick" was the size of one city block and was capable of processing 12,000 tons of anthracite daily. Any attempt at restoration with an eye to historical tourism would have required an inordinate sum

Huber Colliery, Ashley, 2002. (Photo by the author.)

of money and would have needed to consider both its relatively remote location (albeit not far from US Interstate 81) and the presence of an active and extensive stripping operation within one mile. St. Nick was demolished in 2018. As for the Huber (see discussion of the film *Beyond the Breaker* in Chapter Five), despite a comparable cost estimate, an opportunity to convert it into a unique historical site was missed due to a regrettable failure of vision and lack of will on the part of stakeholders in government and business alike. The Huber Breaker Preservation Society fought valiantly for years to save the site, but ultimately its stock of historical and technical knowledge, along with its impassioned pleas, were ignored, and the breaker went under the wrecker's ball in 2014. Its visibility and easy access from a stretch of Interstate 81 south of Wilkes-Barre made the Huber potentially an ideal heritage tourist destination. Its renovation as a historical attraction could have revitalized the town of Ashley and ensured that at least one breaker remained within the entire region (Eckley Miners' Village has a stripped-down replica breaker constructed in the late 1960s as part of the *Molly Maguires* film set and now itself in need of renovation). Consequently, we lost the last chance to save a precious example of the most distinctive architectural symbol of the mining of anthracite coal.

REPURPOSED SITES

Repurposing mine sites means using former mining infrastructure and landscape for new activities such as heritage and tourist attractions, parks and recreation areas, and residential and commercial developments. It is an elaborate and costly process to reclaim a site to stabilize an environment where damaged ecosystems may be allowed to recover, and new activities may safely and successfully take place. Provided they are recognized as such, these repurposed sites become valuable indicators of anthracite history while serving communal and regional needs and stimulating local economies. Other sites simply disappear in the repurposing process as surface structures are removed, and the terrain is returned to nature via re-earthing and replanting initiatives. Some may feel that these initiatives, though environmentally beneficial and aesthetically pleasing, conveniently erase the evidence of a significant and often contentious past; others, however, may encourage and welcome the physical repair and restored use-value of these sites. As we have seen in the context of disaster, the tension between a need to remember and to forget is a recurrent theme in the posthistory of the anthracite region.

This category of repurposed sites excludes buildings not on former mining-related sites. Those include ones originally used by the industry for office or educational purposes. They have been the simplest to repurpose, as, unlike most industrial sites, they have fallen less into disuse or dilapidation and may have required only moderate interior or exterior remodeling to fulfill their subsequent functions.

Opened in 2021, the new Wilkes-Barre Area High School sits on a 77-acre site of the former Prospect Colliery of the Lehigh Valley Coal Company in Plains Township. In 1912, this thirty-seven-year-old colliery set a world record of 104,600 tons for monthly production of anthracite coal at a single facility. Surface mining later continued on the site until the area school board bought it from Pagnotti Enterprises in 2019. The school project remained controversial mainly on environmental

Mining and Mechanical Institute building, Freeland. (Photo: Cynthia A. Carmicle, 2019.)

grounds, as concerns had been expressed over building a school on previously unlined toxic coal ash dumps. A salutary reminder of what may befall a disused building of historical value is the case of the Pennsylvania Coal Company branch headquarters in Dunmore. Built in 1870, this three-story building was last used as a nursing home until falling empty in 2002. After unsuccessful efforts to place the building on the National Register of Historic Places, a fire in May 2016 set by teenage arsonists destroyed most of the building. By contrast, an outstanding example of a repurposed site, especially from an architectural viewpoint, is the MMI Preparatory School building in Freeland. The Industrial School for Miners and Mechanics was founded in 1879 by coal baron Eckley B. Coxe and developed by his widow Sophia Georgianna (*aka* the "Angel of the Anthracite"). Originally located in Drifton, the renamed Mining and Mechanical Institute opened in 1893 in a handsome new building in Freeland, where carefully selected miners enrolled in night school classes. Lack of enrollment forced the Institute to close after World War Two, and a preparatory school replaced it in 1970. Meanwhile, in 1964, the building was reconstructed in keeping with the original style after a fire had destroyed its front wing. Its white dome was salvaged from the wreckage and re-erected. The handsomely restored building continues to suggest the erstwhile power and prestige of the coal industry that had brought it into being.

Abandoned sites that have passed into postindustrial ownership may also become locations for business enterprises and housing schemes. One current example of such a project is at the former Pancoast Mine in Throop, abandoned since 1936 and the scene of a 1911 disaster that left 73 dead. In early 2022, local real estate developer Donald Rinaldi, whose family has owned much of the original mining site since 1972, announced a proposal to build a mix of senior citizen residences and offices on the property. Rinaldi is also currently involved in the residential redevelopment of the former Scranton Lace Company factory, another prominent abandoned industrial site in the same area.

Repurposing projects of any kind must consider the continuing danger of mine subsidence, which remains a common occurrence across the anthracite region and may sometimes generate tensions among landowners, residents, and local authorities. Statewide, by 2014, the DEP Bureau of Abandoned Mine Reclamation (BAMR) averaged 313 subsidence investigations per annum. In the context of residential repurposing, a certain irony attends to the postindustrial construction of housing on former mining properties given a long history of homes, often those of mining families, succumbing in lesser or greater ways to subsidence throughout the industrial era. A degree of risk remains in building new homes, or any new structures for that matter, on potentially unstable land. "Revealing a buried past," writes Bill Conlogue, "a mine subsidence reminds people that history troubles the present" (2).

Repurposing may also take the form of monuments, memorial parks, and those industrial sites restored partly or entirely as historical attractions. Projects of this kind are not always successful, as in the case of the proposed Ashley Planes Heritage Park, planned to arise on over 400 acres of land acquired by the Earth Conservancy in 1994 from the bankrupt Blue Coal Corporation. An extraordinary feat of engineering that remained unchanged in design until it ceased operation in 1948, the Planes consisted of three long slopes up which coal was hauled in cars utilizing a cable system to the mountain top whence it descended to loading docks on the Lehigh Canal. A relatively elaborate scheme, the park project eventually failed because of anticipated costs and an uncooperative corporate landowner—a scenario comparable in both respects to the effort to save the Huber Breaker, whose proposed restoration as a heritage attraction could have linked it directly to those Planes that once carried its coal to market.

Smaller-scale projects are generally more viable and successful because of more compact land areas and lower construction and maintenance costs. Whether sitting on repurposed or purpose-built sites, memorial parks incorporating monuments and other installations offer visitors an opportunity to briefly detach themselves from the rush of the surrounding world to reflect on the daily lives of local miners or on cataclysmic events in the unfolding of the anthracite story. Due mainly to the efforts of the Plymouth Historical Society and the Anthracite Living History group, assisted in their land acquisition by the Earth Conservancy, the Avondale Mine Memorial Garden at the mine site commemorates the September 6, 1869, fire disaster that claimed the lives of 110 miners and boys and led directly to the introduction of safety measures in Pennsylvania anthracite mines. Sitting a short distance below US 11, the garden is a good example of how a space comprising some rough colliery remnants became an attractive historical destination due to local volunteer dedication and effort. In addition to restoration work carried out on the mine tunnel and the placing of information kiosks, including a display of old newspaper accounts of the disaster, an overgrown site filled with debris from illegal dumping was transformed into a tidily planted area of flowers, shrubs, and grass lending a beautiful aspect and a peaceful atmosphere to a place marked by tragic association. One problem, however, faced by isolated and unpatrolled sites such as this one is their vulnerability to anti-social and criminal activity. In 2020, one of the kiosks was vandalized, and all four security cameras were stolen. A related site is the Washburn Street Welsh Cemetery in the Hyde Park section of Scranton, where, in association with the Lackawanna Historical Society, sixty-one graves and a bronze marker commemorate Avondale victims. These related sites resonate with anthracite history enthusiasts, as commemorative ceremonies are held there in September. In this way, the sites and their stories become known to a greater number of people.

Avondale Disaster Memorial Garden. (Photo: Cynthia A. Carmickle, 2019.)

It is not an easy task to tell of the anthracite beyond the region, so it is notable that at the 2012 North American Festival of Wales, organized by the North American Wales Foundation and held that year in Scranton, the saga of Avondale, in which the majority of victims were Welsh, was introduced to a national and international audience.

Dating from 1972, the Lattimer Massacre Memorial is located on the site of a tragedy that occurred on September 10, 1897, when nineteen striking miners marching for equal pay and better conditions were murdered by a posse of Luzerne County sheriff's deputies. Six more died of their injuries; thirty-eight others were wounded. The massacre, which happened on the edge of the town, is marked by a boulder informally known as the "rock of remembrance" or the "rock of solidarity," at whose base are displayed several chunks of coal, a pick, and a shovel. The celebrated National Farm Workers Association leader César Chavez attended its dedication ceremony, and the UMWA/AFL-CIO donated a plaque placed on the boulder. That a memorial to the victims took seventy-five years to materialize has been a matter of lively debate over the years. Memorial services were held from 1898 to 1908, and $10,000 was raised for a memorial, but the initiative stalled; other than in several books on the subject, the Lattimer massacre fell into a black hole of forgetfulness lasting over sixty years. Though still causing occasional controversy and even downright opposition (the site marker has been defaced more than once), the commemoration of the massacre has evolved from focusing primarily on the class identities of the victims to recognizing their ethnic and religious ties equally. Following the dedication and erection of a PHMC marker at the site, a second marker was erected in 1997, on the 100th anniversary of the massacre, nearby in Harwood; unlike the first, its text specifies victimized ethnic groups as comprising marginalized immigrant workers of southern and eastern European origin. Yet, it is unfortunate that the 1997 celebration, a two-day on-site event with an ethnic dinner, a march, and a one-day conference at Eckley Miners' Village, served to perpetuate a bias in that the strong presence of Italian miners on the 1897 march and in the local community was completely overlooked. A Catholic Mass was held at the memorial until 2005 (with an Interfaith service from 2013 to 2019), while commemorative markers and victims' gravestones may be found in three Hazleton cemeteries: St. Stanislaus's, St. Joseph's, and Vine Street.

On US Highway 209, close to the former site of the LC&N Co's No. 8 Colliery in Coaldale, a Miners' Memorial Park consists of a marker in the form of an information board, some chunks of coal on display, and a brick bus shelter once used by miners. On its sides, three replica 1950s-era company slogans, "A Car A Day Means More Pay," "Did You Produce A Car More Today?" and "Everybody's Goal Is Mine More Coal," were painted by local artist and historian Michael Havrischak for the occasion of the memorial dedication in 2000. Havrischak, who also planted flowers around the base of the shelter, recalled that "these men did not have time to stop and smell the flowers during their lives. The flowers came at their funerals." The shelter is an ingenious commemorative structure in that its ordinariness forcefully represents the daily slog of the mine worker coming and going from his shift, while the replica slogans impress on the visitor the constant company pressure on the miner to increase his productivity. Close by the memorial site stands a PHMC marker dedicated to famed labor activist Mary Harris "Mother" Jones, who led a march of 2,000 women from McAdoo to Coaldale in October 1900 in support of a strike.

Though few former colliery buildings across the region remain fit for repurposing, they have the potential to become attractions of historical and educational value. At the site of the Gravity Slope Colliery in Archbald, operated from 1913 to 1955 by the Delaware & Hudson Coal Company (D&H), a nonprofit civic volunteer group, the Gravity Slope Committee, is renovating three structurally sound buildings—Oil House, Shifting Shanty, and Fan House—into a coffee shop, museum, and restored fan house respectively. The Fan House project aims to restore to working order a rare wooden Guibal Fan, the last intact example of its kind, for display as an important piece of equipment once used to ventilate the mine. As of 2022, the Oil House has been partially restored, but the other two buildings remain in disrepair. Though the entire site is largely overgrown, the sealed-up entrance to the mine also is a potentially distinctive attraction. The whole project comes under the wing of Archbald Borough, which has invested municipal funds in it to supplement a matching grant from the National Park Service "Save America's Treasures" program; another grant from the Lackawanna Valley Heritage Authority (LHVA), which oversees a National and State Heritage Area and whose master plan envisages Gravity Slope as an ideal interpretive site of industrial history; and yet another from the Pennsylvania Department of Transportation (PennDOT). The prospect of a symbiotic relation to other tourist and leisure activities lies in the accessible location of the site close to a park in the southern part of the town and at a point adjacent to the Lackawanna River; to the entrance of the Rails-to-Trails portion of the seventy-mile Lackawanna River Heritage Trail system; and to railroad tracks already carrying passenger excursions beyond Archbald to Carbondale at various times of the year. Due to their rarity value, the remaining buildings at Gravity Slope could assume a historical status disproportionate to their size. Gravity Slope is a good example of how a relatively small site could be integrated into a larger-scale heritage project. It could tell the stories of the colliery, especially its employees and mining technology, and of the town of Archbald for so long dependent upon it for employment and economic benefit. Furthermore, given the LHVA includes the Anthracite Heritage Museum and the Lackawanna Coal Mine Tour as partner sites, Gravity Slope could become a corresponding

Awaiting repurposing: Gravity Slope Colliery, Archbald. (Photo: Cynthia A. Carmickle, 2019.)

location in telling the history of how anthracite drove the Industrial Revolution throughout the Lackawanna Valley.

The Anthracite Outdoor Adventure Area (AOAA) near Shamokin in Coal Township is one repurposed site that would not immediately appear to have historical value. The name it has chosen invites us to think again. A long time in the making, the facility opened to the public in 2013. This enterprise has not been without opposition from many area residents who bemoan the fact that access to the area leased by Northumberland County was formerly free of charge. Operated by the county, the AOAA occupies 7500 acres of reclaimed coal lands for its multipurpose trail system stretching along seventy-five miles of old mining roads

Interpretive sign, Coaldale. (Photo: Cynthia A. Carmickle, 2019.)

and forest tracks. The facility, administered by a four-person authority, is designed mainly to attract two- and four-wheel off-road vehicles for recreational activity in a controlled environment. As a large-scale outdoor project, it requires less remodeling or new construction than other historical sites, though it has opened the main building close to its trailhead. It has also installed informational displays—albeit geographical and geological rather than historical—at one of its lookout points, and it intends to provide some historical context for its visitors at a later stage of development. It has also committed itself to environmental recovery; at Boyers Knob, acid mine drainage pools have been filled, water diverted, and crop-falls (surface holes of coal chutes used in pitch mining) backfilled in partnership with the Bureau of Abandoned Mine Reclamation within the state Department of Environmental Protection. A similar area, occupying around 20,000 acres in Schuylkill and Northumberland counties, is Famous Reading Outdoors (FRO). Trading on the recognition value of the Reading Anthracite company's logo as redesigned to incorporate an off-road tire, this facility comprises eight tracts of land. Its self-description online touches on the context of the visitor's trip by promising "majestic views and mountain top meadows to ghost towns and coal mines from our historic past." We may not readily associate the vast majority of recreational dirt bike and ATV riders with interest in visiting museums and other curated historical sites. And such visits may not be on their list of priority leisure activities. Yet, as we have seen in considering the appeal of abandoned and unofficial sites, individual tourists are free to make what they wish of historical sites, to understand and interpret them in subjective, oblique, and sometimes resistant ways. A rider at AOAA or FRO may well grow aware, even unconsciously, of the history of the terrain over which s/he speeds, bringing to mind the vastness of coal company holdings, the elaborate construction of mining roads and rails, and the long-term damage to the land wreaked by the industry.

Most popular among repurposed sites are those located at former mines, one in each of the three main coal fields, where guided tours function as part of a burgeoning heritage industry promoting the anthracite region. All three tours offer a comparable experience—entering an old mine and discovering what it was like to work in one—but each freely interprets its place within anthracite's overall history. These interpretations also depend on the specifications of each site and its links to regional promotional agencies as well as to other anthracite-related sites. Considerable potential exists for creating a symbiotic relationship to other attractions gathered together beneath the same regional umbrella and for using a range of advanced informational techniques (especially online) capable of expanding on traditional print sources. The three tours are the Pioneer Tunnel Coal Mine and Steam Train in Ashland (middle field), the Lackawanna Coal Mine Tour in Scranton (northern field), and the No. 9 Coal Mine and Museum in Lansford (southern field).

One defunct tour that long predates these more recent initiatives is the Brooks Model Mine in Nay Aug Park, Scranton, established in 1902 as a gift from the company of Reese J. Brooks & Son and opened by the city of Scranton in association with the public education program of the Scranton School of Mines. Closed after 1938, the Scranton Chamber of Commerce began to get visitor requests post-World War Two to "see a coal mine," so the site was spruced up and reopened to the public in 1953 in a move anticipating the heritage tourism of subsequent decades. In 1975, a cave-in of part of the roof led to the mine's closure two years later for structural instability, and it has since been sealed by a metal door despite efforts to reopen it in 2002-03 that foundered on updated legal requirements. However, in early 2022 the nonprofit heritage group Underground Miners inspected the mine, found it in reasonably good shape, and announced plans to renovate and reopen the site as a tourist attraction.

Brooks differs fundamentally from the other three mines. Firstly, it was designed to be demonstrative of a thriving industry and could not be designated as a commemorative site. Secondly, it was never a commercial operation, though its miniature design followed the typical features of a working mine: a tunnel penetrating 150 feet and sloping gently to a depth of 20 feet along a wooden walkway lit by incandescent bulbs. Furthermore, it tapped visibly into a vein of anthracite and featured a miner mannequin and a loaded coal car, both of which peculiarly remain inside the now inaccessible interior. Brooks remains open externally to the tourist gaze much as before, while the continued presence since 1948 of the "Pioneer," a Pennsylvania Coal Company Railroad passenger gravity car, and of a marker erected by a division of the Ancient Order of Hibernians confirms the status of Brooks today as a commemorative site.

By contrast, the first former *working* mine to open to the public in 1963 was the Pioneer Tunnel Coal Mine and Steam Train; the site operated as the Pioneer Colliery of the Philadelphia & Reading Coal & Iron Company from 1911 to 1931 as a horizontal (drift) mine driven 1800 feet into the side of Mahanoy Mountain. Unlike its two equivalents, Pioneer—run by a nonprofit organization, the sixty-year-old Ashland Community Enterprises Incorporated—combines its mine tour with a three-quarter mile narrow-gauge steam train excursion taking visitors to the site of a stripping operation on the Mammoth Vein and the remnants of a bootleg mining hole. The entire attraction is a self-sustaining operation generating its revenue from admission ticket and gift shop sales, though it has recently been the recipient of two grants, one from the Federal Bureau of Abandoned Mine Reclamation for a headframe salvaged from a nearby colliery site, the other from Pennsylvania Tourism, a subdivision of the state Department of Community and Economic Development, for the construction of a new locomotive ("lokie") barn. Though lying adjacent to the Museum of Anthracite Mining, Pioneer is fully independent of this museum, now owned and operated by the Borough of Ashland, which took it over from the PHMC in 2006. The museum building, located on former coal company land that was originally deeded to the state, comprises both exhibition space and borough offices, while the PHMC remains the owner of the exhibit collection, which it reviews and inspects annually. Here is a curious instance of two closely related and physically proximate commemorative sites being shared three ways: by private enterprise, borough, and state, among which exist limited interaction and no formal relationships.

Established in 1959 within the bounds of the Continental Mine and worked until 1966, Slope 190 of the Delaware, Lackawanna & Western Coal Company on the edge of Scranton reopened in 1985 as a tourist attraction. Traversing three anthracite veins on a 1300-foot long and 250-foot-deep slope, the Lackawanna Coal Mine Tour, unlike Pioneer and No. 9, is a county-owned and operated facility. It was established mainly because of its proximity to the state-run Anthracite Heritage Museum, of which it is independent, though these two sites appear to be more reciprocally related to each other than the two Ashland sites: Pioneer and the Museum of Anthracite Mining. The tour can take advantage of visitor throughput from the Anthracite Heritage Museum, which is much larger and gets greater publicity than the MAM. The 126-acre McDade Park complex housing both museum and mine tour has its own history as a compromised landscape, as it was reclaimed from sixty-five acres of badly scarred mining lands. Located on the line between the boroughs of Scranton and Taylor, Lackawanna County bought the land in 1970 to create a recreational area. To that end, the U.S. Bureau of Mines made an initial grant of $291,000 toward site reclamation and gave further monies for subsequent revegetation and pond construction. Originally dedicated in 1975 as Keyser Valley Park, it was renamed in 1977 in honor of US Congressman Joseph M. McDade, who had been largely responsible for securing substantial reclamation funds from the federal government. Though here is not its place, the history of an ongoing process of land reclamation in the anthracite region remains to be told.

The No. 9 Coal Mine and Museum in Lansford occupies the site of a former Lehigh Coal & Navigation Company mine that lays claim to be the world's oldest continuously operating anthracite mine, having been worked from 1855 to 1972. Its owner, the Panther Creek Valley Foundation—like Pioneer, a self-sustaining nonprofit organization dependent primarily on site revenue and donations—opened the museum in 1992, began restoring the interior of the mine in 1995, and opened it to the public in 2002. Unlike Pioneer and Lackawanna, No. 9 does not have another site in its immediate vicinity: other than a miners' memorial elsewhere in Lansford, the closest sites are a 1941 monument to anthracite pioneer Philip Ginder in Summit Hill and the aforementioned memorial park in Coaldale, the towns directly east and west of Lansford respectively. Pioneer takes its visitors 1600 feet into the mountain along a horizontal drift while also permitting them to observe a 900-foot-deep pit shaft just above the original cage platform. The museum, which has been placed on the National Register of Historic Places, is housed in a 1924 wash shanty, thus making further use of the original physical plant.

Putting aside differences in their ownership and operational structures, these three tours share a basic set of attributes. All receive valuable promotional support from the publicity agencies of town, county, regional, and state authorities. This support includes, for instance, short promotional videos running anywhere from one to three minutes in length. Yet, neither mine tours nor agencies need to invest extensively in video coverage of their attractions since unofficial material proliferating on the Internet offers, if not always of guaranteed quality, a wide choice of descriptions and depictions to the interested viewer. Yet, despite this ease of virtual access, most would agree that nothing betters the experience of an in-person tour. What draws the crowd and makes these historical sites effectively telling of the anthracite? All offer an image of the past to the tourist gaze within an authentic setting. All invite visitors to immerse themselves further in mining history by offering souvenirs in their gift shops and placing artifacts, photographs, maps, and paintings in their museum and store spaces and at other strategic points around their sites. All have adopted distinctive logos used both on-site and in publicity material: Pioneer's shows a train trip and a mine trip emerging from the words "coal mine"; Lackawanna's, whose slogan is "Go Down in History," sports the tour's name across a miner's helmet opening into a tunnel; No. 9's is a circular design showing a helmeted miner crossed by pickaxe and shovel. No. 9 also makes eye-catching use of the Old Co. Lehigh Premium Anthracite Coal logo, stirring patriotic associations in blue and white with a bull's-eye in red and serving to remind the visitor that this history is still being written since a limited amount of anthracite continues to be produced nearby albeit no longer by deep mining methods.

All tours are guided by persons with extensive knowledge of mining, some of whom are ex-miners. A *performative* dimension is thus central to the appeal and success of the tours in imparting historical knowledge.

Lackawanna Coal Mine Tour visitors with guide. (Image: courtesy of County of Lackawanna.)

Lackawanna's brochure, for instance, invites visitors to "learn from a real miner." To hear stories recounted by such guides dressed for the occasion and wielding requisite tools and instruments creates a powerful theatrical effect. All three tours utilize modified dolly cars, known as mantrips, to convey visitors inside the mine safely and in reasonable comfort, while Pioneer uses open train cars for its ride around the mountain. Visitors even play a gently interactive role in being invited to leave the cars and walk short interior distances, more or less following in working miners' footsteps. In these ways, the tours educate visitors informally in anthracite history while offering an entertaining and somewhat edgy experience, one that plays to an extent on a "fairground ride" effect, as visitors may feel a thrill of fear in venturing onto open "coasters" and "ghost trains" rolling around mountains and dropping into the dark, enclosed spaces of anthracite's own "tunnels of love."

PURPOSE-BUILT SITES

This category comprises museums in new buildings, historical markers, and monuments and memorial parks that have not arisen directly on former coal mining sites. The institutional and commercial telling of anthracite history has resulted in the construction of museums and exhibition spaces financed by private and public funds. Two such facilities exist in the region: the Anthracite Heritage Museum and the Museum of Anthracite Mining. Eckley Miners' Village is a hybrid site, a "living history" village comprising original buildings, a replica breaker, and a visitor center with a museum component, the latter two items dating from the late 1960s and 1980, respectively. The Eckley breaker has drawn criticism as a pale imitation of a working one, but it has accrued symbolic value given that no original breakers now remain in the region. To those dedicated facilities, we may add several anthracite-related displays to be found within the museum collections of historical societies and other cultural organizations across the region: for instance, in Tamaqua, where its historical society occupies a repurposed 1905 bank building, or in Forest City where its society is housed in a former Methodist church.

Visitor Center, Eckley Miners' Village. (Photo: Cynthia A. Carmickle, 2019)

Another repurposed but non-mining related site may be found a little south of the coal region, in the heart of Bethlehem, formerly one of Pennsylvania's principal steel manufacturing centers. The Industrial Archives and Library is a nonprofit organization dedicated to preserving industrial records of various kinds. Founded in 2015, it holds some anthracite materials and plans to extend its mining collections generally. Its headquarters are in a historic building renovated in 2000 and gifted to the organization.

More than a century old, the historical marker program run by the PHMC has produced over 2000 of the familiar blue cast aluminum markers placed in locations across the state. This number includes eighty-nine related to either anthracite or bituminous coal. The markers cover many aspects of anthracite: labor history (e.g., the "Great Coal Strike" of 1902 with signs in Scranton and Shenandoah); businesses (e.g., Abijah Smith & Company in Plymouth, founded in 1807 and, as reads the text of the sign, "considered the first commercially successful anthracite firm"); disasters (e.g., in Sheppton where in 1963 one miner perished and two were rescued); individuals (e.g., Burd Patterson, a pioneer in 1835 of a "slope method for mining below water table," in Pottsville); buildings (e.g., Concrete City, the DL&W housing project in Nanticoke);

Pennsylvania Historical & Museum Commission marker, Eckley Miners' Village. (Photo: Cynthia A. Carmickle, 2019.)

transportation (e.g., Firth Dock, 1828-71, between Pottsville and Port Carbon, built to facilitate the moving of coal along the Schuylkill Canal to Philadelphia); communities and neighborhoods (e.g., Little Lithuania USA in Shenandoah, the name a synecdoche of the entire Schuylkill County population, one that boasts the "greatest concentration of Lithuanian ancestry in the United States"). These strategically placed markers are small but important sites in telling the anthracite story since they are distinctive and eye-catching, may be seen easily by pedestrians and motorists alike, and present a short and simple text describing the historical significance of the subject they represent.

Carefully placed memorials commemorating anthracite miners may be found in many communities across the region. They resemble conventional war memorials in their engraved or enameled inscriptions and honor rolls accompanied by various visual symbols. Sculpted monuments typically represent an unknown miner in a helmeted pose with a pickaxe or shovel in hand, comparable to a soldier standing alert with a bayonet or gun. By investing in such memorials, a community may claim pride in its history and gain a dignified remembrance of the life of its miners. As purpose-built memorials, they offer communities an opportunity to situate them in central or highly trafficked locations where they function as key local sights, an option not always open to memorials placed at designated historic sites that may be more out of the way. Jadviga M. da Costa Nunes divides anthracite region public sculpture into three loosely chronological categories: one, those created by and in honor of private industrial patrons (late-nineteenth/early twentieth centuries), one exception being the John Mitchell monument in Scranton for which miners raised funds; two, those mostly relief sculptures commissioned for government and corporate buildings, such as post offices in Pittston and Mahanoy City (part of a New Deal art project, 1935-1943) and banks such as Miners Memorial in Pottsville (early twentieth century); three, those created by local heritage and advocate groups (later twentieth century). This third category, which embraces the sculpted monuments of the posthistorical period, materialized "from commissions by local groups of former miners and their descendants," (102) writes Nunes, and thus may be seen as examples of vernacular rather than elitist or official memorializing in action. However, "with no future prospects for the anthracite industry and the number of former miners dwindling with each passing year, most likely [we have seen] the last of the public sculptures concerning the industry" (114).

In 2007, in Olyphant, a bronze statue designed by celebrated regional artist and miner's son Frank "Wyso" Wysochansky was dedicated to miners and their families by the town's Coal Miners Memorial Association before around 100 people gathered at a levee by a bridge over the Lackawanna River. Jody Roselle, a reporter for the *Scranton Times*, described the statue: "A short, muscular man stands clutching his pickax while he looks out across the borough as if paused in a moment of dignified reflection. He represents the hard work and determination that this [Lackawanna] Midvalley town was built upon." Communal memorials of this kind are generally financed by voluntary donations from individuals and groups and often in tandem with grants from local or state authorities. In the case of the Olyphant memorial, 500 donors raised $50,000 over three years. Memorials located in communities adjacent or close to each other show that independent communal identity across the anthracite region is as important as its sense of collective identity. For instance, only a few miles separate Olyphant from Blakely, where a "Coal Miners Remembered" memorial on the site of an old skating rink in Blakely Borough Park was dedicated in 2018. It materialized principally from a two-year effort by resident Silvia Passeri, whose father, Robert, an Italian immigrant, died of silicosis ("black lung" disease) at the age of fifty-six. The granite memorial consists of a five-foot miner's statue flanked by wings engraved with over 600 miners' names added by donation, the first memorial in Lackawanna County to do so. It was funded by $21,000 in voluntary donations, a $6,000 county grant, and a $35,000 state gaming grant. While the Olyphant and Blakely memorials confer prestige on each town, they also represent collective solidarity based on common values and shared historical experiences. As Passeri emphasized in her dedicatory remarks, she planned the memorial to remember *all* miners of the region, a statement reminiscent of Olyphant association chairman Gene Turko's one year earlier: "The man in the monument could be any miner, even the sculptor's father."

Elsewhere in the northern field, a comparable memorial may be found in Scranton's Courthouse Square, not to miners but to their hero, United Mine Workers (UMW) union leader John Mitchell. Though the monument dates from 1924 and is thus not a posthistorical artifact, it is a unique example from an earlier era of a memorial to a pro-labor rather than to an establishment figure; besides, on the back of the monument, a relief depicts a miner and his family. The memorial's significance to the labor movement is evidenced by union rallies still taking place at the site. Elsewhere in Scranton, adjacent to the AHM and the Lackawanna Coal Mine Tour in McDade Park, stands a bronze statue, *A Tribute to Anthracite Miners*, sculpted by Scranton native Frank Talarico, who is perhaps

Frank Talarico, *A Tribute to Anthracite Coal Miners* (detail), Mc Dade Park, Scranton, bronze, 2001. (Photo: Cynthia A. Carmickle, 2019.)

best known for his statue of baseball great Ted Williams located at Fenway Park in Boston, Massachusetts. In 1993, at the northernmost point of the anthracite minefields, the Forest City Rotary Club led by Harry Newak set a plaque into a brick wall containing a huge bronze relief by town native Martin Heffron. In Nanticoke, a bronze statue sculpted by Alan Cottrill of a miner at ease with a black lunch pail under his arm was erected on Main Street in 2003. Thanks to a communal effort, a black stone and granite memorial to all miners stands in a tiny park on Main Street in Plymouth; forty-eight local mine disasters, the worst being nearby at Avondale, are commemorated there in inscriptions. In Pittston, a civic Bicentennial Committee nurtured a project resulting in the 1979 dedication of an anonymously sculpted ten-foot-tall granite statue of a miner (also carrying a lunch pail). Carved in large letters, the bottom line of the inscription on the statue plainly reminds us that "We Owe

Him Much." Also in Pittston, a PHMC marker stands close to the site of the 1896 Twin Shaft disaster, where 58 men and boys remain entombed to this day. The Greater Pittston Historical Society commemorated this tragedy on its 120th anniversary in 2016.

In 2017, the downtown campus of King's College in Wilkes-Barre's Public Square became the site of a Miners' Park, a joint project of the College and the Anthracite Heritage Foundation. The Park features a Wall of Honor, displaying almost 2000 miners' names. Beneath the image of a miner run the following lines: "Those years rush back / Like beating wings-- / Long years of strife / When Coal Was King." Around the forecourt stand plinths bearing historical information inscribed on plaques. Inside the main entrance of the adjacent Richard A. Alley Centre for Health Sciences, on a wall along two hallways, a thematically ordered permanent display of anthracite paintings by local artist Sue Hand completes the memorial site. On an opposite wall, we may also view anthracite scenes painted by Margaret "Barney" Sordoni, the original instigator of a plan to establish the Sordoni Gallery in Wilkes-Barre, a project delayed in her time but realized after the 1972 Agnes flood, a disaster that led to extensive civic redevelopment.

In commemorating an anthracite event, historical markers are not necessarily located in the same place as other memorials carrying their own meanings for different sectors of the community involved. Such is the case, for instance, of the commemoration of the No. 2 Baltimore Mine Tunnel explosion of 1919, in which ninety-two miners lost their lives. The main memorial site is on PA (Business) 309 in Wilkes-Barre Township, where a marker erected in 2015 along with a plaque installed in 2019 stand in a grassy plot by the side of the road in a position close to the original tunnel entrance. Elsewhere in the township, in St. Mary's of the Maternity Cemetery in Georgetown, the site of the common burial of twenty-four of the Baltimore victims from the parish, mainly Polish miners, a voluntarily funded memorial consists of a two-ton block of coal bearing a plaque commemorating those men. It is not uncommon to find multiple interrelated memorials to persons, places, or events across a specific delimited area. An event may occur in a specific place, but its impact spreads much further afield.

One of the most striking of all regional memorials is in Shenandoah. Standing in Girard Park, the $250,000 memorial dating from 1995 is "dedicated to the men who worked in endless night." It comprises a triptych of bronze bas-relief plaques on slabs of black granite by celebrated sculptor and Pennsylvania resident Zenos Frudakis (aka the "Monument Man"). An eight-square-foot centerpiece, "The Passageway," depicts four miners exiting a mine shaft. Two six-by-four-foot side panels, "Life Underground" and "Life Above Ground," show late nineteenth-century miners at work in a pit and their families at home. Brick surroundings carry miners' names, while the triangular forecourt's ("black") diamond shape carries a strong symbolic meaning. Elsewhere in the western middle field, an anonymously sculpted life-size bronze statue of a miner stands in the Frackville Mall.

In the same area, in Mahanoy City, we find perhaps the strangest and most chilling of all anthracite memorial sites: a statue sculpted in bronze by Frudakis commemorating a member of the Molly Maguires awaiting execution by hanging. First planned in the late 1990s to stimulate area tourism, *The Day of the Rope* has stood since 2010 in a small space named the Molly Maguire Historical Park, built entirely of brick and stone and separated from private houses by a wall. Wholly green, symbolizing the Irish identity of the Mollies, the statue depicts a hooded man in civilian clothing, his hands and feet bound. He stands before a walled backdrop suggesting gallows. Opposite him, three stone plaques set in a wall carry a detailed account of the Molly Maguires legend. The overall effect—especially of a space lacking any grass or soft earth—is harsh and disturbing, and it is unsurprising that this memorial proved controversial among residents and has attracted, like Centralia, some "dark" attention from quirky Internet sites. Despite its unconventional and forbidding appearance, it is arguably as valid as are more conventional memorials to the historicizing of anthracite since the dubious narratives and controversial interpretations of the Molly Maguires episode have long been a staple of regional historiography.

In the southern field, in Minersville, the local Rotary Club, under the leadership of former miner Joseph T. Walacavage, created a memorial park in 1997. Standing at the intersection of US 209 and PA 901, it consists of a 9.5-foot-high bronze statue on a ten-foot base surfaced with

Zenos Frudakis, *The Day of the Rope*, Molly Maguire Historical Park, Mahanoy City, bronze, 2010. (Photo: Cynthia A. Carmickle, 2021. Image: courtesy of the artist.)

anthracite chunks. Sculpted by Pottsville native Jim Ponter, it portrays a miner with a pick and lantern in hand. Adjacent bronze tablets bear inscriptions, and a surrounding walkway is set with memorial bricks. Four days after seeing his dream of this tribute come true, Joe Walacavage passed away. Also, in this vicinity lies the hamlet of Buck Run, where a memorial depicts a miner standing next to his mule-drawn loaded coal car at a replica entrance to a tunnel. A side note to this monument is that Buck Run was once a renowned model company town developed over forty years from 1900 by visionary colliery owner James Brown Neale. Almost nothing remains of it today.

SIGNS

The historical significance of signs as physical objects, old or new, comes from their messages. Most signs in public places convey factual messages in words or images. Many, however, especially those displaying logos or slogans, allow for associative or figurative interpretations and are particularly interesting to the historian looking beyond the straightforward statement of name, date, or place that constitutes a basic transmission of practical information and historical record. Across the anthracite region, signs indicating a historic site or event have a primarily commemorative function. The PHMC's historical marker network, discussed above concerning memorial sites, epitomizes this function. The presence of an anthracite heritage site may also prompt adjacent businesses to associate themselves with it by name. In Lansford, for instance, we find a sign for the Coal Miners Bar and Grill directly across the street from a repurposed building boasting two full-size commemorative murals.

Signs using distinctive logos or slogans typically indicate names and locations of companies still active in the production and marketing of coal. Their desire to survive and prosper in a postindustrial era marked by fierce competition from other fuel sources as well as by environmentalist opposition to the industry renders all the more important their need to bolster their reputations. Hence the desire for a public image of their business as representing the values of tradition, continuity, and name recognition. The Jeddo Coal Company logo features an image of a chunk of anthracite within a circle, whereupon appears the company name in red lettering over a black background. Suggestive of a wheel, thus of mechanism and transportation, the circle bears the slogan "Aristocrat of Anthracite" along with a single red star superimposed on its base. This company has roots in the Jeddo-Highland Company, dating back to the early twentieth century. From a historical viewpoint, the sign and its accompanying slogan emphasize both the longevity of the company and its appeal to notions of class ("Aristocrat") and superiority, twin attributes that ideally separate it from lesser rivals. Its argument for brand superiority—contested keenly by most of its rivals—may rest on its reputation for longer burning and lower ash-producing anthracite. In an undated promotional flyer, the slogan "65 Years of Experience in satisfying customers" sits beneath the logo. This slogan tellingly capitalizes the first letters of "Years" and "Experience" to emphasize words that we might otherwise expect to see entirely in lowercase. The Reading Anthracite Company sign also presents a circular logo bearing the slogan "Famous Reading Anthracite," the epithet "Famous" appealing indirectly to an illustrious history (in corporate eyes at least) dating back to 1871 as an offshoot of the giant Philadelphia and Reading Coal & Iron Company. The company also exploits the homophonic "red/Reading" to trademark its product by distinctive coloring. The Lehigh Anthracite sign emphasizes the preciousness of its product by presenting a clean-burning black diamond rising from a bed of coal. The accompanying slogan, "Where Coal is King, But *Safety* is #1," goes one better than Jeddo's aristocratic claim by heralding its own "royalty" via a maxim long familiar to the industry. This blue (or black, should we say) bloodline refers to the earlier incarnation of the present company in the giant and once dominant Lehigh Coal & Navigation Company. The sign of Blaschak Coal Corporation near Mahanoy City plays on its ownership of St. Nicholas Colliery by showing a jolly St. Nicholas carrying anthracite in his shoulder bag.

Lehigh Coal Company sign. (Photo: Cynthia A. Carmickle, 2019.)

Blaschak Coal Company sign. (Photo: Cynthia A. Carmickle, 2019.)

Winter happiness in the form of bountiful warmth and plenty of good cheer is the chief message here, while an association with the former St. Nicholas Breaker, widely recognized across the region as one of the largest and most imposing of such facilities, augments the sign's historical value. Visible on its website, Blaschak's contemporary logo of juxtaposed triangles triggers landscape memory subliminally by bringing both a black diamond and a culm bank to mind. In its promotional material, Blaschak also stresses its prominence "since 1937," while a short video claims its coal as the "world's greatest." It is not only the bigger anthracite companies making these claims to historical status. A modest roadside sign locating Shingara and Wynn's Bottom Rock Slope near Trevorton stresses the five-generation continuity of this family-owned underground mine, one of the last of its kind.

A history of local and state politicians supporting the anthracite industry also figures in the messaging of regional signage. For instance, at the Spring Mountain Mine of the Atlantic Carbon Group in Jeansville, a patriotic red, white, and blue slogan declares "Lou Digs Coal," referring to former US Congressman Lou Barletta, a native of nearby Hazleton. After Barletta lost his Senate bid in 2018 and declined to return to Congress, some signs were reworded to read "Trump Digs Coal" in a nod to former President Donald J. Trump's professed support of the domestic coal industry. Barletta and Trump viewed their support of coal primarily as denying the threat posed by climate change and thereby defying leftist environmentalism. However, the connotations of this sign exceed the declarations of well-known politicians throwing their weight behind an ailing industry. To industry employees and residents, especially those in the wider communities peopled by descendants of European immigrants to the coal region, the sign carries an implicit appeal to the strength and virtue of a traditional way of life and work, one now little more than a collective memory, but one they perceive as defended and upheld by political figures like Barletta and Trump. Yet, it masks a nativist, anti-immigrant sentiment that Barletta notoriously espoused in his time as mayor of Hazleton throughout the first decade of this century. On his watch, the city of Hazleton passed an Illegal Immigrant Relief Act in 2005, an ordinance designed to penalize those who rented accommodation to illegals, but one never used and struck down repeatedly by courts of law. This was a decade in which a new population composed heavily of Latino migrants entered the area to take up low-paid and unskilled work in its postindustrial service industry. On the surface, therefore, "Lou Digs Coal" appears to have little or no historical resonance and presumes only a familiarity with Barletta as an influential regional figure. At a subtextual level, though, it functions as a synecdoche for a xenophobic discourse and a set of ultra-conservative values amplified by recent vituperative social and political divisions throughout the United States.

In this respect, "Lou Digs Coal" is a veiled postindustrial manifestation of a familiar story: a deep-rooted history in the anthracite region of systematic anti-immigrant discrimination on the part of coal companies, politicians, civic leaders, and law enforcement agencies. This history includes a deliberate stirring-up of one ethnic group against another. We need only recall a killing in the same coalfield and no more than a few miles from the Jeansville sign under discussion: the 1897 Lattimer massacre of mainly eastern European miners marching for fairer pay and an unfair tax on nonnaturalized immigrants. According to Michael P. Roller, "the violent repression of their mobilization emblemized the racialized class violence that characterized the region's industrial structures throughout the late nineteenth and early twentieth centuries" (34). As for Atlantic Carbon's adjacent sign at Spring Mountain, its logo shows a veined black diamond suggestive of a site map and again exploiting a traditional association of anthracite with the precious gem. This location has a further historical resonance, though the sign perhaps prudently does not refer to it, in that thirteen miners drowned there in 1891 in the No. 1 Mine.

The word "anthracite" triggers so many memories and strong associations in the minds of the regional population that, unsurprisingly, many commercial enterprises use it in their signage. Its use carries a strong sense of history, tradition, and belonging to the region in the eyes of entrepreneurs and onlookers. We may see signs, for instance, indicating the Anthracite Café (Wilkes-Barre), Anthracite Provisions (Shamokin area), Anthracite Car Wash (Tower City), Anthracite Fire Company (Mt. Carmel), and Anthracite Animal Clinic (Ashland). The Clinic presents a set of small images of a mule, a coal car, a railroad, a breaker, and miners; it suggests a full awareness of the weight of regional industrial history. By virtue of its umbrella quality bathed nowadays in nostalgia,

Anthracite Café, Wilkes-Barre. (Photo: Cynthia A. Carmickle, 2019)

Anthracite meat wagon, Northumberland County. (Photo: Cynthia A. Carmickle, 2019.)

legend, and lore, "anthracite" is used strategically in efforts to revitalize the region. These efforts apply notably to the reimagining of former coal towns, especially along their principal and most visible thoroughfares. A case in point is Carbondale, where large signs directly opposite each other on Main Street identify the Hotel Anthracite and the Anthracite Center. Representing a hotel and a commercial space, these signs offer potent verbal reminders of the importance of mining to the city both in its former industrial days and at present when an appeal to anthracite history has become a key element in economic regeneration via touristic development. It is notable that both buildings occupy historic sites, though neither is coal related. Hotel Anthracite is a recently constructed building on the site of the former Irving Theater, while the Anthracite Center is housed in a restored 1928 bank building. Entering the lobby of Hotel Anthracite via its main doors, we are greeted by a large installation in the form of a three-tier chunk of coal. Elsewhere within the premises, we may find displayed a range of coal-related photographs and artifacts reinforcing the link between the hotel's name and local mining history. We may discover a similar extension of association beyond name alone in the Anthracite Center, where plans are in hand to open a "Breaker Boys" cigar club and lounge. In Shamokin, a plan announced in 2020 to build another new hotel using the word "Anthracite" on a former mill's site confirms the name's status as both attractive and effective in urban revival projects.

SOUVENIR MERCHANDISE

This category comprises functional or purely decorative objects that signify anthracite history through simple association. Trade in industrial souvenirs originated in the early stages of the Industrial Revolution in eighteenth-century England. Objects belonging to this trade may be found in museum collections, antique stores, and flea markets, where they hold differing monetary value depending on condition and rarity. They are a significant aspect of material culture both in embodying the design and reflecting the taste of different time periods and correlating to broader social histories. Mostly they are contemporary merchandise items available widely to the general public for purchase in gift shops, museum stores, and online sites. Souvenir merchandise tells of the anthracite, if often at a simplistic or superficial level, by reinforcing the idea of a distinctive regional culture defined by its major industry. To the view that it does not contribute meaningfully to the anthracite narrative, we may respond that its connotative value may prompt consumers and spectators to further their knowledge of history. For instance, I own an Irish-green tee-shirt with "The Mollies Were Men" printed on the front and "Hard Coal Country Pennsylvania" on the back. Its visibility when worn in public may conceivably stir the curiosity of someone with limited regional knowledge to speculate on the meanings of the color coding or slogans (especially the irony of the gendered reference) and perhaps to wonder who the Molly Maguires were, what constitutes Pennsylvania's hard coal country, and where it may be located. A few more examples found readily online: a "Breaker Boy" coffee mug printed with one of Lewis Hine's famous photographs; a "Coal Cracker" drinking glass printed with the image of a loaded coal car and a shovel; a humorous "Coal Region Food Groups" tee-shirt, depicting four pie-chart slices with "beer" on the side, thus tempting the unsuspecting gourmet to sample such delights as pierogies, halupka, bleenies, and kielbasa, and thereby to learn more of anthracite culture and its lasting ethnic traditions (Slavic in this instance). We may add souvenir utensils and clothing, such as caps or children's miners' helmets complete with lanterns, assorted knick-knacks, paper products (miner's "scrip" and certificates, stickers, posters, books, brochures), audio and video tapes or disks, and ethnic group- or town-specific auto license plates, such as were produced and marketed for the Anthracite 250th Anniversary celebrations. All have a role to play, however tangential or simplistic, in making anthracite history and culture better known.

Souvenir merchandise, Eckley Miners' Village. (Photo: Cynthia A. Carmickle, 2019.)

One type of souvenir is of particular and more lasting interest: carved anthracite in various forms and shapes. I return to this type in Chapter Four, as its finer examples belong to the art of sculpture in the work notably of C. Edgar Patience and Frank Magdalinski. Collectors particularly seek out pieces, writes Bill Thornbrook, "lathe-turned or carved-in-the-round, often finished with chip-carved sections that lend a contrasting texture to the polished surfaces." More common are mass-produced souvenirs, typically in the form of jewelry, shaped miniature lumps of coal, replica figurines of industrial items, and mining scenes such as the proud but weary miner, old breakers, and overflowing coal cars. Today, most of this merchandise on the market is not fabricated from pure anthracite but rather from composite materials, adds Thornbrook, "cast from a slurry of resin-infused coal dust that has been molded and hardened . . . . By contrast, genuine hand-carved anthracite usually exhibits formal simplicity, but is always jet-black and often polished to a hard sheen."

HISTORICAL ARCHAEOLOGY

Established in 1968, the Society for Historical Archaeology defines its field as "the study of the material remains of past societies that also left behind some other form of historical evidence." Anthropology, history, geography, and folklore contribute their scholarship to a field that addresses the modern world and is thus applicable to urban and industrial environments. Historical archaeology combines the practice of conventional excavation with the unearthing of documentary records of various kinds. It also enters into communal life by recording oral histories. Michael Roller affirms that "the materiality of archaeological evidence and the communal effort required for its execution can provide a venue rich for public engagement" (25). The anthracite region presents historical archaeologists with an ideal opportunity to transcend the object-centered work of traditional industrial archaeologists by engaging with community members in posing often difficult questions about their views on immigration, work, race, and class. Following this line of questioning, historical archaeologists carefully avoid labeling their subjects as passive victims of chronic exploitation by the industrial or commercial powers that have held sway over them. On the contrary, writes Stephen W. Silliman, they strive to reveal "the ways that those laboring accommodated, resisted, made use of, and lived through labor situations" (149). An emphasis on the role of agency within the working community, an aspect sometimes ignored in anthracite region history, becomes a key part of the contemporary historical archaeologist's work.

On this basis, the interdisciplinary Anthracite Heritage Project (AHP) of the Department of Anthropology and Historic Preservation Program established in 2009 at the University of Maryland undertakes fieldwork in both archaeology and oral history. Its goal is both to uncover aspects of the past via established methods and, writes Paul Shackel, a co-founder of the Project, "to address issues related to inequities in the community, past and present" (1).

The AHP concerns itself with the lives of new immigrants to the anthracite region, especially in the Hazleton area of Luzerne County, where the Latino community may lack coal mining in its historical profile but belongs nonetheless to the economy, geography, and culture of the region. Natives of the Dominican Republic predominate in this community, followed by those from Puerto Rico and Mexico. The AHP works to develop the idea of a universal and inclusive heritage that embraces those new immigrants as much as it does those members of the established ethnic groups. To the possible objection that coal has never been a factor in the acculturation of this new group, we may respond that the nature of much of their work is a postindustrial equivalent of laboring in an anthracite industry that once occupied the sites of many of these newcomers' workplaces physically and that subjected its employees to similarly demanding conditions and relatively low levels of pay. Other than some archaeological work carried out under the requirements of Section 106 of the National Historic Preservation Act, the AHP is the only project of its kind to have been launched in the anthracite region. Following an initial ethnographic survey designed both to gather information and to stimulate local interest, the Project began archaeological investigations in 2011 on the exact site of the 1897 Lattimer massacre. Consistent with one of the Project's guiding principles, to investigate the politics of remembering and forgetting, a primary goal was to reawaken the memory of the massacre and explore its protracted and often contentious narrative by canvassing the views of current residents. Collaborating with the New Jersey-based Battlefield Restoration and Archaeological Volunteer Organization (BRAVO), the Project crew used metal detectors to locate cups, buckles, and bullets from the time of the incident. In 2013, further excavations took place in what is today known as Pardeesville, focusing on two sets of worker housing: company-built homes reserved for "native" miners (American, British, German) and peripheral enclaves of shanties for the "foreign" (mainly Italian and Slavic) element. This aspect of the Project highlighted a disparity in the standard of living quarters, which reflected discrimination against and disadvantage to that denigrated element. One knock-on effect of the Project's gathering momentum and increasing involvement of community volunteers was that it afforded fresh opportunities for recording oral histories. Since 2015, the Project has moved its field site to Eckley Miners' Village, where research is ongoing. The focus is again on peripheral housing occupied by "inferior" immigrant groups in the past to highlight the persistence of similar disadvantages to the new immigrant community in the area today.

The AHP archaeological program is an annual six-week field school bringing together, on average, six college undergraduates and six Hazleton

Area high school students under the direction of graduate students in anthropology from the University of Maryland. Among the high school participants in recent years have been several of Latino backgrounds selected from the Hazleton Integration Project/Hazleton One Community Center, a non-governmental organization providing social services for underprivileged youth in the community. Some of the excavated items from the Project sites, according to Shackel, include "pipe stems, shell-edged whiteware, and marbles [plus] a few religious items that the Latinx students could connect with, like part of a rosary, a portion of a porcelain crucifix, and a medal with a figure inscribed of Papa Pio IX (Pope Pius IX)" (9). These religious objects, he adds, "helped to make a connection between the values of the new Latinx immigrants and the historic immigrants" to the region.

However, there is another side to this story insofar as a comparison of the new immigrant community in the area with those of traditional immigrant groups in the past reveals several important differences. Despite much hardship and discrimination at the hands of the original settler groups, those largely Irish, Italian, Polish, and other Slavic immigrants came in successive waves to settle in the region and become an established part of the regional community. They understood the need to learn English to work in the mines and communicate across non-English-speaking ethnic groups. By contrast, a substantial proportion of the new Latino bloc in the old eastern middle coal field centered on Hazleton does not intend to settle in the area. Though a good number do settle in the area and become homeowners and community businesspersons, the new Latino community is, in many respects, self-contained and transient. Many of its members are sojourners in the area, working four- to five-day weeks and staying in temporary lodgings before returning elsewhere on weekends, many to New York City, some even back to the Dominican Republic. Many do not, therefore, feel a need to learn English, as their daily interaction is largely within their own Spanish-language group. Furthermore, their work lies almost wholly in the distribution rather than the manufacture of goods, offering a stark contrast to that of the original immigrant groups, which lay directly in the production of anthracite and products associated with that overarching industry.

INTERPERSONAL ACTIVITY

ORAL HISTORY

Since Allan Nevins pioneered the modern tape-recorded method at Columbia University in the 1940s, oral history has been a powerful tool for historians. For the industrial and labor historian, the wealth of testimonies "from below" has been especially rewarding and instructive. At the same time, advances in recording technology have greatly facilitated the oral historian's work. Though oral history is a rich source of valuable material, it is a method that demands sensitivity and rigor if it is to be an effective and reliable element of historical inquiry. It may take the form of a monologue whereby a narrator offers an uninterrupted life history, but it usually takes a more structured interview form, though considerable overlap exists between the two. In a standard exchange between narrator and interviewer, the questions of the narrator's integrity and the reliability of his memories always hover in the background. The issue of reliability applies equally to the interviewer and transcriber, who are usually one and the same. Subjective by definition and reflecting the narrator's worldview, oral history does not answer readily to the factual record. It should be understood, like most historical inquiry, as an interpretive event throwing light, often imaginatively and with license, on events and circumstances of the past. When all is said and done, the issue of accessibility remains important, for unless an oral history is transcribed into print form or converted from tape into digital format, as is increasingly possible for owners and curators of collections, it risks being overlooked by its potential audience especially if its original recording and written transcription sit undisturbed in a box or on a shelf.

For the anthracite historian, oral history is a particularly valuable means by which to let working-class voices be heard; voices, especially of women, that for many decades were unknown ignored, repressed, or even suppressed by a social and industrial system that gave little or no credit to proletarian acts of speech. Edited or not, anthracite oral histories mostly appear in the pages of periodicals, of which the majority are academic journals. One example is a 1990 panel at Eckley Miners' Village on "Anthracite Mining Unionism and the UMW" featuring current or former miners and moderated by James Abrams, Folklife Coordinator of America's Industrial Heritage Project. This edited discussion appeared in *Pennsylvania History* in 1991. While this type of publication is far preferable to an undisturbed tape or transcript lying in a box somewhere, it has a limited audience beyond a circle of specialist historians.

Book form remains the most substantial and visible means of presenting oral histories as a bedrock upon which to address a range of broader socioeconomic and political issues. In anthracite history, four major examples of this approach are *Anthracite People: Families, Unions and Work, 1900-40* (1983) by John Bodnar; *Growing Up in Coal Country* (1996) by Susan Campbell Bartoletti; *When the Mines Closed: Stories of Struggles in Hard Times* (1998) by Thomas Dublin; and *Sewn in Coal Country: An Oral History of the Ladies' Garment Industry in Northeastern Pennsylvania, 1945-1995* (2020), edited by Robert Wolensky. Of these four titles, *Growing Up in Coal Country* is the only trade publication (of the other three, two are from academic presses and one from the PHMC), and it has the most immediate appeal to the general reader. Basing her book on sixteen personal interviews plus more than twenty taken from the PHMC's collection and others, Bartoletti's blend of oral history and archival research allowed her slowly to be able "to piece together what life was like for the children of coal country in northeastern Pennsylvania . . . nearly one hundred years ago" (9). While the author ranges widely over aspects of daily life in the coal region, her unifying theme of youthful experience lends a poignant tone to the book and lays a quasi-fictional patina over the narrative.

Bodnar's book was the first to focus on the anthracite region. Based on 1981 interviews he conducted in the Nanticoke/Plymouth/Glen Lyon area of Luzerne County, plus four others conducted in 1977-78 by Angela Staskavage, James Rodechko, and Kenneth Hughes, Bodnar shows how oral histories may form a strong backbone of evidence for the period and events under investigation. In acknowledging the help of his main sources and a network of further connections arising from them, Bodnar also confirms how oral history can productively engage a large number of people, many of whom might otherwise never volunteer their stories or find a way in which to place them on the historical record. The interviewees' memoirs focus on the period from the 1920s through the 1940s when the anthracite industry began its downward slide. Their stories pay particular attention to the bitter labor wars in the northern field from 1933 to 1936 when the breakaway United Anthracite Miners of Pennsylvania (UAMP) struggled both against the combined power of the UMW and the coal companies and for the principle of job equalization in response to the effects of the Great Depression and declining production in area pits. Bodnar insists that the miners' quest for job equalization should not be seen as surprising since "cooperation and sharing were the means by which they had always met the exigencies of industrial life" (14). By drawing on recollections of that period by miners, their womenfolk, and those who were children, these oral histories forcefully and consistently confirm that "the attitudes of most workers were rooted, ultimately, in the loving concern that united both family and neighborhood and also in the tensions which pervaded these relationships" (15). Moreover, these attitudes were by no means newfangled, as the memoirs "reconstruct the strong web of the family and communal relationships that sustained them, *as they always have* [my italics], during difficult times" (2). Nor, adds Bodnar, were these attitudes peculiar to the anthracite region working class: "In every instance where an industry flourishes, people construct a social system of family groupings and communities, incorporating values and behavior patterns shaped by that industry's economy and dependent upon its good health and continued existence" (1).

Dublin bases his book, which includes some examples of George Harvan's celebrated anthracite photography, on ninety interviews done from 1993 to 1996 with residents of the Panther Valley around the towns of Lansford, Coaldale, Summit Hill, and Nesquehoning. The author conducted most of the interviews; Walter Licht and Mary Ann Landis did several others, including some with outmigrants from the region to model home developments in Fairless Hills and Levittown, which lie northeast of Philadelphia, and to northern New Jersey. Twelve narratives structure the book: six by men, seven by women (one joint account) in various occupations. They reveal a pattern of former life in the area that was both deeply gendered and more complicated than it may have seemed from a superficial viewpoint. The philosophical underpinnings of the book and its invitation to understand a broader process of deindustrialization owe much, for Dublin, to the influential work of social historian Herbert Gutman behind which in turn lie the inspirational words of Jean-Paul Sartre: "The essential . . . is not what life has done to people, but what people do with what life has done to them." In this spirit of inquiry, oral history becomes more than the passive recounting of experience; it becomes the active voice of individuals who, through the work of memory, may come to terms with their past, help others do the same, and reshape their sense of the present.

Wolensky states that his method draws on historical sociology, labor history, and union studies; he cites the work of Alessandro Portelli in the Harlan County, Kentucky, coal region as a particular influence. In *Sewn in Coal Country*, building on his earlier book *Fighting for the Union Label: The Women's Garment Industry and the ILGWU in Pennsylvania* (2002), Wolensky draws on eighty-four interviews with sixty-three subjects representing factory workers, managers, owners, and others. Institutional history is secondary here to the stories themselves, though Wolensky emphasizes the role of unionism and invites further thought on the practice of oral history. The resulting book of sixteen narratives organized into fifteen chapters with one joint interview springs from the Northeastern Pennsylvania Oral and Life History Project (NPOLHP), which Wolensky had founded in 1982 as the Wyoming Valley Oral History Project (WVOHP). Wolensky's primary motivation for creating this project was his ILGWU interviews with celebrated unionists Min and Bill Matheson; his secondary motivation was the Knox disaster. Other anthracite-related oral history projects undertaken by various hands under the NPOLHP umbrella are Glen Lyon (early 1970s), Wilkes-Barre (1975, later combined with WVOHP); Laurel Run Mine Fire (1985); and Hazleton (1970s-80s).

One of the two main repositories of anthracite oral history is at Penn State University, where the Special Collections department of the University Libraries houses the NPOLHP. It includes the collection created between 1975 and 1985 by anthracite historian and regional native

Harold W. Aurand. Under his supervision, Aurand's undergraduate students at Penn State Hazleton conducted eighty-six interviews with miners and their families in the Hazleton area. The original audiocassettes have been copied onto compact disks. The other main repository is in the state capital, Harrisburg, within the Pennsylvania State Archives. Quantitative data on the extent of these holdings varies between those found in Matthew S. Magda's *Oral History in Pennsylvania,* a 1981 guide to these collections, and those in a 2005 online update from the PHMC. Five anthracite region collections may be found in the archive, including Bodnar's project in Nanticoke and Dublin's project in the Panther Valley. Of the other three, the Eckley Oral History Project, undertaken in 1972 and 1975, consists of fifty interviews with a total duration of over thirty-seven hours. Described by the PHMC as a "folklife project done by [the] University of Pennsylvania to document retired miners and miners' widows," it was one part of work carried out on the life and culture of Eckley in preparing for the establishment of the site's museum in 1975. A joint undertaking of the PHMC and Wilkes University faculty and students, the Nanticoke Women Oral History Project dates from 1977-78 and consists of fifty-four hourlong interviews of women "whose economy was based on anthracite coal mining and factory work." The ethnicity of these women is Polish, Russian, Irish, German, and Welsh. The value of such projects to the historian is affirmed by Magda's description of the interviews as dealing with a wide range of subjects: "immigration, 'old-country' life, family life, inter-ethnic relations, community life, education, ethnic customs and foods, women's roles, and attitudes toward marriage, careers, child-raising, mine work, and religion." Another joint undertaking, by the University of Scranton and the PHMC Ethnic Studies Program, the 1973 Scranton Oral History Project comprises fifty-nine interviews over fifty hours with "the Welsh, Irish, Polish, Scottish, Italian, Slovak, Ukrainian, Hungarian, and native-stock population of former coal miners who resided in the anthracite coal-patch towns surrounding Scranton." Magda's description lists a dizzying number of subjects covered in over seventy tape reels of these life histories. Some oral histories also reside in the collections of regional historical societies. One example is a 2015 collaboration between the Greater Pittston Historical Society and Misericordia University. Some of its results were published online at the university, as in an essay by student participant Rebecca Schnable entitled "A View from Pittston: The End of Anthracite in the Wyoming Valley," in which she draws on three oral histories she did on the project. James Kozloski remembers a 1943 cave-in that destroyed Pittston High School; Sally Scott recalls another cave-in that took a young girl's life in 1944; Gayle Gromala describes her reactions as a child to the Knox disaster of 1959. Schnable quotes selectively from their histories in the body of her essay.

Public folklorists Michael and Carrie Nobel Kline were commissioned by the Schuylkill River National and State Heritage Area (SRNSHA) to carry out an ethnic heritage study of Schuylkill County that involved documenting the survival of diverse cultural practices and traditions. Their fieldwork in 2004-05 within a small cross-section of the county involved collecting oral histories as well as musical performances (a specialty of their company, Talking Across the Lines: Worldwide Conversations) and compiling an extensive photographic archive. Their work in the county is held at the SRNSHA headquarters in Pottstown and the Pottsville Free Public Library. Though the Klines' project is not overtly historical, it opens a wide window on the continuity of much Schuylkill County history by revealing the high degree to which ethnic diversity and customs persist in the area and, by implication, across the entire anthracite region. In their project report *Come to the Old Country: A Handbook for Preserving and Shaping Schuylkill County's Cultural Heritage* (2005), the Klines, who have lived and worked in many states including West Virginia and have "seen ethnic diversity . . . depressed places . . . coal towns," declare that "never before have we seen the vitality and wealth of ethnicity that makes up Schuylkill County . . . This leaves [the county] with a rare wealth . . . Maybe it's a hard coal thing. Family, religious and ethnic tradition helped people endure the suffering that came with anthracite mining." They point out that "members of most, if not all of Schuylkill's immigrant groups went to West Virginia as well to work in the soft coal. But you have to look pretty hard to find pockets of ethnicity remaining there" (11). One caveat they issue is that older rather than younger generations are responsible for this remarkable cultural survival; their report moves beyond their findings to propose a plan for amenities and activities that would ensure the unbroken transmission of this precious heritage to successive generations.

In the same way as religion in its various sectarian denominations once helped to define life in the mining cities and towns, ethnicity has always been a central element in the history of the anthracite region. In *Coal Dust on Your Feet: The Rise, Decline, and Restoration of an Anthracite Mining Town* (2013), her historical ethnography of Shamokin/Coal Township, Janet MacGaffey states that while ethnicity may have diminished importance in the region today, it remains a vibrant cultural phenomenon. Ethnicity is not simply a matter of historical preservation of older social structures; rather, it is processual, changing form and function to fit its shifting historical context. MacGaffey asserts that while ethnicity was once critical in structuring people's lives around the need for survival, safety, and solidarity in a coal mining-dominated environment, "in the twenty-first century [it] is transformed from what it was in the early years of the town to become primarily a social identity option" (xviii). Moreover, ethnicity now has a significant economic function insofar as ethnic arts, crafts, foods, and festivals have become commercially viable in helping to revive a depressed regional economy. The production and marketing of these ethnic commodities form part of a newly constituted heritage culture designed to stimulate tourism as one way to replace the coal and manufacturing industries that were formerly the anchors of the region's traditional economy.

ASSOCIATIONS

Historical societies across the region, many with long traditions of communal presence, remain important bodies for the pursuit of anthracite history since they may own extensive archives and artifacts relating directly or indirectly to coal mining. These societies offer focal points for the activities of anthracite history enthusiasts. For instance, the Lackawanna Historical Society in Scranton touches on anthracite history in much of its relation to the Lackawanna Valley Heritage Area. It does so via programs in partnership with other organizations (e.g., in the Avondale disaster commemoration events), a game show involving school history groups, and individuals' inquiries of a genealogical or other kind. Several groups, organized informally or more formally, exist as associations dedicated to pursuing anthracite region culture and its heritage.

One former club reminding us of the vanished traditional workforce is the Last of the Panther Valley Deep Coal Miners. Founded in 1972 when Lansford No. 9, the last deep mine in the valley, closed for good, it brought together twenty-two former Lanscoal workmates. The club held an annual banquet open to members of the public, at which members shared stories from the mines in a convivial atmosphere of fellowship and commemoration. At the closing of No. 9, each club member took home a lump of coal from which he would cut a sliver on each occasion that one of his peers passed away. He would proceed, in turn, to lay his sliver in the form of a cross on the casket of the deceased miner. Interviewed by Chris Parker in the August 27, 2000, issue of *The Morning Call* (Allentown), Frank J. Karnish, former president of the Panther Creek Valley Foundation, which administers the No. 9 historical site, referred to the club members as "typical of every miner that ever worked in the Panther Valley or anthracite fields . . . Those individuals not only represent the Lanscoal miners, they represent just about every coal miner in the Panther Valley . . . They maintain a very important camaraderie." By 2000, only three miners survived: Michael Sabron, Stanley Stanek, and the last member Paul Paslawsky, who died in 2004. However, a handful of former area LC&N miners survive today. Designed in 1976 by Stanek, the Lansford Miners' Monument was erected in Kennedy Park the following year. Stones salvaged from the former LC&N main building form a wall bearing two plaques showing images of miners at work; between them is a cross fashioned from anthracite with a name plaque below. Nearby sit two anthracite chunks; beneath one is buried a time capsule. Jadviga da Costa Nunes points out that "unlike earlier traditional monuments raised on tall pedestals, this memorial (and all the "memory sites" that followed) has a low base that engages the viewer at a more egalitarian eye level" (109). The monument was rededicated in 2016. In *The Face of Decline* (2005), Thomas Dublin and Walter Licht write at length about these commemorative activities in the Panther Valley, ones that were accompanied by the publication of a primarily historical monthly paper, the *Valley Gazette*, conceived and edited from 1972 to 2004 by local journalist Ed Gildea. The paper also featured the photographic work of George Harvan, who, together with Gildea, wrote Dublin and Licht, "made the *Valley Gazette* a resource for their community's response to the closing of the mines. In the process they came to champion the establishment of [the No. 9 Mine and Museum]" (197).

Other groups have formed expressly to create monuments or to restore and preserve anthracite sites and artifacts. Following a 1991 project on the Huber Breaker conducted by the Historic American Engineering Record (HAER), a National Park Service program, the Huber Breaker Preservation Society was formed to work toward saving the breaker as a historical site with educational and tourist potential. Despite the group's best efforts, the breaker was demolished in 2014; thereafter, the society redirected itself toward creating and funding a memorial park on the colliery site. With the park established successfully, the society now maintains a website/Facebook page "honoring the memory of those who helped fuel the Industrial Revolution" and serving as an open forum for exchanging anthracite heritage information.

Underground Miners is the popular name for Abandoned Mine Research, Inc., founded in 2002. This group is particularly interested in salvaging and restoring old mining equipment. Otherwise, its main interest is in photographing and documenting old mine sites as well as giving related presentations. Additionally, in the early 2000s, it completed seven public tours averaging thirty participants, but this side of their activity has been discontinued for the moment. The group has some affinity with fashionable "dark" tourism, but though it seeks access to derelict and often perilous sites, it is a highly trained and well-informed band of individuals whose emphasis is less on transgressive thrill-seeking than on serious anthracite investigations.

National associations also contribute to the pursuit of anthracite history through their local chapters. One organization with similar technical interests to Underground Miners is the Society for Mining, Metallurgy, and Exploration (SME), whose Penn-Anthracite section covers the entire eastern part of the state and some adjacent areas in New Jersey. A national association involved in all forms of mining, its origins are firmly in the anthracite region, as it derives from the American Institute of Mining Engineers founded in 1871 in Wilkes-Barre. Its mission, as stated in its 2020 Strategic Plan, is "to be the voice of the mining profession in the region." One of its goals is to promote STEM education at primary and secondary levels by providing classroom materials and instruction wherein history plays a part, as in the mine tours it organizes for young people. The four-season regional section meetings of the society often carry a historical theme.

Other associations exist in formal partnerships with established institutions or organizations to take advantage of cooperative venture potential, name recognition, shared publicity, and supplemental funding. In Wilkes-Barre, working with King's College, a Catholic school established to educate the sons of miners, the Anthracite Heritage Foundation (AHF) is a nonprofit corporation founded by James Burke and Don Sanderson. Governed by a board of trustees, its educational mission is to offer an ongoing program of events, including lectures, concerts, film screenings, and exhibitions. The primary target audience is area public, private, and parochial school students, though most events are open to the general public. However, given the considerable challenge of stimulating interest in anthracite history among the younger generation and many of its teachers (with several notable exceptions), the foundation foresees the greatest impact from promoting entertainment that appeals to the sophisticated audiovisual literacy of youthful audiences. One example of this approach was the presence of 500 Pittston Area High School students at two screenings of David Brocca's 2019 documentary *Knox Mine Disaster: The End of Anthracite*. Following the model of the Ellis Island Foundation, the AHF has also developed a computer-based questionnaire designed to invite descendants of miners to enter information about the lives of their forebears. Another achievement has been to create the downtown Wilkes-Barre miners' memorial and permanent display of artwork by Sue Hand, largely by a donation from the late James Burke, a prominent local booster of anthracite heritage who, as Chief Financial Officer of Paramount Pictures, had helped to commission for the studio the 1969 feature film *The Molly Maguires* shot on location in the region.

Not to be confused with the AHF, the Anthracite Heritage Alliance was created in 2008 by the Delaware and Lehigh National Heritage Corridor (D&LNHC) to be active across the anthracite region. It was an ambitious scheme to join with two other national heritage areas (LHVA and SRNSHA), eight federal and state bodies, sixteen watershed and conservation groups, one electric utility company, and four anthracite heritage partners in establishing a network of volunteers throughout the region to educate the public about coal-related environmental issues and to promote anthracite history and culture in various ways. However, the AHA no longer functions in its original form, as the D&LNHC chose not to continue its involvement at a regional level. The politics of national versus regional may have come into play in a turn of events that also suggests an inherent problem in efforts to promote and sustain anthracite culture since, beyond the region's borders, the same level of interest, enthusiasm, or commitment is understandably absent. The AHA may have struggled with its initial ambitiousness, as its elaborate partnership scheme may have been difficult to sustain efficiently and harmoniously. One of its instigators, retired mining engineer Michael Korb, keeps the project alive on a smaller scale via a Facebook page named "Anthracite Coal National Park," the name being inspired by unsuccessful prior efforts—notably in 1964 by Genevieve Blatt, who served in a Democratic administration and as a judge in the Commonwealth of Pennsylvania—to establish federal park sites in the coal region. Korb hopes that the original alliance project may eventually resume.

FESTIVALS AND GATHERINGS

Capable of drawing sizeable crowds, festivals and gatherings are ideal ways to introduce a broad cross-section of the general public to anthracite history and culture. The main purpose of such events may be entertaining, educational, or ceremonial, though the first two and occasionally the third are commonly combined on a single occasion. In the cases of the Patch Town Days at Eckley and the Coal Miner's Heritage Festival in Lansford, the organizers hold these events on or close to historical sites already existing as tourist attractions so that attendees may easily take advantage of the opportunity to visit established features such as museum spaces and mine tours. Held over two days in June, the Patch Town Days festival offers guided tours and musical and theatrical performances foregrounding aspects of anthracite history. The voluntary Eckley Players group has been staging costumed and history-themed performances each year since 1999. In the interests of diversity and an accurate historical reflection of the community, a single ethnic group is featured each year: Irish, Slovak, and Italian, for instance, have been showcased in various ways. The Coal Miner's Heritage Festival takes place in July and is promoted by the Panther Creek Valley Foundation, which administers the site's permanent attraction, the No. 9 Coal Mine and Museum. It typically attracts around 1500 visitors, who may view historical displays and enjoy artistic performances during their attendance. At the same site on Memorial Day weekend, a car show and picnic are held; on Labor Day weekend, another picnic takes place upholding a communal tradition of miners' picnics dating back to the early twentieth century.

Based in Shamokin and founded in 1999, the Northumberland County Council for the Arts and Humanities (NCCAH) administers a fine art gallery and auditorium in the old Shamokin High School building as well as the Greater Shamokin Heritage Museum located above the County Library in the historic American Legion Building. With a slogan "Celebrating History and Heritage in the Anthracite Coal Region," the museum includes a range of anthracite exhibits. An original anthracite festival, tied to the coal industry as late as the early 1980s—its parade still featured coal companies, retired miners, and UMWA representatives—had died out by the early 1990s due to postindustrial indifference. The NCCAH revived it in 2005 as the Anthracite Heritage Festival of the Arts. Over two days in May, the event offers art exhibits, live entertainment, and train/trolley/city tours bolstered by the irresistible (and indispensable) attraction of food and other refreshments. One tour engages with anthracite history by taking its groups to view where the first area coal was mined and to visit Mother Cabrini Catholic Church (formerly St. Edward's, lost to fire in 1971), the first church in the world to have been electrically lit by Thomas Edison's improved three-wire system. Visitors may view altars made of oak-trimmed anthracite and an anthracite lectern commissioned in 1972 for the rebuilt church and installed as a tribute to the area's mining heritage. According to its Facebook page, the Anthracite Heritage Festival "was created to enhance the quality of life, economic development and tourism in and around the coal region area through the promotion of the Arts while reconnecting with our heritage." By drawing together the arts, economic development, and heritage consciousness, this statement typifies a symbiotic approach adopted widely across the region and now deemed essential in any efforts to preserve and sustain anthracite history and culture.

The first Molly Maguires Weekend occurred in Pottsville in 1996 and recurred annually in various locations until 2005. Organized by the Schuylkill County Council for the Arts (SCCA), the initial event offered drama, storytelling, poetry, a symposium, and a Molly Maguire tour in conjunction with one developed in the 1980s by the then Schuylkill River Greenway National Heritage Area Association. A former SCCA director emphasizes the value throughout the festival of "bringing the descendants from both sides of the story together to share the stories from their personal family perspectives." Special events included reenactments of the Molly executions staged in Tamaqua (1998) and the grand jury investigation of James McParlan staged in the Schuylkill County Courthouse in Pottsville (2003). Elsewhere in Schuylkill County, the Independent Coal Miners' Picnic takes place in Hegins each year in August. A brainchild of the late David A. Lucas, this gathering celebrates the tradition and survival of small-scale, family-based mine operators in that area and honors all former and present anthracite and bituminous coal miners. The Picnic has become a rallying point for those who continue to earn their living by mining coal, whether on their own or as employees of corporations. The annual production for the picnic of a mug inscribed with individual miners' names demonstrates a simple souvenir's commemorative value.

Each January sees a celebration of coal culture during Anthracite Mining Heritage Month (AMHM). Coordinated by Robert Wolensky, this month-long series of lectures, forums, performances, and exhibits offer a blend of the academic gathering and the community cultural event. Centered on the northern field, AMHM brings together as sponsors many regional institutions and organizations, from colleges and historical societies to local associations and independent artists. As the series has grown, it has begun to invite the occasional participation of interested parties from further afield, such as the National Museum of Industrial History in Bethlehem.

Academic institutions are established venues for conferences and other scholarly gatherings. Regarding anthracite history, the annual "History of Northeastern Pennsylvania: The Last 100 Years" conference held at Luzerne County Community College in Nanticoke deserves special mention. In keeping with the mission of the college "to provide cultural enrichment programs for the people of Luzerne County and Northeastern Pennsylvania" and with the purpose of the conference "to make the people of this region aware of their history and heritage," the college's Social Science/History department organized an unbroken sequence from 1989 of twenty-eight meetings until the coronavirus pandemic forced a temporary halt in 2020. Many papers on anthracite history and culture have been presented over the years and published in conference proceedings. Similar mention is due to the annual symposium held from 1982 to 2011 in Easton by the National Canal Museum in conjunction with Lafayette College. Masterminded by late historian and curator Lance E. Metz, these symposia included many contributions on anthracite history, also published in proceedings, which reinforce an integral connection between the histories of the area canal/railroad systems and the coal industry reliant on them for transport of its product to external markets.

Annual ceremonies are held to commemorate the tragedies of Avondale, Lattimer, and Knox. Though these occasions are suitably solemn in tone, they also serve to celebrate the lives of those involved. Beginning in 2004, the annual Avondale commemorations reached an apogee on September 8, 2019, the 150th anniversary of Avondale, when around 100 persons gathered at the disaster site in Plymouth Township. Descendants of the victims read their ancestors' names aloud to the accompaniment of a tolling bell before each pinned a carnation on a ceremonial wreath. Wilkes-Barre musician Don Shappelle performed "The Avondale Ballad." Following the formalities, the participants repaired to the premises of the Plymouth Historical Society for a social gathering. On the previous day, a corresponding ceremony had been held in Scranton's Washburn

Street Cemetery, where sixty-one victims, all miners of Welsh heritage, are buried. The program included a description of the site, the dedication of a new marker listing the names of each victim buried there, a short memorial service, a reading of the victims' names by descendants and local students, and the performance of Welsh songs. The special three-day commemoration also included a conference at the Anthracite Heritage Museum. A Knox Disaster Memorial Committee organizes the formal commemoration of the Knox disaster. These formalities began one year after the disaster, in 1960, when local people, including victims' families, arranged for a Sacred Mass to be held in St. Joseph's Catholic Church, Port Griffith, now the Baloga Funeral Home, adjacent to the Knox memorial and marker. Following the closure of St. Joseph's, the annual Mass has been held since 2009 in St. John the Evangelist Catholic Church, Pittston. A public commemoration has been held at the memorial since the 1980s; since 1999, a PHMC marker has stood in the same location. This ceremony is followed by a short walk to the disaster site.

In addition to these regular gatherings is a one-time regional celebration that, despite huge logistical challenges, proved to be a great success. In 2018, under the chairmanship of fifth-generation mining family member and self-titled "last of the anthracite photographers" Scott D. Herring, the Anthracite 250th Anniversary, seven-and-a-half years

Memorial Day, *The Knox Mine Disaster*, film, 2019. (Image: courtesy of David Brocca.)

in the making, saw the participation of 236 groups plus eleven tourist train/trolley operators. The cultural focus was the unique identity of the "People of the Black Diamond" since there is no other anthracite culture identifiable as such to be found anywhere in the world and nothing comparable in any bituminous coal regions. Falling within the historical record, the start date of 1768 was established where none had existed before. It was chosen to commemorate a land purchase by the Connecticut Company that established five townships in the Wyoming Valley: Kingston, Wilkes-Barre, Plymouth, Pittston, and Hanover (Nanticoke). Another key factor in creating the festival was the strong collectors' culture in the region that opened up a raft of possibilities for commemorative items to be produced for the occasion. These ranged from automobile license plates (over 3000 produced) to DVDs, booklets, calendars, posters, Christmas cards, tee-shirts, coasters, and customized town signs. Four symbols (miner with mule, coal train, canal, and hex) were chosen for use in the festival's diamond logo design, which appeared consistently on signs and memorabilia. Events throughout the region included parades, exhibitions, firework displays, musical and dramatic performances, film screenings, baking and brewing demonstrations, and road and rail excursions. It is noteworthy that the Board of Directors (fifteen persons plus Herring) funded the entire project independently, as it wished to avoid any dependence on public funds or any corresponding pressure on participants to observe unwished-for bureaucratic procedures or to accede to certain content expectations. This decision was also an implicit indicator of ingrained and widespread suspicion of an appointed or elected government in the anthracite region.

Notwithstanding this skeptical view of the role of government, the cultural importance of anthracite to the Commonwealth of Pennsylvania was proven in 2016 when the third Saturday of July entered the state statute book as Anthracite Heritage Day. Following a constituent's suggestion, the passing of the statute followed a resolution by five state senators from northeastern Pennsylvania, of whom one, Lisa Baker, said that "anthracite is a bedrock part of our heritage story. It is a prominent part of our past, a distinct part of the present, and an intended part of the future." Another senator, David Argall, anticipating the core identity value of the 2018 Anniversary festival, pointed out that "coal is more than just an important local natural resource. The coal region is defined by a work ethic and way of life."

INTERNET SITES

While online initiatives in anthracite history are to be commended, it would appear they appeal primarily to individuals who already have a lively interest in regional history. Yet, in its unlimited reach, easy access, and sophisticated interactivity, the value of the Internet can barely be overstated. Taken as a whole, online initiatives demonstrate via their differing approaches that valuable new resources exist in further making a regional historical record. Moreover, they may succeed in drawing into the historical debate those who do not ordinarily turn to the established literature or conventional cultural events such as lectures or exhibitions. This applies especially to younger people for whom traditional historiography may hold scant appeal. I revisit this particular educational challenge in my concluding chapter.

The Anthracite Coal National Park website, edited by Michael Korb (www.facebook.com/AnthraciteHeritageAlliance) has almost 9000 followers. Adapting the defunct AHA's mission statement to an online presence, Korb describes "the challenge of preserving and telling a nationally significant story" with a triple focus: natural resource conservation; cultural resource conservation, interpretation and enhancement; and marketing of anthracite heritage. A printed publication from 1992, *Anthracite History Journal*, founded by Eric McKeever, switched to a now defunct online version (www.minecountry.com) in 2000. Another early venture, https://coalpail.com (formerly Nepacrossroads.com), set up an online forum. With almost 10,000 members today and popular with domestic anthracite fuel users, it carries a historical section. More recently, the *Anthracite Coal Region of Northeastern Pennsylvania*, comprising a Facebook page, a corresponding website (www.anthracitecoalregion.org), and a Blogspot, was set up in 2013 by Melissa R. Meade, a media and communications professor in Pennsylvania and a native of the coal region. The site, which has almost 10,000 followers, "collects, aggregates, and makes publicly available cultural, historical, media documents, personal memories and comments" of regional residents; its goal is "to build a community archive of these materials and include location-based digital mapping technologies." In this way, writes Meade, "community members become public storytellers and producers of media." A comparable site is *Anthracite Miners and the Pennsylvania Coal Region* (https://www.facebook.com/PennsylvaniaAnthraciteMiners), which boasts over four thousand followers. Public historian Jake Wynn set up a website (https://wynninghistory.com) and Blogspot that extend beyond anthracite to include other historical topics. J. Stuart ("Stu") Richards, of Orwigsburg, Pa., an author and musical performer prominent in anthracite cultural circles, set up https://coalregionhistorychronicles. blogspot.com. Less interactively but with a regional enthusiasm and a deep cultural understanding equal to the abovementioned sites, www.coalregion.com emerged in 1997 from online exchanges among friends in Schuylkill County. It presents itself lightheartedly by offering "a collection of nostalgia and regionalisms" and "the kinds of things you don't see in history books." Its sections include recipes, a "CoalSpeak" dictionary, lists of coal towns and famous persons from the region, an image gallery, and extensive links to other regional websites. Several other smaller sites focus on specific interests. One (www.anthraciterailsandtrails.com) concerns "the region's fascinating geography, topography, geology, and history." Its main focus is on mapping anthracite region railroads. Counting around 3700 members and including a personal blog with over 1000 followers, *Abandoned Anthracite* (www.facebook.com/AbandonedAnthracite) offers "a variety of rogue photography aimed towards the history and beauty in the hard coal region." Hosted by a single person, it is yet another good example of the degree to which anthracite history is being preserved and encouraged online by enthusiastic amateurs and their close associates. An oral historical project operating via an e-mail address, "Anthracite Ancestry," is a segment of the *History Bytes* online newsletter (www.HistoryBytes.org) supplementing the quarterly print journal of the Lackawanna Historical Society. Functioning similarly to an archive set up by the Anthracite Heritage Foundation in Luzerne County, it invites submission of mining family-related stories.

Another of this kind is *Anthracite Unite* (https://anthraciteunite.com). To revive the radical tradition of the anthracite region, it describes itself as "a voice for the working class" by offering "an approach that is unapologetically anti-racist and pro-worker." With clear relevance to new low-paid immigrant newcomers to the region, it seeks to build "the working-class power necessary to stand up to modern-day coal barons." As befits a site that understands the political dimension of history and how it impacts the struggles and needs of the present day, it includes historical content in the form, for instance, of an article by Karol K. Weaver ("Thinking about Ashland") on the closures of Ashland State General Hospital, an institution founded to specialize in treating mining injuries, and of the former Sunbury Community Hospital after it became part of the University of Pittsburgh Medical Center (UPMC) Susquehanna system. Weaver, the author of a book (2011) on the history of women medical caregivers in the region, questions these closures especially given a shortage of communal hospital capacity during the coronavirus pandemic, and poses another question, one as vital today as in the heyday of the coal industry, of how to provide adequate care for and to ensure the physical welfare of the regional population. Her piece relates incidentally to the historical significance of abandoned sites within the region and the popularity among "dark" tourists of exploring disused or derelict industrial structures and public buildings.

Remembering anthracite takes many different forms, and its modes of recall are wide-ranging. We may go as far as to state that any means by which anthracite history is remembered functions as a mode of recall in the broadest sense of the term: one that cues or triggers either random reflections on or deliberate recollections of the past. Any mode succeeds thereby in bringing single or multiple aspects of anthracite history to the forefront of the mind. An act of remembrance may be conscious and purposeful, or an unconscious and involuntary act of memory stimulated, for instance, by language or visual perception. Such remembering may occur privately among individuals or small groups—for instance, in the informal perusal of a collection of books, images, or souvenirs—or publicly, as in an organized commemorative event such as a disaster anniversary or an annual mining festival. There is, therefore, a considerable overlap between the modes discussed above and the representational forms discussed in the following chapter, which covers the highly diverse telling of anthracite via the media of literature and the arts.

CHAPTER FOUR

REPRESENTATIONAL FORMS

LITERATURE

Anthracite history may be represented by any literary genre with an aesthetic dimension. This criterion excludes only official historical records and similar documentation of a strictly factual kind. Our immediate sense of what constitutes "literature" implies the production of short and long fiction, poetry, drama, essays, and biographies—each of these genres capable of playing a part in representing history. In answering, folklorist Simon J. Bronner writes, "questions about the everyday life and traditions of historic communities," (473) "literature" also includes writing of a more personal kind such as journals, diaries, correspondence, and transcribed oral histories. Above all, it includes historiography (the writing of history by historians). We now broadly accept that historians, in writing an account of history, construct a story from a set of historical facts in ways that resemble the practice of creative writing. In doing so, they may use literary methods and techniques such as plot, tone, and figurative language. Equally, they may take their share of poetic license to help render their historical narratives more persuasive and appealing to the reader. But then, nothing is new under the sun: Herodotus, Tacitus, and Edward Gibbon, to name but three eloquent masters of historical writing, employ a range of literary techniques, including an imaginative reconstruction of events. In "The Decay of Lying," writes Oscar Wilde, ever alert to the claims of art on reality, "the ancient historian gave us delightful fiction in the form of fact." The writing of history invites its practitioners to employ a wealth of expressive language and structural ploys in the same way as the writing of historical novels, often manifesting itself as "faction" in postmodern literature, requires extensive and careful research to be effective and convincing. Furthermore, it would seem impossible to interpret history objectively since interpretation is, by definition, a subjective act; historians view the past in ways that are greatly—some may argue, always—influenced by or weighted toward particular values, belief systems, and ideological positions.

HISTORIOGRAPHY

Historiographic texts indubitably remain the dominant literary representation of anthracite region history, principally via scholarly publication in academic journals and books. Since the 1960s, the literary turn in historiographic practice allied to the impact of radical social and political movements (the two being interrelated via their grounding in critical theory) has opened anthracite history to postmodern historical methods and insights. A case in point is using oral history as a basis for a historical study (see Chapter Three). The work of the Wolensky family on Knox and the ILGWU, of Bodnar in the Nanticoke area, of Dublin in the Panther Valley, and of Bartoletti across the region exemplifies an oral historical method that facilitates and liberates stories told largely "from below," ones that are mediated carefully by the authors' contextual knowledge and their skill in framing them in book form.

In charting the posthistorical discourse of anthracite, we may observe that relatively little historiographic work emerged during the 1960s and 1970s when a clear historical perspective was being formed. Much like the populace, scholars sought to understand the nature and consequences of the region's drastic industrial and socioeconomic decline. In any case, little research based on new interpretive models had been done or had materialized at that time. Nonetheless, several books—by Broehl, Barrett, and McCarthy on the Molly Maguires and by Greene and Novak on Lattimer and the Slavic community—were already setting the stage for innovative investigations of these topics. A work of political history indirectly relating to the story of the Mollies is *Before the Molly*

Maguires: The Emergence of the Ethno-Religious Factor in the Politics of the Lower Anthracite Region, 1844-1872 (1976) by William A. Gudelunas, Jr. and William G. Shade. The authors argue that the political crises of the 1850s in the anthracite region played out less around the issues of slavery and labor resulting in the Civil War than around conflicts of religious identity rooted in sectarianism and ethnicity. Despite originating in a 1956 University of Pennsylvania thesis unpublished until 1979, Theodore Bakerman's *Anthracite Coal: A Study in Advanced Industrial Decline*, covering the period from 1930 to 1953 and focusing on economics and demographics, anticipates the seminal work on the regional decline by Dublin and Licht published fifty years later. Nor may we overlook *When Coal Was King: Mining Pennsylvania's Anthracite* (1970) by Louis Poliniak. Though its text consists largely of sections describing the industry in action, it is narrated, as its title indicates, in the past tense, "tells the story of early development and takes the reader through the hey-day of mining in the Anthracite Region" (30) and includes sections on life in the mine patch and episodes of labor unrest from 1849 to 1925. As an illustrated thirty-two-page booklet, its format of historical information presented simply to the reader in word and image is comparable to the later emergence and ongoing popularity of glossy photo-book series (by Arcadia, America Through Time, etc.) tied to regional people and places. We should not underestimate the appeal of such publications to a general audience eager to learn about aspects of anthracite history but reluctant, perhaps, to engage with the greater demands of reading a scholarly disquisition.

After a slow but steady beginning during the first two posthistorical decades, the 1980s and 1990s witnessed a surge of anthracite historiography that runs parallel to the growth of a heritage industry in turn informed and stimulated by new methods and techniques, notably digital, of documentation and interpretation. Amid an outpouring of specialized studies, a more general book marks a historiographic milestone of this period. *The Kingdom of Coal: Work, Enterprise, and Ethnic Communities in the Mine Fields* (1985) by Donald L. Miller and Richard E. Sharpless stands as the first comprehensive history of the anthracite industry to appear in the posthistorical period. *The Kingdom of Coal* epitomizes a growing concern among anthracite historians to transcend narrower economic or industrial studies by grounding their work equally or more in social, political, and labor histories. Other distinctive works followed this pattern. Anthony F. C. Wallace, an anthropologist and Bancroft Prize winner for *Rockdale: The Growth of An American Village in the Early Industrial Revolution*, his 1978 study of a Pennsylvania cotton manufacturing community, turned his attention to the anthracite region in *St. Clair: A Nineteenth-Century Coal Town's Experience with a Disaster-Prone Industry* (1981), an account of a small Schuylkill County town from 1835 to 1880. In the spirit of "small is beautiful," Wallace's microcosmic examination of life and work in St. Clair embraces, by extension, the entire anthracite region where coal companies and community leaders alike failed repeatedly both to see the economic limitations of their single-minded reliance on the production of coal and to heed repeated warnings over safety in the mines. In *Anthracite Aristocracy: Leadership and Social Change in the Hard Coal Regions of Northeastern Pennsylvania, 1800-1930* (1985), Edward J. Davies examines the contrasting evolution of social and economic structures in two much larger coal-centered cities, Wilkes-Barre and Pottsville, where the elite leadership organized itself and acted in ways leading to vastly different outcomes for their respective communities. Burton W. Folsom, Jr.'s *Urban Capitalists: Entrepreneurs and City Growth in Pennsylvania's Lackawanna and Lehigh Regions, 1800-1920* (2001) is a related work tracing comparable narratives to those of Davies and especially one that unfolded in the city of Scranton. One of Folsom's chapters addresses the crucial differences in economic leadership between Scranton and Wilkes-Barre, two cities separated by a mere sixteen miles but, in another way, worlds apart in leadership values and attitudes.

Following on from Bodnar's oral-historical analysis of bitter 1930s labor struggles in *Anthracite People*, and taking a similar ethnic slant, if one more concerned with class conflict than Gudelunas and Shade in *Before the Molly Maguires*, Grace Palladino's *Another Civil War: Labor, Capital, and the State in the Anthracite Regions of Pennsylvania, 1840-68* (1990) examines what she calls "The North's Civil War," a fierce struggle between employers and workers across the region from 1840 to 1868.

Focusing similarly on the history of political violence, *The Kelayres Massacre: Politics and Murder in Pennsylvania's Anthracite Country* (2014) by Stephanie Hoover analyzes the 1934 shooting of Democratic marchers outside the house of Republican boss "Big Joe" Bruno in Kelayres, a small Schuylkill County mining community south of Hazleton. Thoroughly political in tone as befits its author, a co-founder of regional activist group Anthracite Unite, Mitch Troutman's *The Bootleg Coal Rebellion: The Pennsylvania Miners Who Seized an Industry, 1925-1942* (2022) emphasizes the power of collective action. His study focuses on bootlegging in Schuylkill, Northumberland, Carbon, southern Columbia, and upper Dauphin counties, a guerilla activity that a government survey suggested may have had 14,000 practitioners during the Great Depression and one that prompted the subsequent legal establishment of small, independent coal companies across the region.

Some of the most progressive anthracite region historiography has focused on tragic events involving needless loss of life, such as mining disasters and violence against or purportedly by workers. The drama of such occurrences and their conflicts and controversies render their historical representation open to many competing interpretations. The appeal of these contentious events to deep historical scrutiny has already been made apparent in the cases of Knox, Centralia, and Lattimer. These tragedies have produced their share of provocative studies. Reflecting the Wolenskys' sympathies with the cause of labor, their *Knox Mine Disaster, January 22, 1959* (1999) revealed a web of corruption among coal companies, miners' unions, and organized crime that contributed directly to the disaster. Simply to consider the titles of DeKok's first and Kroll-Smith/Couch's books on Centralia—*Unseen Danger* (1986) and *The Real Disaster Is Above Ground* (1990), respectively—confirms the political and economic complexities accompanying a long, painful, and bitterly contested destruction of the town as well as the investigative commitment of those authors. In the same manner as his work on Knox, Robert Wolensky (*Tragedy at Avondale*, 2008, co-authored with Joseph Keating) goes beyond the simple recounting of the 1869 disaster to address a variety of related social and industrial factors—such as ethnic rivalry, political maneuvering, and resistance to mine-safety laws—that permits a better understanding of an event that has long been shrouded in mystery and suspicion.

The Lattimer massacre has also proven to be a controversial subject. The mass murder of unarmed striking miners had been largely forgotten—conveniently to some, it would seem—until historian Edward Pinkowski wrote a pamphlet on it in 1950. Thereafter, little effort was made to memorialize the victims until philosopher-theologian Michael Novak, himself of Slovak descent, published *The Guns of Lattimer* in 1978. In choosing to write his book, Novak credited Pinkowski's pamphlet as well as *The Slavic Community on Strike* (1968) by Victor Greene, who touches on the massacre as part of his broader concern with the anthracite region. In his introduction, Novak discusses his methods, which include attempting to meet the standards of professional historians regarding the factual evidence, drawing inspiration from literary sources such as *Hordubal*, Czech author Karel Čapek's 1933 novel about an immigrant miner, and interiorizing the experience of the event via real (Luzerne County Sheriff James L. Martin) and fictional characters ("Benedict Sakmar" in separate interwoven chapters). In *Remembering Lattimer: Labor, Migration, and Race in Pennsylvania Anthracite Country* (2018), Paul Shackel delves beyond Novak's distinctive account to address, for instance, the causes of the long delay in memorializing the victims and to remind us that the process of commemoration may be far from straightforward and may be subject to protracted ideological conflict: "There are varying and competing narratives that struggle to control the discourse of the event . . . A memory [only] becomes public when a group has the resources and power to promote a particular past." (58, 60)

No saga in anthracite region history has proven to be more controversial and long running than that of the Molly Maguires. Based on an earlier model of clandestine gangs seeking revenge on evicting landlords in Ireland, the Mollies were allegedly a guerilla group of the 1860s and 1870s that carried out acts of violence and sabotage against coal company owners and their mine bosses in retaliation for their oppressive practices especially in the period up to and during the "Long Strike" of 1875. The plain facts remain that many Irish Americans, whether identified correctly or not as Mollies, were tried and convicted largely on the testimony of James McParlan, a Pinkerton detective who had been detailed to infiltrate the group. Another fact is that twenty Mollies were executed by hanging between 1877 and 1879, ten on one day in 1877. Beyond those facts, a lack of substantial evidence has meant that much remains unclear regarding the guilt or innocence of this outlaw band. For a century and a half, the enigma of this episode has produced no shortage of colorful speculation and substantial analysis.

The historical discourse on the Mollies began almost immediately with Allan Pinkerton's account in 1877, claiming McParlan's heroic role in bringing evil men to justice. Reinforced by Cleveland Moffett in 1894 and Arthur Conan Doyle in his novel *The Valley of Fear* (1915), this damning portrayal of the Mollies held sway until the 1930s when Anthony Bimba and J. Walter Coleman, emboldened by the self-confident leftist politics of that period, separately presented them in a more sympathetic light. This more positive viewpoint suffered a setback at the beginning of the posthistorical period; in 1964, in *The Molly Maguires*, Dartmouth College professor Wayne G. Broehl, Jr. reverted weightily and eloquently to a damning assessment of the Mollies by uncovering new documentation and conducting his own research in Ireland. In 1964 again, Arthur H. Lewis, a coal region native and former *Philadelphia Inquirer* reporter best known as a nonfiction writer with a penchant for quirky true-crime material, supported a renewed vilification in *Lament for the Molly Maguires*, though his verdict on the Mollies remains noncommittal. As a basis for the 1969 Hollywood movie *The Molly Maguires*, Lewis's book proved to be a catalyst for the popular revival of interest in the story. In 1969 again, two amateur historians in the region separately offered further revisionist versions of the story. Despite criticism of their historiographic methods from several professional reviewers, Thomas F. Barrett in *The Mollies Were Men* and Charles A. McCarthy in *The Great Molly Maguire Hoax*, succeeded once more in stirring up debate. Barrett's book, written in the form of an episodic and quasi-fictional narrative revised and completed by his son (also Thomas) in 2003, argued that the trials were a complete travesty of justice. McCarthy, in particular, drew a great deal of local publicity following his effort to address the topic at a large public gathering in Wilkes-Barre in the summer of 1968. Pointing to ninety years of suppressed affidavits and records in the case, he portrayed the alleged Mollies leader John ("Black Jack") Kehoe as a nonviolent representative of Irish American workers agitating legitimately on behalf of his community. He argued further that no organization called the Molly Maguires had ever existed in the anthracite region, the whole idea having been a grand hoax by Reading Coal & Iron Company President Franklin D. Gowen. McCarthy's view is that Gowen equated membership of the fraternal Ancient Order of Hibernians, to which Kehoe had been appointed Schuylkill County delegate, with that of alleged Mollies and thus justified a process of eliminating anyone in active opposition to his power. McCarthy's skeptical viewpoint continues to influence historians, notably Anne Flaherty, a great-great-granddaughter of Kehoe, who established the Kehoe Foundation in 2013 to support yet further studies of the Molly Maguire story.

The stage was set for other academic historians to enter the fray. In 1971, within a broader study of the rise of the United Mine Workers union in the late nineteenth century, Harold W. Aurand contended that the economic collapse of 1873 and the weakening of the Workingmen's Benevolent Association left the anthracite miners in desperate plight with no representation and with no choice eventually but to take matters into their own hands. By 1982, in "The Mythical Qualities of Molly Maguire," an article co-authored with William Gudelunas, Aurand had concluded that the key to sustained interest in the Mollies story lay precisely in its mythical status within the region and in an open-endedness inviting highly partial accounts. Despite the respected position of Aurand as a regional historian, this was not enough for Kevin Kenny, who, in *Making Sense of the Molly Maguires* (1988), called for "a formulation that extends beyond the rather obvious question of the biases historians bring to their evidence and moves to the deeper questions of the biases and distortions inherent in the evidence itself." (6) While unlikely to be the last word on this saga, Kenny's book stands as the most balanced analysis yet of this strange and dark episode in American labor and anthracite region history. However, in 1991, having been drawn to the topic fifteen years earlier by Lewis's book, Patrick Campbell, grandnephew of executed Molly Alec Campbell, published *A Molly Maguire Story*. Dissatisfied with Lewis's findings, Campbell reemphasized the ethnic angle by arguing that the Mollies were but one group of men among many victims of prolonged and concerted anti-Irish sentiment in the region.

Due to the specialized nature of anthracite historiography, its production centers understandably on publishers within or proximate to the region in question. Established academic presses are active in this respect. Penn State University Press in University Park (main campus of the University) published the Wolenskys' studies of the ILGWU; the University of Pennsylvania Press in Philadelphia published Miller and Sharpless's *The Kingdom of Coal*; Susquehanna University Press in Selinsgrove, barely beyond the western fringe of the coalfield, published two sociologically weighted books by Aurand: *Population Change and Social Continuity: Ten Years in A Coal Town* (1986) and *Coalcracker Culture: Work and Values in Pennsylvania Anthracite, 1835-1935* (2003). The first concerns Hazleton and anticipates some themes of subsequent work by Shackel and others in the developing Anthracite Heritage Project. The second helps our understanding of how a distinctive regional identity had been formed among its inhabitants, who "speak in a unique idiom [and] more importantly . . . share a set of belief patterns that informs their behavior." (7) In Harrisburg, the PHMC published Bodnar's *Anthracite People* and the Wolenskys' two books on Knox. In New York State and not far north of the anthracite region, in Binghamton and Ithaca, respectively, the State University of New York Press published *Democratic Miners* (1994) by Perry K. Blatz, while at the academic home of the Industrial and Labor Relations School, Cornell University Press published Dublin's *When the Mines Closed* and Dublin and Licht's *The Face of Decline*. An even closer connection is with the (Center for) Canal History and Technology Press (CHTP) based at the National Canal Museum in Easton, slightly southeast of the coal region but intimately bound to that region's history by anthracite's use in iron and steel manufacture in the Lehigh Valley as well as by the canals and railroads that transported coal southward toward Philadelphia. Founded in 1981, the CHTP continues to exist, though currently inactive. In addition to publishing the proceedings of the museum's annual symposium, this press has brought out at least six anthracite-related titles. Unsurprisingly, three deal with aspects of the Lehigh Coal and Navigation

Company: *The Coal Miners of Panther Valley* (1995) by regional photographer George Harvan; *Death of a Great Company* (1986) by W. Julian Parton, who emphasizes the decline and fall of LC&N and the broader issue of deindustrialization; *Coal on the Lehigh, 1790-1827* (2001) by Michael Knies, who concentrates on the beginnings and early development of the illustrious "Old" enterprise. To these titles, we may add the independently published *History of the Lehigh Coal & Navigation Company's Room Run Gravity Railroad* (2019) by Vince Hydro, who has also authored a book on coal baron Asa Packer's family. Two CHTP books with a sociological and labor history slant are Wolensky and Keating's aforementioned *Tragedy at Avondale* and Wolensky and William A. Hastie's equally searching *Anthracite Labor Wars* (2013) about tenancy (subcontracting and leasing), Italians, and organized crime in the northern field from 1897 to 1959. Another CHTP title centering on labor relations and unionism is *The "Great Strike"* (2002), a collection of essays by various hands on the momentous and consequential 1902 strike that saw a walkout by 150,000 mine workers across the anthracite fields.

Unfortunately, two significant publishers in one regional city—the Anthracite Museum Press in Scranton and the University of Scranton Press—are no more. Producing only three titles, the short-lived Anthracite Museum Press was a venture of the museum's governing Board of Associates with the cooperation and support of the PHMC. The press received grants from the federal Institute of Museum Services, the PHMC, and the Board of Associates. Subsequent funding shortfalls appear to have been the main reason for the demise of the press. Its first two titles date from 1984: *Hard Coal, Hard Times*, a collection of essays by fourteen contributors that came out of a 1982 symposium at the museum on "Ethnicity and Labor in the Anthracite Region" and was edited by then Anthracite Museum Complex director David L. Salay; and Ellis Roberts's *The Breaker Whistle Blows*, a collection of twelve essays on mining disasters and labor leaders. The wide range of subjects covered in these two volumes attests to the rapid expansion of anthracite historiography in the early part of that decade. The third book, *The Anthracite Miner: The Photographs of George Harvan* (1986), edited by Salay and Adrienne Horger, anticipates two corresponding publications concerning Harvan, *The Coal*

Miners of Panther Valley (1995) and *Miner's Son, Miners' Photographer* (2001), as well as the key presence of Harvan's work in Dublin's *When the Mines Closed*. From 1988, led by founding director Fr. Richard W. Rousseau, S.J., the University of Scranton Press committed itself strongly to regional material. By the time the university closed the Press down in 2010 for budgetary reasons, it had brought out eight anthracite-related titles comprising anthologies of poetry (Blomain, *Coal Seam*, 1996) and drama (Mosley, *Anthracite!*, 2006); a documentary film tie-in (Currá/Matkosky, *Stories from the Mines*, 2002); photography (Dinteman, *Anthracite Ghosts*, 1995); economic and business history (Folsom, *Urban Capitalists*, 2001); Healey, *The Pennsylvania Anthracite Coal Industry 1860-1902*, 2007); transportation (Karig, *Hard Coal and Coal Cars*, 2006); disaster (Munley, *The West Side Carbondale, Pennsylvania Mine Fire*, 2011). Much of this varied output dates from the final five years of the press under the energetic and imaginative leadership of Jeffrey L. Gainey, whom the university had recruited from the University of Notre Dame Press in 2005 as Rousseau's successor.

The historiographic breakthrough of the 1980s and 1990s has been largely maintained through the first two decades of the twenty-first century. A comprehensive work comparable to that of Miller and Sharpless twenty years earlier is Dublin and Licht's *The Face of Decline: The Pennsylvania Anthracite Region in the Twentieth Century* (2005). Though the authors confine their study to the twentieth century and slant its supporting evidence toward the Panther Valley, an area that Dublin had researched extensively for *When the Mines Closed*, they achieve a rare balance of social and economic history that accounts definitively for the slow and inexorable decline of the anthracite industry. Taking his cues from an emphasis on labor history in the work especially of Dublin and Licht, Palladino, and the Wolenskys, Walter T. Howard's *Anthracite Reds: A Documentary History of Communists in Northeastern Pennsylvania during the 1920s* (2 vols., 2004) was quickly followed by *Forgotten Radicals: Communists in the Pennsylvania Anthracite, 1919-1950* (2005) in which Howard revises the conventional view of local Communist Party activity as determined and delegated by Soviet Russia. He argues for the emergence in the anthracite fields of small and largely decentralized groups of "authentic American radicals," who took issue both with the direction and dogma passed down stiflingly from Moscow and with the often-misapplied power and influence of the domestic miners' union. *Anthracite Roots: Generations of Coal Mining in Schuylkill County, Pennsylvania* (2005) by Joseph W. Leonard, III, represents a continued investment in the telling of anthracite history by native authors strongly identifying with the region. Formerly a coal miner and a professor of mining engineering, Leonard's highly personal account based on five generations of his family's involvement in coal mining functions persuasively as a synecdoche of the experience of all largely unsung heroes of the mines.

In the more recent period of historicizing anthracite, we see an expansive interdisciplinary approach in the work of many younger scholars. At the intersection of health care studies, ethnic studies, and women's studies, the aforementioned *Medical Caregiving and Identity in Pennsylvania's Anthracite Region, 1880-2000* by Karol Weaver lays bare the patterns of female neighborhood caregiving at times when and in places where the application of medical science was backward, inadequate, or subject to hostility. This line of inquiry is particularly apt, as industrial first aid in the United States originated in 1899 in Jermyn, Lackawanna County, where Dr. Matthew Shields pioneered methods of treating injured mine workers. Another study of decline from socioeconomic and political standpoints is *Anthracite's Demise and the Post-Coal Economy of Northeastern Pennsylvania* (2015) by Thomas J. and Jacqueline M. Keil. The authors point to a triple phase of deindustrialization in the coal region from the mining industry through the garment industry, which had employed droves of regional women in the wake of wholesale job losses among their menfolk, to other kinds of manufacturing introduced unsuccessfully to replace the declining garment trade. Bill Conlogue's *Undermined in Coal Country: On the Measures in a Working Land* (2017) combines history, ecology, psychogeography, and literary criticism to interlock long-standing narratives of anthracite extraction, subsidence, and surface instability in an unusual and contemplative text that employs figures of those narratives as incisive metaphors of our current condition. An English professor at Marywood University in Scranton, Conlogue probes a breakdown of cultural and educational values corresponding to the physical void and frequent collapse, or break-down, of the anthracite grounds beneath our feet. Though his overall tone is anxious and pessimistic, he defends the worth of the embattled liberal arts tradition, especially via literary texts, in unsettling what appear to be solid and comfortable points of view. To the author, "Life on the coal measures demands that I discover what extends beyond appearances, beneath surfaces . . . I learn that surface life hides histories stacked beneath me, times that have long supported what I do." (93)

Original work also appears in scholarly articles driven by this fresh interdisciplinary spirit. Three examples will suffice. "Living in Anthracite: Mining Landscape and Sense of Place in Wyoming Valley, Pennsylvania" is co-authored by Peter Goin, a photographer/videographer with a special interest in altered landscapes, and historian Elizabeth Raymond. Their piece reflects a shared interest in how landscapes transformed over time produce new contexts of meaning wherein alternative stories are inscribed. Of the once ubiquitous culm banks, for instance, they suggest that "for the descendants of the miners who produced them, these derelict scenes constitute monuments of a sort. Culm banks are, if nothing else, mute testimony to the bone-breaking work of immigrant ancestors. Their now familiar contours are part of the vernacular landscape." (38) "In the Shadow of the Coal Breaker: Cultural Extraction and Participatory Communication in the Anthracite Mining Region" is by Melissa R. Meade, a communication scholar and, as a coal region native, an author personally invested in matters of regional ethnicity and identity. In a manner similar to fellow area native Conlogue, Meade unearths the lasting consequences of a relentless historical process both of the industrial removal of anthracite from the earth, leaving scars and holes behind, and of a physical, mental, and cultural hollowing-out of the regional population. The author's research included conducting "a community participatory communication forum" around the demolition of the St. Nicholas Breaker, which quotes the striking language of one of her contributors: "People were mined as well as coal and communities left empty like the mines after the resources dried up." Meade identifies a disintegration felt on both physical and psychological levels, "the *affective reality* was anticipated nervously in the community—a future without the last remaining artifact that aggregated miners' labor into one mass." (389, 385) Mining a similar vein, Andrew Long's visual essay "The Afterlife of Extraction in the Coal Region: An Exploration into the 'Land of the Living Dead'" adopts a psychogeographical approach, as he reports on his "drift" through the anthracite in an attempt "to investigate what it means to live in the region now." These three essays, plus books such as Conlogue's, demonstrate a growing interest among anthracite scholars in how residents react to and try to adjust to the damaging realities of postindustrial life in the region.

FICTION

Novels and short stories are effective vehicles for telling history. That which historical fiction may lack in historiographic method, detail, or documentation, it makes up in its appeal to the "common reader," who may be disinclined or ill-equipped to explore conventional history books. The pleasures of fiction—such as exciting plots, fascinating characters, and stylish prose—can bring history alive in surprising ways. Any reader's response to literature is subjective in some measure, and responding to fiction may be especially so, given the reader's literary taste, level of critical skills, and degree of emotional investment in a text. Historical fiction must pass the test of reader satisfaction more than its strict historical accuracy, since a fictional text is less beholden to verisimilitude than nonfictional. If we accept that all history telling is storytelling of a kind, then novelists and historiographers alike share the task of constructing a convincing narrative based on their interpretations of the past. The quality of historical fiction reflects the extent of its author's knowledge of the period in question (language, dress, customs, landscape, etc.) and his ability to evoke it artfully and vividly. It also reflects an author's understanding of audience expectations, as some readers will look for a high degree of historical specificity, while others will be satisfied by broader brushstrokes on the generical canvas, such as the introduction of fictional rather than real-life characters or of a relatively imprecise period setting.

Whether we define historical fiction narrowly or broadly, the anthracite region has its share. Fiction about life in the region had long been written, though it grew scarcer once "King Coal" vacated his throne. After a fallow period of stunned forgetfulness in the 1960s and 1970s, anthracite fiction began to reappear slowly in the 1980s, gathering pace in the following two decades and falling off again only in recent years. Two coming-of-age novels by writers who grew up in the region appeared in 1986. Set at the turn of the twentieth century, Jan Kubicki's *Breaker Boys* tells of tensions between Polish and Welsh mining communities playing out inevitably against a backdrop of terrible working conditions and conflict between employers and workers, a scenario permitting the author to introduce the haloed figure of Mother Jones into his plot. Although overwrought at times in its characterization and tending to the didactic in its descriptiveness, Kubicki's novel is a curious postmodern example of literary naturalism. During the period in which Kubicki's novel takes place, this movement—epitomized by Émile Zola's celebrated French coal mining novel *Germinal* (1885)—flourished in the United States in the works of Theodore Dreiser, Frank Norris, Jack London, Upton Sinclair (*King Coal*, 1917), and Stephen Crane. The latter wrote a notable article on the anthracite region, "In the Depths of a Coal Mine," for *McClure's Magazine* in 1894. Set in the summer of 1925, *The Patch Boys* is by Pittston-born and Scranton-reared Jay Parini, who has since authored numerous acclaimed works of fiction, nonfiction, biography, and poetry. Parini bases his novel on the life of his father, a miner. The hero, a son of Italian immigrants, has the (mis)fortune to fall in love with a Protestant girl while labor strife and gangsterism in the coalfield envelop them.

The work of Catherine Gourley, like that of Bartoletti, confirms the increasing importance of women writers from the region and of their telling of women's history as a major part of the anthracite story. Known also for her nonfiction, especially that dealing with women's lives and issues, and her works for children and young adults, Gourley published her first novel, *The Courtship of Joanna*, in 1988. Set in the 1880s and evoking the Irish immigrant community from which the author is descended, it tells in first-person diary form of sixteen-year-old Joanna, a country girl who enters service in a more affluent fellow-Irish family in a mining town. There, despite her misgivings about her new environment, she falls in love with a miner.

Telling the story of Owen Roderick, a Welsh American boy aged twelve at the outset, and influenced by the earlier novels of Kubicki and Parini, *Flames and Embers of Coal* (1990) by Ellis W. Roberts (author of *The Breaker Whistle Blows*) depicts episodically many notorious events in the anthracite region from the 1860s to 1930, such as the Avondale disaster, the Scranton riots, the Great Strike of 1902, and the Pancoast fire. A quasi-fictional memoir by a retired physician, *The Coal Cracker* (1997) by John Devers has the character Pat Devlin reveal "the proud but strange camaraderie" of the citizens of Mt Carmel. In 2002, William G. Williams published *The Coal King's Slaves*, a novel set in the late nineteenth century. *Anthracite History Journal* founder Eric McKeever brought out two similar volumes that draw heavily on a folkloric tradition of storytelling, his own *Tales of the Mine Country* (1995), an assortment of anecdotal pieces and reminiscences of Shamokin in the 1930s, and *Panther Valley Tales* (1997) by Tamaqua native James Haldeman. By refusing to romanticize his novel *Coal Cracker Blues* (2003), which contrasts memories of a youthful idyll in 1950s Shamokin to his view of a depressed postindustrial town, James Stevens exemplifies the risk taken by a contemporary writer seeking a realistic portrayal of the anthracite region today. His novel garnered a cool reception in some quarters from those who felt his portrayal of present-day life in the town to be unduly negative. Also hailing from Shamokin, thriller writer John R. Lindermuth published *Schlussel's Woman* (2003), a novel about vaulting ambition and doomed love set in the early nineteenth-century anthracite fields. Lindermuth, who has also published on regional railroad history, based *Digging Dusty Diamonds: A History of the Pennsylvania Coal Region (2013)* on contemporary newspaper articles and genealogical records.

Other women writers followed Bartoletti and Gourley in the late 1990s and early 2000s. Geraldine Glodek's *Nine Bells at the Breaker* (1998) turns on issues facing the Polish American mining community in the period before World War One. Lucia Dailey's *Mine Seed* (2002) traces the miners' struggle for rights in the Scranton area, from a shooting of workers in 1871 to the Great Strike of 1902. Christine Goldbeck, erstwhile editor of the *Anthracite History Journal*, brought out *A Tribute to O'Hara and Other Stories* (2000), a collection of short stories whose eponymous piece honors Pottsville's most famous literary son John O'Hara. Meanwhile, in 2000, Bartoletti contributed to the anthracite fiction field with *A Coal Miner's Bride: The Diary of Anetka Kaminska, Lattimer, Pennsylvania, 1896*. A title in the popular "Dear America" series of historical fiction in diary form published by New York outfit Scholastic, Inc., and aimed at the intermediate reader, this story of a thirteen-year-old "mail order" bride begins in Poland and ends with the Lattimer massacre. Bartoletti's concern for historical accuracy is supported by a note at the end, a set of archival photographs, a Polish-English glossary, an ethnic recipe, and a coal-mining song. Most recently, *The Road to Lattimer* (2019) by Virginia Rafferty adds a further chapter to the fictional treatment of the massacre. Rafferty's book plus several others, mainly fictional, related to the anthracite story have appeared under the fifteen imprints of Sunbury Press, a wide-ranging independent trade publisher based in central Pennsylvania.

In particular, fiction for young adults and children may be more successful than the conventional historiography of school textbooks in bringing the canvas of history to life in their minds. Gourley's and Bartoletti's novels are adult works that may appeal to readers of any age group. Other novels are more expressly written for a younger audience. From the very beginning of the posthistorical period comes *Rebels in the Shadows* (1962) by Robert T. Reilly. Nothing further appears until *Breaker* (1998) by N.A. Perez set around the 1902 Great Strike, while *Molly Justice* (2001) by Steve Varonka was published by his own Coal Hole Productions. Before ceasing operations in 2004, Varonka's company also published three short story collections by himself, plus James A. Goodman's *Two Weeks Under: The Sheppton Mine Disaster/Miracle* (2003), a nonfictional account of the escape in 1963 of two out of three miners trapped underground for two weeks. The title's use of "miracle" invokes a spiritual-cum-supernatural interpretation that has dominated but also dogged accounts of this event. Along with over thirty others at one point, including Goldbeck, Glodek, and Patrick Campbell, Varonka belonged to the Coal Region Book Nook, an online group of anthracite authors, researchers, editors, publishers, book dealers, and artists formed by McKeever in the late 1990s as an extension of his Mine Country publishing venture. As well as providing a forum for shared interests in coal region culture, the group had a regular presence for several years at area heritage events.

The Sheppton disaster, which remains shrouded Mollies-style in a degree of mystery and speculation, gained further nonfictional attention from regional author Maxim W. Furek in *Sheppton: The Myth, Miracle and Music* (2015), which was self-published on Amazon. In 2021, Furek published another book on the subject, focusing more on the musical history surrounding the band that hit nationally with a song about the disaster. Similarly self-published, we find *The Black Rock That Built America: A Tribute to the Anthracite Coal Miners* by Gerald L. McKerns, published by Xlibris in 2007. Self-publishing and print-on-demand initiatives of this kind have become increasingly common over the last twenty-five years and show no sign of diminishing. While many books produced in this fashion may be of questionable literary or historical worth and may compromise the reputation of their authors in some people's eyes, the efficiency and relative ease of this method cannot be ignored, especially in a shrinking and fiercely competitive traditional book market. Such publications represent, as do myriad websites and blogs, a viable and possibly sole alternative to traditional publication for some anthracite region historians, poets, and novelists. These publications occasionally present otherwise scarce opportunities for telling anthracite history by writers often new to the subject. For instance, *This, Their Friendship's Monument* (2020) by Melanie Akren-Dickson, self-published on Amazon, is a genealogical study based on the discovery of an autograph album kept by her relative Mary Boyd, in an anthracite patch town from 1881 to 1896.

DRAMA

As the main section below on Performance confirms, the production of drama contributes widely to the telling of the anthracite story, though less so as published literature, since the readership for plays is relatively small. There are few plays in print from the posthistorical period other than six in my own *Anthracite!* anthology and in a publication of Bloomsburg Theatre Ensemble's (BTE) *Hard Coal: Life in the Region* (2005). My anthology comprises six plays—by Jason Miller, Michael Cotter, Genia Miller, BTE, Jack McDonough/Bob Shlesinger, and Deborah Lou Randall—discussed below as theatrical performances.

POETRY

As with drama, poetry is a minority taste these days, yet it can tell of the anthracite in ways distinct from fictional or nonfictional prose. The art of poetry invites its practitioner to create memorable insights into regional life via flashes of illumination from an interiorized perspective. A striking, even startling use of imagery and tone, a sensitive perception of the physical world, and a heightening of significant moments drawn from everyday experience characterize much anthracite poetry. Such poems mainly find their way into literary magazines since poetry books with anthracite themes are relatively few. As with fiction and historiography, little poetry emerged in the 1960s and 1970s. That period, a time to reflect inwardly on industrial collapse and to register a transformed environment and culture, finally gave way to a minor outpouring of poetic language and an unlocking of memories that, for many reasons, both private and public, had long been neglected or repressed.

Following the appearance in 1981 of *Anthracite*, a volume of poems by Scranton native Paul Kelley, *Anthracite Country* by Jay Parini came out in 1982: a tripartite collection of which the first comprises sixteen coal region poems based heavily on Parini's memories of growing up in Scranton. Beyond images of the collieries, some related scenes of pollution are part of Parini's remembered landscape, such as the river in "The Lackawanna at Dusk": "In whirlpool eddies, odds / of garbage and poisoned fish / inherit the last red hour of light." (19) *Coalseam* (1996), edited by Karen Blomain, remains a definitive anthology of anthracite region poems. It includes works by fourteen authors, including several, all regional natives, with national and international reputations: Parini, W.S. Merwin, Harry Humes, and Anthony Petrosky. Merwin's selections are drawn from an early volume, *The Carrier of Ladders* (1971); "Burning Mountain" is about a culm bank on fire, but the poet's evocation of its implacable menace holds good for all coal region fires, above or below ground: "It consumes itself; but so slowly it will outlast / Our time and our grandchildren's, curious / But not unique: there was always one of these / Nearby, wherever we moved, when I was a child." (16) Among many volumes of poetry, Humes has published *Robbing the Pillars* (1984) and *Pennsylvania Coal Town: The Girardville Poems* (2004), the second with photographs by Lincoln Fajardo. From that volume, "Mine Settlement" evokes the lurking fear of collapsing homes: "Nor did we name the abandoned tunnels beneath us, / their rotting timbers, drip of acid water and gas / dissolving the edges of what we most believed." (21) In a prefatory interview by Kevin McCloskey, Humes explains why he continues to evoke his hometown of Girardville in his writings: "It is my primary landscape, and I try to remember it and recreate all its wonderful smells and beat-up detail. I feel very lucky to have this connection to the voices, faces, the abandoned tunnels." (8) On return visits to the town, adds Humes, "sometimes I just wander its streets and alleys. Lots of ghosts, you bet. I drive up to my father's old mine, Packer Number Five, and look at its ruins . . . The whole damn town . . . never gives up its hold on me. It never stops giving me ideas for stories, essays, and poems. It never stops breaking my heart." (13)

Born in Exeter, Anthony (Tony) Petrosky won the 1982 Walt Whitman Award for his first volume *Jurgis Petraskas* (1983), which covers four generations of Petrosky's Lithuanian American family. "A Pennsylvania Family" highlights the familiar scenario of a miner wanting better for his offspring: "Old man Petraskas worked the mines / until he died and refused to let his sons / do the same. They worked the stills, / delivering what finally saved them, / the whiskey." (5) More recently, Scranton native John E. McGuigan published *Part of a Geography* (2003). In a publisher's note, Jennifer Hill Kaucher describes McGuigan's poetry as "rooted in memories of his childhood home and its landscape . . . of 'dark coal pits' and dust, the chant-like chug of trains." The lulling title of "Evensong in Summer" leads ironically into a dark, frightening world wherein his constant hearing of indecipherable colliery names—"Storrs. Marvine. Cayuga."—feeds an anxiety that plagues even his childhood dreams: "Sometimes I woke / in the middle of the night / trapped inside a lunch pail / swinging from the fist / of a black-faced man." (22)

Though Anton Piotrowski's poetry does not belong to the posthistorical period, its public rediscovery does; in 1998, Harold E. Cox of Wilkes University edited a collection of his poems. A Polish immigrant to Nanticoke, Piotrowski had been a breaker boy and wrote around the turn of the twentieth century. His verse, some of it lost and some surviving in fragmented form, had circulated freely within the local Polish community throughout the twentieth century. Jule Znaniecki, a local historian, assembled the disparate body of Piotrowski's work into a bilingual edition with English translations by several hands. As Cox points out, the poetry captures "much of the flavor of everyday life" and "is part of the story of both the Polish immigrant community and the anthracite coal industry of a century ago." (7) In one stanza of "Gas in the Mines," Piotrowski eerily personifies a "phantom" sneaking around: "Deep in the shadows he walks / In every gangway he stalks / Lurks in spots not easily detected / Ready to attack the unsuspected / Such a dreadful foe." (29)

Unlike anthracite historiography, which continues to be a fertile field more than sixty years after Knox, the output from traditional literary genres has decreased since a boom period from the early 1980s to the early 2000s. Though fiction occasionally appears, it is difficult to explain why this reduction has happened. One reason, perhaps, is that younger writers now lack their predecessors' personal connection to the coal industry and regional culture, formerly passed down through successive generations of family members. Without that connection, there is less interest in the subject and less incentive to explore its creative potential.

PERFORMANCE

Performance is fundamental to human experience; we all are performers of one kind or another when we do things in the presence of others and elicit reactions from them to those actions. At a more formalized level, the performing arts—theater, music, and dance—are equally fundamental to almost every society in history. Their essence lies in a live exchange between performer and audience, having the potential to generate emotional, physical, and intellectual responses. Film is a performing art too; its difference lies in the fact that, like recorded music, the performance itself is not experienced live, though in a movie theater setting, for instance, a live exchange still takes place in the reactions of viewers individually and collectively to what they hear and see unfolding on the big screen.

The performing arts play a major part in telling anthracite history for the above reasons. It is also because they reach large numbers of people gathered together at any one time and communicate meaningfully with them in ways that do not necessarily demand sophisticated or specialized knowledge of their subject matter. They are ideal vehicles for attracting tourists through heritage promotion, so they feature prominently in cultural events such as festivals and commemorations. It is important that performances correspond to a sensitive and accurate telling of history and that they seek as far as possible to avoid an expedient watering-down of their content to match commercial expectations. If we treat history primarily as a cultural commodity, then we limit and may damage its scope. An approach seeking to balance artistic integrity and audience expectation is key to the role of the performing arts in successfully telling history to the greatest number of persons.

THEATER

Theater tells of the anthracite in dramatic stories, and storytelling is a basic social desire and need. Much of anthracite history is the story of struggle—to feed and clothe families, earn a living wage, exercise one's rights, and be accepted from the outside—and theater enlivens this story by representing elements of conflict and change among individuals and communities alike. By the same token, communal bonds have always been strong in anthracite country, and theater offers a mirror to the region by portraying those communal bonds in action. This is evident from what happens onstage and within the audience. Live theater demonstrates the strength of those bonds by bringing strangers together at one time and in one space to experience dynamic interactions between performer and audience; in the process, those interactions may have a transformative effect on each. Audiences recognize and appreciate the characteristic language, humor, customs, and habits of the coal communities being presented to them. As a creative interpretation of history, theater becomes an effective means of renewing and transmitting collective memories. It does so principally, though not exclusively, via the language given to individual characters in a play, the sum of which represents a substantial part of the history of specific social groups and communities. A further strength of theater lies in its totality, whereby its disparate elements—words, facial expressions, body language, costume, make-up, sets, lighting, sounds, and music—combine to form a powerful spectacle. This heady combination creates a memorable experience in which the history and culture of the hard coal region come alive for the brief time of a performance. That which audience members of any age group or background take with them from the experience may prove valuable in the form of memories revived, or fresh knowledge gained. Anthracite drama falls into several major categories offering various perspectives on regional history. Often there is considerable thematic overlap within plays representing everyday communal life, ethnic identities, labor struggles, mining accidents, and other momentous historical events.

The Bloomsburg Theatre Ensemble created two plays presenting episodic views of coal communities' everyday life. Designed as a production to tour regional schools, the single-act *Patchworks: Life and Legends of the Coal Towns* (1997) consists mainly of stories, songs, and first-person narratives. Set around 1900, the play depicts a day in the life of a typical Slovak mining family and allegorizes a search for the American Dream among immigrants to the region. Using flexible staging to establish a rapport between actors and audience, its two versions played to almost 80,000 regional children in a convincing demonstration of how theater may teach anthracite history to young people in imaginative and entertaining ways. Despite the success of this production and the publication in the same anthology (*Anthracite!*) of five other plays, it is all the more regrettable that few other efforts regionally seem to have been made to use anthracite drama as an educational tool. *Hard Coal: Life in the Region* (1999) is an expanded and more technically complex version of *Patchworks* produced expressly for mainstage production at the ensemble's

Bloomsburg Theatre Ensemble, *Hard Coal: Life in the Region*, play, 1999. (Image: courtesy of BTE/Marlin Wagner.)

Alvina Krause Theatre in Bloomsburg. Set in both past and present, the text consists of authentic source materials such as letters, newspaper accounts, and oral histories. With the acting ensemble playing multiple roles, the play fuses public and private stories in a blend of fantasy and realism that shows a discernibly Brechtian use of words, music, dance, film clips, and photographic projections.

Nobody Hears a Broken Drum (1970), the first play by Jason Miller, who went on to win a Pulitzer Prize for his play *That Championship Season* (1972), stands as one of the earliest posthistorical anthracite dramas. It gave its author his first taste of success in a brief off-Broadway run. Set in an Irish mining community in the southern field during the 1860s-1870s, the play is a two-act collection of thirty scenes lasting five minutes or less representing diverse aspects of daily life in the mine patch. The action covers several milestones in the regional history of that period, such as the origin of miners' unions and the Molly Maguires episode. Offering a critique of the role of the Catholic Church in these struggles, the play also touches on inter/intra-ethnic rivalries and themes of immigration and patriotism in the context of the Civil War. Another early play is *Don't Go to the Mine* (1974), a one-acter by Charles K. Stumpf, who enjoyed a long association with the dramatic wing of the Hazleton Art League. The play morphed into *Black Diamonds* (1976), a "mini-pageant" and "musical production of anthracite folktales and ballads" originally written for the official opening of Eckley Miners' Village as a heritage site. Sympathetic to the cause of the miner and the labor movement, this organic text has enjoyed numerous rewrites and revivals over the years. *Coaltown Breaker* by Michael Cotter (1975) remains the only play dealing directly with regional mining disasters. It is based loosely on the 1963 saga of three miners trapped for two weeks in the Sheppton mine, two of whom were rescued. Though the plot focuses on the unfolding of that specific historical event, notoriously "the ninth biggest story in the world" in that year, its more generic title indicates Cotter's wish for his play to address broader ideological and moral issues largely via the prolonged dialogue among the trapped men. Tracing some strange aspects of the survivors' documented accounts, the play also touches on the religious superstitions and gruesome speculations that have clung to the Sheppton story over the years.

The lengthy struggle of anthracite miners for fair pay and conditions is a recurrent theme in many plays. *The Fire Down Below* (2002), co-authored by Jack McDonough and Bob Shlesinger, is a two-act dramatization of the hearings of the arbitration commission set up by President Theodore Roosevelt to investigate conditions in the anthracite fields that gave rise to the Great Strike of 1902. Much of the play's dialogue closely follows testimony given by, among others, the celebrated pro-labor attorney Clarence Darrow; by coal baron George Baer's attorney Wayne MacVeagh; by UMW leader John Mitchell; by two miners, a mine boy, and a factory girl. In the interest of the dramatic experience, the playwrights introduce a good deal of humor and poetic license; for instance, several characters appear who did not testify in Scranton, such as Baer and Mitchell's trusted aide Elizabeth Morris. Furthermore, in *The Fire Down Below* (2002), his companion book to the play, McDonough stresses his readers' need to accept his subjective and creative approach to the story. The play was first produced at the Lackawanna County Courthouse in Scranton as part of the centenary celebration of the 1902 strike. The authenticity of the courthouse performances resulted from their taking place almost exactly one century after the original hearings and in the very same courtroom, No. 3. With the characters of the commissioners (non-speaking parts except for Chairman George Gray) seated in the judicial box and audience members seated in the jury box and packing the rest of the courtroom space, the producers were thus able to create an extraordinary resemblance to the events that inspired the play. Miners' hero Mitchell reappears in *Johnny!* (2000) by Katherine Ashe, a verse play with built-in potential for adaptation as an opera or musical. The winner of a play competition for a celebration of labor held at Scranton Cultural Center, its expansive, stylized, counter-realist mode of presentation, not unlike BTE's coal-themed productions, was intended to offer a contrast to the documentary quality of the film *Stories from the Mines* with whose appearance it had broadly coincided. The grinding toil and vulnerability of the child laborer are central to *Breaker Boy*, a short story by Catherine Gourley that she adapted as a radio play for the PBS network in 1986. Similarly, the title of *Once a Man, Twice a Boy* (1994), written and performed by Joe Lucas, repeats the coal country saying that a breaker boy becomes a miner only to return later in life—and often disabled—to the kind of menial work on which he started. A dramatic monologue featuring thirty characters and based on a five-generational history of Lucas's own mining family in Schuylkill County, the play has been performed many times in Ireland, England, Florida, California, off-Broadway, and in various Pennsylvania locations. Between 1987 and 2002, another regional writer, Thomas P. Dempsey (*aka* T. Martin Gilhooley), wrote a series of short plays about the anthracite region that have been performed at area museums and, in one case, partially underground at the site of the Lackawanna Coal Mine Tour.

The ubiquitous Mollies saga drives the action of several anthracite plays. Its story of the bitter struggle between coal companies and renegade miners offers ample Manichean conflict of a kind conducive to a powerful theatrical experience. Most of the playwrights using the story have family roots in the region, so their dramatizations are invariably sympathetic to the Mollies and hostile to the mining establishment. Unrelated to Jason Miller, Genia Miller's first play was *Spirit of the Molly Maguires: A Carbon County Legend* (1993). Inspired by Patrick Campbell's *A Molly*

Maguire Story and employing a semi-documentary approach, the play focuses on key events leading to the arrest, conviction, and execution of the prime suspects on June 21, 1877. The main storyline concerns the fate of the "Mauch Chunk Four," notably their leader Alexander Campbell. Miller wrote an alternative version of the play subtitled *The Schuylkill County Story* that focuses instead on the "Pottsville Six" led by the so-called "King of the Mollies," John "Black Jack" Kehoe. The involvement of women in the Mollies story is an important element in Miller's play and even more so in the work of Deborah Lou Randall. *Daughters of Molly Maguire* (2000) was the first version of a play in which Randall sought to combine her knowledge of the saga with an urge to explore her Irish American origins. Discovering new connections in a history of conspiracy and cover-up, *Are You a Daughter of Molly Maguire?* (2001) was a rewrite of the play that enabled Randall to meditate further on female empowerment and the functioning of private and public memories. The play changed again into *Molly Daughter* (2002), an uninterrupted fifty-minute one-woman performance that combined and elaborated elements of the previous two versions. As Randall says of her play: "[It] had three different life forms over a three-year period . . . The story kept calling me back to it [and] continues to . . . ." (Mosley, xxiii) Three other writers—John Kearns, John P. Rooney, and Bobby Maso have also dramatized the story. Kearns's *Sons of Molly Maguire* (2007), set in Mahanoy City, ran in New York City in 2007 and Dublin in 2017. *Irish Echo* critic Joseph Hurley called it a "generally effective blending of pageant, mime, kitchen sink realism, and even flights of poetry." Coming out of Belfast, Northern Ireland, Rooney wrote *The Sons of Molly* as a three-part radio play: "The Detective," "The Organisation Man," and "The Hanging Day." It aired in the British Broadcasting Corporation's (BBC) "Afternoon Play" series in 1996. Regional actor and historian Maso's *The Day of the Rope* (2017) is a brief drama portraying the last three days in the lives of ten convicted Mollies. In 2009, Maso and the Eckley Players wrote and produced *Tragedy at Avondale* based on the eponymous book by Wolensky and Keating. More recently, Scranton-area playwright K. K. Gordon has written a play, *For the Least of Them*, on the life of the "Labor Priest," Rev. John J. Curran of Wilkes-Barre.

MUSIC

Music is a universal art form known to every society. When northeastern Pennsylvania was first settled, and immigrants from many countries came in successive waves to work in coal mining, they brought their traditional folk music. In its original forms and its American adaptations and developments, music was at the heart of regional life. Often accompanied by dance, music was performed and heard daily in every part of the mining community: in homes, churches, bar rooms, at picnics and festivals, on marches, and at rallies. It stirred people to action, accompanied their labors, lifted their sagging spirits, soothed their everyday pains, shared their common experiences, and celebrated their pride and togetherness. Due to a common language, the best-known songs had English, Welsh, Irish, or Scottish origins, but countless others survived in German, Italian, and any of several Slavic tongues.

Miners performed mining songs at work above and below ground. Those songs, whose lyrics often preceded their musical settings drawn from a range of stock tunes, were part of a rich oral tradition that had been brought to the region from the old countries and were circulated by itinerant miner minstrels (or "bards") who, fiddle or guitar in hand, took this repertoire from patch to patch. The lyrics of these songs tell vividly of moments in anthracite history, especially as many were cast in ballad form, of which the strong narrative drive was a perfect way to capture the tales of people, places, and events. By the early twentieth century, changing social patterns and growing mobility had weakened an ingrown traditional music while emerging modern technologies of mass communication, such as radio and phonograph records, took over the function of providing popular music for the masses. The old songs and their system of oral transmission were now in danger of disappearing or, at best, being drowned out by the new, reproducible sounds of Tin Pan Alley, "hillbilly," ragtime, blues, and jazz. It was then that folklorist George Korson decided to intervene "at the eleventh hour," as he put it, seeing that members of the mining communities now preferred more easily disseminated and mass-distributed popular songs to live performance from the regional canon of folkloric material. Hostile to commercial recordings and fearing the loss of a tradition, Korson began a mission to save it from slipping into oblivion. He published *Songs and Ballads of the Anthracite Miner* in 1927; an expanded version became *Minstrels of the Mine Patch: Songs and Stories of the Anthracite Industry* (1938), his definitive work. In 1946, Korson embarked on the second and crucial part of his mission by going down the mines to record songs in Pottsville, Wilkes-Barre, Buck Run, Tamaqua, Shenandoah, and Centralia. These recordings were first released by the Archive of American Folk Song of the Library of Congress in a set of five 78 rpm records in 1947, on a vinyl LP album in 1958, and a CD in 1997. They remain the mother lode of anthracite mining songs. Formerly held by the D. Leonard Corgan Library at King's College, the Korson Collection, donated to the Library by Korson in 1965, is now housed in the Archive of Folk Culture at the Library of Congress, though the Corgan Library holds copies of much of the original material. Korson, who has received detailed attention from Angus Gillespie (*Folklorist of the Coal Fields: George Korson's Life and Work*, 1980) and Archie Green (*Only a Miner: Studies in Recorded Coal-Mining Songs*, 1972), deserves to be remembered as a lone and towering figure in the collection of traditional anthracite (and bituminous) folksong. The posthistorical revival of performances of this music by folk groups and contemporary singer-songwriters may belong to an evolved definition of the folk genre, but it is almost entirely due to Korson's pervasive influence and cannot be understood or fully appreciated without referring to his pioneering work.

A younger generation of anthracite region performers grew out of the folk music revival of the 1950s and 1960s in the USA and the British Isles, a groundswell that encompassed the unearthing of songs from both rural and urban traditions as well as the composition of new material often with a radical activist sentiment. The political nature of much "protest" folk music of the period corresponds well to the re-emergence of the old miners' songs, as amid their earthy humor, they express the frequent hardships and oppression as well as the communal and unionized solidarity of the heavy industrial worker. A recovery of anthracite history via new and revived songs emerged slowly and only blossomed in the work of solo artists after the turn of the twenty-first century. The Irish Balladeers, a Scranton-based folk group, were ahead of the game, releasing *The Molly Maguires* album in 1968 on a New York state label specializing in Irish music. The group consisted of brothers Chuck, Bob, and John Rogers plus their brother-in-law Ted Andrews on vocals, their father Charles, Sr. on accordion, and Eddie Lennihan, a popular Scranton musician, on banjo and guitar. The album cover photograph shows the group standing in front of a coal breaker. They conceived the record as an alternative vision of the Molly Maguires designed to offset the expected presence of negative Irish stereotypes in the eponymous Hollywood movie in production locally at that time. Two of the album's fourteen songs are originals: "Sons of Molly" and "The Knox Mine Disaster." The latter song's liner notes state that it "is included to show that even a century later, with all our modern advancements, nothing has been developed to prevent these terrible mine disasters." Seven other songs stem from the anthracite region, the remainder being well-known Irish ditties. Two songs recorded by Korson ("When the Breakers Go Back on Full Time" and "The Shoofly") are included, though for an ensemble that began performing in 1966, their sound, writes Green, is understandably closer to contemporary folk music in the popular Irish style of the Clancy Brothers than to "any of the rough-hewn Celtic-based singers encountered by Korson." (427) A quarter-century elapsed before a similar group, The Donegal Weavers from the Wilkes-Barre area, released *Last Day of the Northern Field* (1992), an album inspired by the watershed moment of the Knox disaster. Formed in 1980, the group consisted of Ray Stephens, Emmet Burke, Dr. John D. Dougherty, George Yeager, and Joseph P. Jones. They made the album expressly to remind people of regional coal mining history at a time when many still preferred to forget about it. Among the nineteen songs on the album, "Sons of Molly" reappears as a nod to the pioneering Irish Balladeers, as do two of the Korson recordings, "Old Miner's Refrain" and the aforementioned "Breaker" song. Five group originals include the eponymous song and "Sugar Notch Entombment," the latter described in the liner notes as "a dark humored look at the ... 1879 mine cave-in at the Lehigh & Wilkes-Barre Coal Company #10 Slope." Speaking to a reporter, Jones revealed the extensive combing of press archives by Stephens and himself in coming up with a song that would capture "the true feeling as well as the true happenings" at Sugar Notch. In the work of these two groups, we see the result of a vital template that Korson had created for the revival of anthracite mining songs, one that embraced songs not only on specific events, such as the Avondale disaster but also on everyday life in the region. As Gillespie writes, "from the very beginning, [Korson] intuitively understood that folklore is best presented in the context of the entire way of life of a small community." (58) Both groups thus had a platform upon which, in contemporary acoustic folk style, to revive a large body of traditional songs, to add some modern commercial material (two songs by folk-country star Merle Travis on the Donegal Weavers' album), and, most importantly, to showcase their original compositions.

In 1970, Wilkes-Barre/Scranton area pop-rock band The Buoys had their sole chart hit with the controversial "Timothy," whose gruesome allusions to the fate of men trapped in a coal mine appeared to allude to the 1963 Sheppton disaster. The song's composer Rupert Holmes insisted nonetheless on a pure coincidence; in writing it, he was unaware of Sheppton and took his inspiration instead from the classic country-and-western coal mining song "Sixteen Tons" and some macabre elements in the 1959 movie version of Tennessee Williams's play *Suddenly, Last Summer*.

Following in the innovative footsteps of Bob Dylan in the 1960s, the focus of attention in folk circles shifted from ensembles to acoustic-based singer-songwriters. It is solo artists of this kind who have carried the baton of anthracite revivalist music into the present century: Jay Smar, Lex Romane, Van Wagner, and Tom Flannery. Grandson of a Slovak miner from Coaldale, Schuylkill County native Jay Smar incorporates the light, shuffling steps of Appalachian flatfoot dancing into performances that are self-accompanied on guitar, banjo, and fiddle. His repertoire of coal mining songs extends beyond Pennsylvania to those of the bituminous fields of West Virginia. Smar believes that coal region songs are "so engaging that, if performed properly and professionally, can make you feel what the people of that time frame were feeling . . . Frustration . . . Physical and mental pain due to hours in the mines . . .

Women trying to keep their family clothed and fed on little money . . . Anxiety . . . Poverty . . . And [in a particularly well-chosen metaphor] not finding a light at the end of the tunnel." In 2009, to rekindle interest in Korson's work and to present contemporary songwriters following in that tradition, Smar compiled and performed ten *Heritage & Coal Mining Songs of Northeast Pennsylvania*, an album of material written by himself and fellow artists Wagner, Flannery, Lorne Clarke, and Josh Pratt. Smar's updating of the canon allowed him, for instance, to include his own song "The Fires of Centralia" as well as Clarke's song on the 1966 Aberfan disaster in Wales written in homage to the Welsh American population of the anthracite region. Wilkes-Barre native Lex Romane's main contribution to this tradition is also in the form of an album, *Diggin' Dusty Diamonds* (2004), a fourteen-piece collection comprising six of his compositions about anthracite coal mining plus other songs about mining and trains by Jean Ritchie, Merle Travis, Dwight Yoakam, Peggy Seeger, Billy Edd Wheeler, and Norman Blake. In his liner notes, Romane states that after having researched the Korson collection, written his own take on the Knox disaster, and performed some traditional mining songs in the early 1970s, he returned to the subject in 2002, rewriting "Knox Coal Mine Disaster" and penning several other mining songs before releasing his album. In addition to being a musician deeply inspired by his Pennsylvanian heritage, Columbia County native Van Wagner is also an environmental studies teacher, a historical essayist, and a former underground miner at R&R Coal in Schuylkill County. His penchant for creative interpretations of industrial history embraces songs about anthracite mining, iron milling, and lumbering. Mining songs may be found on the numerous albums he has released over the last twenty-five years and in *Coal Dust, Rust & Saw Dust* (2009), a book accompanied by a double CD set where appear, among other songs, "Hard Coal," "Lattimer Massacre," "Bootleg Miner," "Hard Coal, Hard Times," and "Miner's Wife." Author of ten plays, Scranton native Tom Flannery emerged as a singer-songwriter in the 1990s. Prompted by stories he heard from family members, Flannery wrote a song cycle dealing with his family's share of the coal mining heritage. After struggling with preserving his link to this past, the songs eventually "welled up out of nowhere" to form *The Anthracite Shuffle* (2000), a highly personal album of thirteen songs plus one by Lorne Clarke and one co-written with Clarke. Flannery's "The Knox Mine Disaster 1959" offers yet another view of that fateful event and its consequences for the region to add to those in similar songs by the Balladeers, the Weavers, and Romane. As Flannery explains in his liner notes, "What I hope comes through more than anything else is pride. So many people around here seem to turn away from their anthracite heritage as if it is something to be ashamed of . . . Perhaps seeing the town referred to as a 'long dead coal town' over and over again sends them to the Wal-Mart to buy a shovel that will bury the past once and for all . . . To hell with that. These men and women and children are heroes to me. All they asked for was a fair shake, and when they didn't get it, they pushed back. Hard."

Mention should also be made of a Schuylkill County duo, Thomas D. "Big Tom" Symons and John S. "Stu" Richards, who perform anthracite mining songs as the Breaker Boys; formerly, they were joined by the late Chuck Barr, who had made his name in eastern Pennsylvania as a rock 'n' roll singer in the 1950s. Richards is also the author of a photo book, *Early Coal Mining in the Anthracite Region* (2002). Though the album consists of more than mining songs, *Where the Coal Trains Load*, a thirty-one-track compilation of contemporary field recordings in Schuylkill County by folklorists and musicians Michael and Carrie Nobel Kline, is the closest reprise of Korson's great project to have taken place in the anthracite region. As a part of their extensive fieldwork in 2004-05, the Klines recorded these multi-ethnic musical performances in homes and churches within a demarcated area of the county.

These various artists of the last half-century have valiantly kept anthracite history alive through song. Accomplished and popular performers, they are often to be seen at regional heritage events. Yet they lack regular venues in which to perform their music. A handful of folk clubs in the region have come and gone, while the general public has a limited taste for authentic local material in a genre that no longer claims to spring directly from a collective consciousness other than as a historical reminder, a "memory realm" (*lieu de mémoire*) in Pierre Nora's term. Consequently, after a rush of solo talent in the early 2000s on a path cleared earlier by the Balladeers and the Weavers, no younger performers with a similar sense of belonging have come along to keep this particular flame alight. Its future remains uncertain.

Another genre of popular music capable of conveying aspects of anthracite history is the stage musical. An early posthistorical piece on the Molly Maguires, *Black Diamond*, written by Brad Smoker with music by Glen Morgan, was produced at Lycoming College in 1966. Thirty years later, a much bigger production on the same theme premiered in two theaters outside Philadelphia. *The Molly Maguires,* with music and lyrics by Sid Cherry and a book by William Strempek, had been developed over six years at the BMI Lehman Engel Musical Theatre Workshop in New York City. Despite further development in an off-Broadway workshop in 1999 that saw the addition of some Irish dancing under the fashionable spell of *Riverdance*, it eventually failed to make it to the Great White Way. It was brought to the F.M. Kirby Center for the Performing Arts in Wilkes-Barre in 2007 by producer Jim Burke. Despite some stirring music and a daring attempt to present James McParlan as a more sympathetic figure, its presentation as a work *still* in progress (rudimentary set design, orchestra and cast sharing stage space, some script reading by actors, and a mood unrelieved by any lightheartedness) garnered decidedly mixed reviews. Two years later, Burke's attempt to present it in Scranton did not succeed.

Rock music is of negligible relevance to the telling of anthracite history, though the apocalyptic overtones of the Centralia disaster played a part in the naming of the album *Centralia* by the hardcore punk/heavy metal-influenced American band Car Bomb. The town of Centralia is the setting for Squonk Opera's *Inferno* (2003, originally titled *Burn*), a Dantesque vision of the Centralia fire expanding to a dark parable of postindustrial America. Squonk, a Pittsburgh-based company, situates itself beyond any conventional understanding of operatic form. Mixing performance art with wildly diverse elements of theater and music, the company remains almost impossible to classify. In a bizarre audiovisual mélange including shadow puppetry, *Inferno* "moved Squonk clearly into the realm of experimental theater," wrote one reviewer, while another called the show a "full-scale modern rock opera" with a score drawing on classical, jazz, rock, and world music. Yet another critic likened the show to a postmodern version of a seventeenth-century masque.

Anthracite history is represented in classical opera by *A Coal Region Opera: A Pick, A Candle, & A Kiss* (1992), a story of forbidden love between a coal magnate's daughter and a miner at the end of the nineteenth century. The dilemma at the heart of any artistic enterprise based on a minority historical interest was foremost in the mind of the opera's composer Paul W. Miller, who told a press interviewer that "it may be a beautifully and delicately crafted endeavor, but it's also a business . . . It had to be accessible to the audience." Miller thus introduced jazz and folk music elements into an otherwise conventional operatic score. With a libretto by Karen A. Hube, seven main actors, a chorus of the Pennsylvania Theaterworks Company, and a twelve-piece orchestra, *A Coal Region Opera* was staged in Wilkes-Barre, Pottsville, Jim Thorpe, and at Carnegie Hall in New York City before a 1993 tour took it to the annual American Music Festival in Bonn, Germany, and the environs of Prague, Czech Republic.

Teacher, conductor, and composer, the late Patrick J. Marcinko II, a specialist in Eastern European choral music, especially the form sung in Church Slavonic, paid a personal homage with *A Coal Miner's Tale: An Epic Soundscape* (2010), a composition for a forty-piece group, the Upper Valley Winds. This neoclassical piece depicts life in Marcinko's native Lackawanna Valley, where his father was a miner. Stressing the need for an appropriate commemoration, he told a press interviewer that he felt "a wind ensemble would best represent the spirit of the miners" and that it was "important to have this tribute and memorial and some closure for the miners."

In winning a Pulitzer Prize in 2014 for her oratorio *Anthracite Fields*, MacArthur Fellow Julia Wolfe's extraordinary achievement was to draw widespread attention to the subject of anthracite history and culture in musical circles and to do so in an experimental work blending classical and folk influences. The piece pays tribute to the people of the coal region, even though they may be an unlikely audience for such an avant-garde composition. A Philadelphia-area native with roots in the coal region, Wolfe describes her extensive preparation and design of the project: "I went down into the coal mines, visited patch towns and the local museums where the life of the miners has been carefully depicted and commemorated. I interviewed retired miners and children of miners who grew up in the patch. The text is culled from oral histories and interviews, local rhymes, a coal advertisement, geological descriptions, a mining accident index, contemporary . . . everyday activities that make use of coal power, and an impassioned speech by John L. Lewis, the head of the United Mine Workers Union." Structured in five parts, *Anthracite Fields* is performed on CD (2015) by six members of the Bang On A Can minimalist composers' collective (of which Wolfe is a co-founder) and the Choir of Trinity Wall Street, New York. This instrumental and vocal collaboration begins by producing intermittently explosive sounds of catastrophe; the opening section, "Foundation," is at first ominous and intimidating. Then comes a seemingly endless litany of miners' names honoring accident casualties from 1869 to 1916, a roll call drawing additional force from naming *only* those with a first name "John" and a monosyllabic family name. The recitation of this somber list begins to mingle with airy female voices introducing a "primal" section on the formation of coal before resuming the chant now of exotic multisyllabic names. Built around the words and rhythms of children's rhyming games, the varying tempo of "Breaker Boys" suggests both youthful energy and an inescapably furious pace of work interspersed with brief moments of rest and respite. As anthracite photographer Ray Klimek writes elsewhere of breaker boys in Lewis Hine's famous images, one of which is reproduced in the booklet accompanying the CD, "They appear tragic or impish like extras from a silent film or Dickensian urchins . . . If they're icons of a particular injustice they're also typical adolescents . . . [with] a sense of play and even a form of resistance." Evoking a historical recording, a scratchy sound leads into the third part: Lewis's speech calling for improved conditions and fairer compensation for miners and their families. A recitation of floral names based on an interview with a woman raised in a patch town forms the fourth part, "Flowers," reminding the listener both of the natural beauty of the unscarred coal region and of how residents nurtured that beauty against the grime and ugliness surrounding them. Bursting in with funky guitar and barreling piano, the final part, "Appliances," recalls the relentless pulse of electric power generated by coal-fired plants—and how we so often take this utility for granted in our daily lives.

VISUAL ARTS

PHOTOGRAPHY

The art of photography has proven invaluable to the telling of the anthracite. Uncovering history in a succession of discrete and momentary images, its unrivaled capacity to document the world around us and to be easily reproduced has enabled it to establish a comprehensive record of regional life and industry. Arguably *the* art of the industrial revolution, photography developed alongside anthracite production from the early nineteenth century onward. It has produced countless images of people, places, and objects in ways that may powerfully affect the viewer. From the weary expression on a miner's face to a shaft of sunlight across an abandoned culm bank, photographic images of anthracite often have a beauty and dignity that belie their sources in routine scenes of grime, toil, and hardship.

A minor tradition existed for almost one hundred years up to the 1960s in the work of several photographers who took commissions from the coal and associated industries, from the press on assignments to the region, and governmental agencies of one kind or another. Key figures in this practice were George Bretz, William Rau, Frances Benjamin Johnston, John Horgan Jr., Watson Bunnell, and George Harvan. Apart from Harvan's, their work lies outside the posthistorical parameters of this book, but no account of anthracite photography in the last sixty years may be satisfactorily given without acknowledging their influence. Fortunately, their accomplishments have been covered in scholarly articles, in books such as *Illustrating an Anthracite Era: The Photographic Legacy of John Horgan Jr.* by Gwendolyn E. Percival and Chester J. Kulesa (1995), and in occasional exhibitions such as *Anthracite Photographer/Photographers of Anthracite* held at the Anthracite Heritage Museum in 2018 in conjunction with the Anthracite 250th Anniversary celebration. Most of these "classic" anthracite photographers were natives of the region, but outsiders also came with cameras and commissions in hand. Lewis Hine may not have been the first, but he remains the most illustrious. Having abandoned school teaching to become an investigative reporter for the National Child Labor Committee (NCLC), this small man toting a big box camera traveled indefatigably across the country to document children at work. In 1910, his mission brought him to northeastern Pennsylvania, where he took his celebrated pictures of breaker boys. These iconic images were among the first to draw attention to the harshness and injustice of life in the coal fields; they helped to instigate workplace reform and set a standard for socially responsible and moving visual representations of life in the region.

Beginning in the mid-1930s, one initiative springing from President Franklin D. Roosevelt's New Deal was at the Historical Section of the Farm Security Administration (FSA), where Roy Stryker gradually assembled an extraordinarily gifted team of photographers to document the lives of ordinary Americans during the Great Depression. The team produced 270,000 pictures from 1935 to 1943. Though much of the work was carried out in rural communities, Stryker sent photographers into the anthracite region, especially the small towns dotted amid its mountainous terrain. In 1938, Sheldon Dick visited the Shenandoah and Pottsville areas to produce a notable set of photographs—one shot, for instance, of the Maple Hill Mine captures the play of light in an almost painterly fashion. Dick's images went beyond typical industrial images of the workplaces; in line with Stryker's mission, he also captured everyday scenes of residents in their homes and social venues. In 1940, the FSA working with the Office of War Information (OWI), sent Jack Delano to document the region's contribution to the war effort by way of the accelerated production of coal. Delano had already done a Works Progress Administration/Federal Art Project study in 1938-39, at one stage having lodged with a mining family in Schuylkill County, a mission that earned him a place on the FSA roster. His photograph of a Polish family on the deck of its home in Mauch Chunk (Jim Thorpe) has gained iconic status; another shot, of a street in Coaldale, captures perfectly the coexisting yet contrasting features of the region: town life in the foreground, culm bank in the middle ground, and forested ridge in the background. Between 1941 and 1943, another OWI photographer, William Perlitch, concentrated on shooting war production rallies involving active servicemen working alongside miners in Scranton, Hazleton, Wilkes-Barre, and Mt. Carmel. As had Dick and Delano earlier, Perlitch not only took pictures of miners engaged in routine work but also captured townscapes, street scenes, and private homes to convey a fuller picture of life in the region.

Another notable OWI project that furthered the industrial and social documentation of the region was a series by New York freelance photographer Nelson Morris to accompany a propagandistic story about ordinary citizens aiding the war effort. Rediscovered in the Library of Congress archives by researcher Annie Bohlin in 1982, these thirty-eight finely composed photos, of which fourteen appeared in *Click* magazine in July 1942 without crediting Morris (as was then a common practice), offered an unusual insight into regional working-class and immigrant life by portraying Czechoslovakia-born miner Andrew Scavnicky at work in the No. 7 Jeddo-Highland mine near Hazleton and at home pursuing leisure and spending time with members of his family. In 1992, all thirty-eight images were exhibited at the Sordoni Gallery in Wilkes-Barre as *Scavnicky: Portrait of an Anthracite Family*. The exhibition was guest curated by Bohlin, who was finally able to credit Morris for his work. We may also mention Wilkes-Barre native Ralph E. De Witt (1885-1979), who took up photography as a boy and, in 1938, established a studio in the old Corn Exchange building in Wilkes-Barre. Though best known as a portrait photographer, De Witt shot pictures of the coal industry and its communities from the 1910s to the 1940s. A selection of his anthracite images—the most renowned being a shot of boy workers playing touch football in front of a Kingston breaker in 1920—was shown in a 1976 retrospective at the Sordoni Gallery.

Given the period of their involvement, the work of most of the above photographers revolved around documenting scenes of an *active* anthracite industry. However, the work of George Harvan (1921-2002) is of particular relevance to the present study since his photographs from the late-1940s to the 1990s bridge the industry's history and posthistory. Harvan's work has rightly been recognized in several books and online

George Harvan, *Last Car of Coal*, Lansford, b&w photograph, 1972. (Image: courtesy of National Canal Museum, a program of the Delaware & Lehigh National Heritage Corridor, Easton, Pennsylvania.)

publications. In 1998, the CHTP brought out *The Coal Miners of Panther Valley* under Harvan's name. Thomas Dublin, whose own book *When the Mines Closed* is graced by Harvan's photos, contributed an introductory essay to the Harvan book before proceeding with Melissa Doak to curate a retrospective online edition of *The Journal of MultiMedia History* entitled *Miner's Son, Miners' Photographer: The Life and Work of George Harvan* (2001), which included 280 of his photographs. Having taken up photography in Japan during World War Two service, Harvan worked as a press photographer on returning to the Panther Valley before going freelance and winning assignments from the LC&N Company to document its mining operations from 1949 to 1954. The scope of his images was necessarily limited by his company brief, but the experience allowed him to learn how "to photograph people working in a black hole," a difficult task: "My main goal was not to lose the deep mine atmosphere by printing too light. There is a lot of black down there and somehow you have to come to terms with it." (15) By the time he turned his lens on the last of the Panther Valley miners in the shape of Lanscoal, the small and short-lived independent company of twenty miners working the old No. 9 Mine in Lansford from 1960 to 1972, he was free to imbue his work with greater spontaneity and expressiveness. He succeeded in conveying the pride and self-respect of his miner friends while framing their last-ditch enterprise within a broader context of postindustrial loss and decline. In his later years, he continued, among other projects, to shoot anthracite pictures—of retired Lanscoal miners, of surviving breakers, of mine rescue efforts, of Centralia and elsewhere. Harvan's work compares well with that of a line of FSA documentary photographers that includes the illustrious names of Walker Evans and Dorothea Lange, and his work might well have won him a place alongside them in its pantheon had he been willing to move to the big cities when good professional opportunities came his way. His decision to stay amid his roots in the anthracite region gave "a continuity to his life which . . . shaped his photography" and explains why his later mining photographs are so natural and unobtrusive. His personal bond with the miners meant that as one of their group, as "quintessentially the insider," in Doak and Dublin's phrase (21), they readily placed their trust in him and his camera.

Another notable transhistorical body of photographic work is that of the Lukasik brothers, Stephen N. and William R., who, from 1949 until recent years, produced over one million prints and negatives covering the greater Pittston area from their studio in Dupont. Among images in an archive maintained now by William Lukasik, Jr., are definitive ones of the Knox mine disaster and many other anthracite scenes. They were also the official photographers for the ILGWU in the Wyoming Valley.

A familiar pattern emerges on entering the posthistorical period, one of little photography being done systematically in the anthracite region for around thirty years other than by Harvan in his late period and by the Historic American Engineering Record (HAER). In 1969, the National Park Service joined with the Library of Congress and the American Society of Civil Engineers to establish HAER as an accompaniment to the Historic American Buildings Survey (HABS), which it had established in 1934. The HAER photographic archive includes historic and contemporary images that complement written texts and delineated drawings. HAER projects focused on design, function, and operational details. It sent several staff photographers to document the Locust Summit breaker in a period after 1968 before later commissioning three Pennsylvania-based industrial photographers to do further work. Pierce Bounds, the official photographer of Dickinson College in Carlisle from 1983 to 2010, photographed the fan complex (demolished in 2014) at the former Dorrance Colliery in Wilkes-Barre, which had closed in 1959 in the wake of the Knox disaster. In 1990, architectural historian Dorothy Allen Silva photographed the former Marvine Colliery in Scranton, which had closed in the 1970s. In the early 1990s, Muhlenberg College professor Joseph E.B. Elliott, lauded for his work documenting the regional industrial heritage, shot scenes for HAER in and around the former Huber Breaker in Ashley, where he returned to make more photographs before it was torn down in 2014. In 2002, he was re-commissioned by HAER to photograph the St. Nicholas Breaker, though the Library of Congress has only recently taken up this work. Elliott, whose work "resides at the nexus of documentation and art," has also photographed other lost breakers, including Sullivan Trail, Hazleton

Joseph E.B. Elliott, Spring Mountain Colliery, b&w photograph, c. 2000. (Image: courtesy of the artist.)

Shaft, and Locust Summit; those images are in the collection of the National Canal Museum in Easton.

Several outsiders worked in the region, notably Bernd and Hilla Becher, Renée Jacobs, and Walter L. Dinteman. Renowned for their images of industrial buildings and structures, the Bechers, German photographers and conceptual artists, came to the region in 1974-75 and 1977-78 to photograph wooden headframes typically found at small-scale independent mines, mostly in the southern field. As they state in the introduction to the 1991 book on their exhibition at the Dia Center for the Arts in New York City, "the mine-head constructions for hauling the coal to the surface, called tipples, are made from simple materials, adapted to the particular topography, the location of the coal beds, and the conditions for removal of the coal" (Introduction). The distinctiveness of their work lies in their preference for often documenting quirky, even ramshackle structures found in remote mountain locations rather than on huge, fully mechanized breakers associated with big company operations in the valleys. As the Centralia fire became national news in the early 1980s, photojournalist Jacobs spent six months in the town beginning in 1983, documenting the plight of its citizens—mostly younger ones—and their responses, positive or negative, to the options facing them of either staying put or moving away with governmental support, a painful choice that came to a head in the 1984 buy-out vote that opted for relocation. Working in a blend of Dorothea Lange's FSA and Henri Cartier-Bresson's "momentous" styles, Jacobs matched her images with interviews to produce a photo essay that captured the desperate situation in which the townspeople found themselves. The majority welcomed Jacobs's presence among them, as they realized that responsible and sensitive coverage could prove instrumental in making their dilemma known further afield. *Anthracite Ghosts* by Walter Dinteman (1995) unveiled a distinctive portfolio of photographs taken on weekend visits to coal country between 1970 and 1973. Dinteman's work represents the first truly posthistorical anthracite photography; his images, full of a nostalgic atmosphere, are predominantly of industrial ruins rather than human subjects and suggest a landscape shorn not only of mining activity but of mine workers too. These photographs show that the anthracite landscape had transformed within two decades from declining industrial activity to one largely of disuse and abandonment. Yet, they represent more than absence and loss; these desolate, empty scenes accrue posthistorical aesthetic value in their strange formal beauty. Accompanying the large, soft-focused final image is a caption: "I wandered over the snow-covered coal site. The snow had melted on parts of the culm bank, revealing a thin black outline of the mountainous dump. In the distance, a breaker formed a black silhouette in this scene reminiscent of a Japanese ink-brush painting." (99)

Non-native photographers continued to be drawn to the region in the early years of the twenty-first century, which saw a lively renewal of interest in this devastated landscape. In 2001, New Jersey native Carl Weese, a specialist in photographing drive-in movie theaters, shot a series of images in Trevorton and Coal Township that, alongside photos he had made over several years in Centralia, resulted in a 2007 show, *Coal Country*, at the Camerawork Gallery in Scranton. Following his work in Centralia, Weese photographed another lost place: Wadesville, in Schuylkill County, a community slowly being swallowed up by a strip mine. In *Modern Ruins: Portraits of Place in the Mid-Atlantic Region* (2010), Shaun O'Boyle includes twenty-four photographs on the theme of coal, accompanying those on the themes of public institutions, arsenals, and steel. His depiction of the anthracite region ranges widely: houses, signs, statues, park benches, machinery, breaker interiors/exteriors, culm banks, and townscapes. O'Boyle's work in this volume, especially the chapter on state hospitals and penitentiaries, parallels the rise of urban exploration and "dark" tourism in that decade. In his introduction to the book, Geoff Manaugh concludes: "Neglected ancestors, simultaneously preserved and repressed, O'Boyle's ruins persist as shadows of rock and metal on the peripheries of cities, giving shape to a past we thought we'd long forgotten." (xii)

During this period, two photographers with deep roots in coal country returned to shoot its postindustrial scenes and, in so doing, rediscovered aspects of their own relationship to its checkered history. Ed Dougert is from Philadelphia, but his family was from Shenandoah; growing up, he spent much time there. Acknowledging the influence of Harvan, he revisited the region in 1999 to make a set of black and white photographs that appear in *The Black Land: Remnants of the Once & Great Anthracite Coal Industry* (2003). Disavowing any sociological, environmental, or historiographic purposes, Dougert offers "a photographic interpretation of the land and what happened here." Noting the "strange beauty" of this land, his photo essay "pays homage to the discarded black hills and small towns left behind." (1)

In 2007, the Sordoni Gallery presented an exhibition, *Black Deserts/Welsh Tips: Photographs by Ray Klimek*. He has since updated the title of this project online to *Transatlantic Seam: Black Deserts and Grudging Grass*. He writes in the exhibition catalog that his work "addresses the value of underused and overlooked places. In particular, it explores the postindustrial landscape as a site of flux and fantasy continually shaped and reshaped by the interaction of natural and cultural processes." He explains: "Just a few yards away from my childhood home in Exeter was an abandoned colliery and tip commonly referred to as the Black Desert, an unofficial appellation that later became the title for my project on the area as a whole." In this project, Klimek's first major one, he presents comparative geography of mining landscapes in northeastern Pennsylvania and south Wales. In color images focusing on culm banks ("slag heaps" to the Welsh), Klimek shows how geological, industrial, and social histories have been shared by the two regions. "It's possible," he writes, "to see a continuum between the coalfields, a primal connection spanning continents and populations. The story goes that a great seam of coal runs from Pennsylvania to South Wales." Furthermore, "in the nineteenth century, Welsh miners migrated to Pennsylvania where they found a landscape that was strangely familiar." Equally though, he raises questions of difference between the two regions in their topographical detail, methods of reclamation, and approaches to heritage culture. In this way, Klimek encourages "a dialogue about the legacy of mining and the future of the landscapes upon which it has left its traces." He explains his choice to shoot in color as springing from a desire "to catch the chromatic richness and variety of areas that have traditionally been represented in black and white." He also wanted "to question an old documentary assumption that color is fundamentally decorative . . . The contrast between green grass and various shades of spoil, for instance, is not merely formally interesting. It also indicates reclamation, the passage of time and patterns of use, in short content that might go unnoticed in a black and white image." For Klimek, this project is organic and ongoing. In his essay, *Black Desert: Nineteen Remnants*, he uses his early memories of the region, Hine's breaker boy images, texts of historical markers, and snippets of press reports to meditate on the former landscape, on its potential as a play space, and on what it has become. He argues that "precisely to the degree that capital has already transformed the landscape on a global scale, it's important to address what happens to these landscapes in the aftermath of their usefulness."

Klimek's coal region images are the catalyst for a subsequent project, *Carbon*, in which he explores the transformative visual potential of the element. In one excursion, "Carbon Analog," influenced by NASA's analogical photography, he defamiliarizes his coal region scenes by reimagining them as extraterrestrial landscapes in a radical shift of perspective toward abstraction, surrealism, and futuristic vision, a measure of his continuing

Ray Klimek, *Hughestown*, Pennsylvania, photograph, digital C print, 2002. (Image: courtesy of the artist.)

interest in the "intersection between history and fantasy." He cites the influence on his coal-related work of regional artist Franz Kline, especially regarding Kline's movement from representational landscapes to abstract forms. In another excursion, "Archipelago," Klimek uses Google Earth images of culm banks to reimagine them as islands detached from their surroundings. However, he insists that for him, "abstraction . . . is never a goal in itself." Rather, he conceives of it and landscape "as intimately related and representing a continuum rather than a set of distinct views or practices . . . An object on one scale becomes a landscape on another and displaces the viewer from a comfortable anthropocentric view to an unfamiliar and challenging terrain." A further excursion, "The After Archive," presents a series of images of objects that Klimek found returning to the demolished Huber colliery site in Ashley, where he had made some of his earliest photographs. He writes, "The sense of ruin in these pieces represents neither death nor regeneration but a diversion, a metamorphosis beyond planning and intent. Taken together, they constitute a catalog of loss, an inventory of abandonment, and a reverie on the passage of time." Fourteen years after he began his anthracite photography, Klimek has conjoined these evolved projects in a 2021 exhibition at the Sordoni Gallery. Certain aspects of Klimek's work may be compared to photographs in *Remains to be Seen* (2020) by Hudson Valley-based photojournalist and documentarist Travis Fox. Marking out a curious space between ground-level and conventional aerial photography by using a camera mounted on a drone, Fox's book explores an American landscape of abandonment and dereliction from a fresh perspective. He includes several shots taken in Old Forge. One shows culm banks marked by ATV tracks, the juxtaposition of their tracer lines and the piles of tailings lending an abstract, elemental, highly textured quality to the scene. Another one, equally disorienting but of peculiar beauty, captures rust-colored water due to the presence of iron oxide from acidic mine drainage into the Lackawanna River.

In 2002, Scranton native Tim Butler's exhibition *Untangling My Roots* at the Everhart Museum in Scranton explored the effects of industrial pollution and how individuals perceive them. In shots taken with an underwater camera in the polluted Lackawanna River and at various derelict mining sites, Butler plays on the visibility and stability, or lack

Ray Klimek, *Swoyersville*, Pennsylvania, photograph, digital C print, 2002. (Image: courtesy of the artist.)

thereof, of lines above or below ground and water in the anthracite region. In this respect, his concern with what is seen or concealed, how it shifts over time, and on which levels it may be understood relates to the notion of "coal measures," a term used technically to describe the formation of stratified coal seams and sedimentary rocks during the carboniferous period but colloquially to designate the entire fabric of the anthracite field, as Bill Conlogue employs it in *Undermined in Coal Country: On the Measures in a Working Land*. Butler furthered his investigations in another show, *Anthracite Attic: Scars and Dreams of the Industrial Era* (2004) at the Lackawanna Historical Society in Scranton. To probe the relationship between "dreams" of the past and "scars" of the present, he projects slides of historical subjects onto the textures of extant physical surfaces and then inserts those compound images into everyday objects of latent memory value, such as goods and chattels stored in an attic. Butler explains: "The images are then lighted from within the objects. In the half-light of these pieces, I hope to suggest a very scattered, yet collective history of the region."

From a coal mining family, Tamaqua native Scott Herring is not a professional photographer, has never been hired by a coal company to document its operations, and declines to market his photographs. Selections from his personal inventory of images, which number more than 170,000, are consequently on rare public view. An exception was during the Anthracite 250th Anniversary celebration in 2018, which Herring chaired, when his *Hardcoal Chronicles, 1973-2013* were displayed at the Anthracite Heritage Museum in Scranton, marking his fortieth year as a fiercely independent anthracite photographer. A passionate proponent of anthracite history who started with a Kodak Instamatic camera, Herring aims to continue to document as much as possible without concerning himself unduly with matters of artistic detail. He wishes only for his treasure trove of mining images to be available to those involved in restoration work or other cultural heritage projects.

Specializing in glossy pictorial books on local history, Arcadia Publishing has enjoyed great success since its founding in 1993. The anthracite region and its communities have received their share of attention from this publisher, and among its titles, we find two of relevance here: *Lost Coal Country of Northeastern Pennsylvania* by Lorena Beniquez (2017) and the aforementioned *Relics of Anthracite in Northeastern Pennsylvania* (2018) by Michael G. Rushton. While these works depend heavily on color photography for their appeal and carry limited textual commentary, we should not underestimate their contributions to the telling of the anthracite insofar as they are highly marketable and accessible to general history enthusiasts with a particular interest in that which the visual record may reveal.

In naming their works, these various photographers choose words suggestive of all that the anthracite industry has left behind. Dougert's and Klimek's "remnants," Rushton's "relics," O'Boyle's "modern ruins," Beniquez's "lost . . . country," Butler's "attic" and "roots"—the former suggesting a place where a jumble of forgotten things wait dustily to be rediscovered, the latter something hidden and tangled but strong, like the anthracite culture and its people. These *remainders* are also *reminders*. Potent triggers of memory, the photographic evidence of these places and objects allows us mentally to go beyond what physically remains to imagine everything else around them that once constituted the bustling life and work of the region. These spirits of place are Dinteman's "ghosts" conjured up by a rusting piece of machinery, a burned-out breaker, or an abandoned yet still loaded coal car.

PAINTING/DRAWING/PRINTMAKING

As in photography, a tradition of anthracite painting exists in which key names are George Luks, John Willard Raught, Nicholas Bervinchak, and Franz Kline. This tradition has been documented notably by curator and art historian Richard Stanislaus. The hard-nosed realism of Ashcan School painter Luks, raised in Pottsville, reflects his experience of an upbringing in an anthracite mining community. In a modern reworking of the industrial sublime, impressionistic landscapist Raught painted breakers in the 1910s and 1920. That he viewed this phase of his career as a testament to the miners' hardship is clear from a 1922 statement: "To me, the coal breakers are tragic notes in our beautiful valley, for they bring to mind the many horrors that have taken place in this region when in those underground depths human lives have been blotted out by hundreds, in awful darkness and despair." Already he foresaw the importance of committing their images to canvas: "In a short time, the coal breaker in this locality will be only a memory." (16) Starting as a church muralist, Mahanoy City-born Bervinchak's renown rests on his etchings, oils, and watercolors depicting everyday regional life in a social realist mode. Working mainly during the fall of the industry, Kline introduced simplified forms into the growth of his celebrated abstract expressionist style, which owe much to the dark, stark shapes of the mining environment of his Wilkes-Barre upbringing.

In the field of wood engraving, a striking body of coal region images was done for the WPA art project in the late 1930s and early 1940s by Scranton native Michael Gallagher, who was also the co-inventor of the carborundum process, a method allowing for greater gradations of light and dark in printmaking. Though born in 1915, Blakely native Frank "Wyso" Wysochansky, son of a miner who died in a mining accident when Wyso was twenty-one years old, is an artist of the posthistorical period, as he developed his talent only after the mid-1950s while earning his living as a cartoonist. Recognized as a fine artist in the following decade, he worked until his death in 1994, producing over 5000 pieces in watercolor, oil, crayon, pen-and-ink, as well as metallic-looking sculptures made from found objects. "Wyso" typifies the homegrown folk artist of the coal country, staying close to the regional roots that imbue his art. In a homage to Wyso's work, a mural in Mt. Carmel done by four students in a Keep Pennsylvania Beautiful internship program depicts five miners in a pose of camaraderie and bears the slogan: "Together We Can Make A Difference."

A specialist in depicting industrial relics from railroads to grist mills to aircraft, Frederick Bartlett II (1940-97) made detailed drawings of colliery scenes and coal breakers. He began to draw these subjects in 1969 and by 1972 had sketched twelve mines. He came to national attention when many of his drawings of breakers and railroad stations were featured in *When Coal Was King: Breakers and Depots*, a Smithsonian Institution exhibition of his work in 1973-74. His meticulous method involved photographing whichever remaining structures he happened to come upon before making a rough pencil outline and then finishing his image (according to his website) "in free hand pen and ink . . . either as a series of dots (stipple technique), line drawing, or a combination of the two." Each original drawing could take him between 100 and 800 hours, a dedication to his art in which, he said, "my hope is to preserve a small remembrance of what once served well in the past."

Bartlett's interest in preserving the history of breakers through art is an influence discernible in the extensive work of Luzerne County painter Sue Hand, who also acknowledges Kline's work as inspiring her to express herself. A thoroughgoing artist who likes to create serial work, Hand personifies a dedication to preserving anthracite history. She speaks of an "obsession," an "addiction," of being "compelled" to tell this story urgently since much time has already been lost. Combining acrylic and collage on stretched canvas, *The Anthracite Miners and Their Hollowed Ground*, completed in 2007, consists of 300 hexagons, of which 200 are now on permanent display indoors at the King's College miners' memorial site in downtown Wilkes-Barre. The title's play on "hollowed"/ "hallowed" suggests the miners' respect, if not reverence, for the spaces where they earned their living. Hand's art is highly symbolic. Her use

Sue Hand, *Sullivan Trail*, acrylic/collage on stretched canvas, 2007. (Image: courtesy of the artist.)

of hexagons gives a honeycomb shape to her canvases and represents the interlocking nature of industrial and social life in the region. Each canvas rests on a point, thus evoking the instability of the mines and the "honeycombed" land beneath which they were dug. She layers her paint to reproduce the effect of multiple seams of coal. In a manner comparable to mixed-media artists discussed below, Hand takes care to depict anthracite history and culture in appropriate material ways, as if regional memory is somehow contained in its geological, atmospheric, and manufactured matter. She embeds "real coal" and a "historical 3-D object (nails, rope, etc.)" into each composition and strives to find ways of painting dust, smoke, and haze. To this end, she opts for low chroma colors—dull, dirty, and earthy. Each hexagon contains collaged historical images "related to a single concept involved with mining," and this collaged history "influences the abstract composition for each separate canvas." She employs verbal allegory, too: each hexagon carries a meditation on suffering, pain, and justice in the form of a verse from the *Book of Job*. Hand's choice of metaphor in her statement on the first project reveals her ongoing commitment to this subject matter: "My obsession has quieted, but it has not ended. It has merely gone underground. I fully expect it to emerge again, like another convoluted vein of the black diamonds." It has now done so. Her sense of a vanishing history that needs to be recorded lies in the epithet "faded" she chooses in the title of her most recent project, *Coal Breaker Communities . . . Faded Memories*, whose focus on people of the coal communities, based on family photographs furnished by her art students, renders it more personal than her previous project. Each canvas, painted in thickly layered aquarelle acrylics, "depicts a certain breaker in a certain community with people from that community or near it depicted in a shadowy manner." To portray this ghostly past remains a pressing matter for Hand, who is "constantly on the hunt for more breaker references as well as family photos." She is in a self-avowedly artistic race against time.

Working in the same folkish vein as "Wyso," in a style that has been described as "primitive pop," the self-taught Jack Savitsky (1910-91) focused on painting and drawing the industrial and agrarian life that he knew in and around Lansford. He depicted especially the figure of the coal miner, his own occupation for almost forty years. Afflicted by the black lung disease that forced him out of work, he took up art in 1960. Later, he adapted his materials to accommodate his growing physical incapacity abandoning paint for pencil, pastel, and ink marker. The work of "Coal Miner Jack," indirectly influenced by Slavic folk art in its approach to line and repetition, has a simple, colorful, good-humored quality that appeals to viewers conditioned by common exposure to popular cultural forms such as the poster and the cartoon. Another folk artist is Bob McCormick. *Almost Touching: Shades of a Coal Town Childhood* (2017), the first two words of the title coming from Harry Humes's poem "My Mother at Evening," is a set of bright canvases representing McCormick's memories of growing up in Ashland during the 1950s and 1960s. His watercolors, acrylics, and mixed media appear in a style he calls "Modern Primitive" to define his naïve figuration blended with geometric abstractions and optical illusions. Human figures go airborne; huge breakers have a hallucinatory presence; buildings are unmoored or tilted from the vertical. These characteristics, plus a dreamlike quality and a nostalgic investment in communal memory, bring to mind some of Marc Chagall's famous surrealistic reminiscences of his Russian village origins. Many of

McCormick's paintings seek to capture night scenes in the coal region. One such example is *Down, Down, Down*, its title paying homage to mine patch minstrel Bill Keating's 1927 barroom ballad recorded by George Korson at Pottsville in 1946. The artist states, "in this piece, I envisioned the men treading tiredly out of the mine and coming down the hill to Mary's warm and well-lit establishment." (17)

Specializing in Irish American historical paintings, Maine-based Robin Savage has produced a seven-by-nine-foot oil canvas, *The Anthracite Coal Region*, in a modified Cubist style. It presents multiple allegories of coal region life. While not specifically concerned with depicting coal-related subjects, New Jersey native Tom Birkner's *The Long Drive* is based on multiple trips to the anthracite region from 1999 onward. These paintings represent "the vitality of memory, nostalgia, and perception" in the "bluesy resignation of the depressed town." Rust Belt lyricism of this kind, to which coal-themed art is related, may be compared to the work of a group of photographers who have established the "Rust Belt Biennial," its first manifestation having been at the Sordoni Gallery in Wilkes-Barre in 2019.

Bob McCormick, *Down, Down, Down*, watercolor, 2015. (Image: courtesy of the artist.)

On one occasion unrelated to coal, a regional disaster furnished designers and artists with an opportunity to commemorate the anthracite industry through public artworks. That cataclysmic event, the Great

Flood of June 1972 caused by Tropical Storm Agnes, devastated the Wilkes-Barre area along with many others in the state. In the reconstruction of Public Square in downtown Wilkes-Barre, the city-based architectural firm of Bohlin, Powell, Brown, Larlin, and Cywinski conceived a series of locally themed petroglyphs (postmodern versions of primitive rock carvings) to be sandblasted onto granite blocks forming the new pavement of the Square. Between 1974 and 1979, Frank Grauman designed a twelve-square collage carved by sculptor Regis Milione that depicts generically a coal breaker, company houses, a miner's helmet, and a birdcage with a canary.

As does this work and many other memorial sculptures located the length and breadth of the anthracite region, the art of mural painting represents aspects of anthracite history in highly visible public spaces; as such, it has the potential to engage many more viewers than works often confined transiently to gallery or museum spaces. We have noted the Kline reproduction mural in Mt. Carmel. In the city of Pittston, where downtown revitalization efforts

Bob McCormick, *Bearcat Rides the Nine O'clock Flyer*, watercolor, 2014.(Image: courtesy of the artist.)

began twenty-five years ago and which among self-revitalizing coal towns has shown an unusual dedication to public artwork of all kinds, Dwight Kirkland, aided by Michael Colley, screened and spray-painted a heritage mural on the side of a dental office on Main Street. Unveiled in 2013, it has three sectional themes: anthracite mining, garment manufacturing, and railroading. In the mining section, two miners surround four boys with a breaker in the background. By evoking the interrelationship of these industries in the history of Pittston, the mural represents a phenomenon common to many other anthracite region cities and townships. Also in Pittston, on one side of the Boden Building, we find an idiosyncratic interpretation of the Knox mine disaster painted by street artist Christian Mendez, whose work shows the influence of leading 1980s neo-Expressionist artist Jean-Michel Basquiat. In addition to an unnerving rendering of a miner's agonized face, Mendez includes details such as a canary serving as a mine barometer, the number 63 denoting a breaker boy's daily pay in cents, and the names of the twelve victims of the disaster inscribed on twelve coal cars. In the small town of Jessup, Heather Evans created a mural adorning a railroad overpass. A trained Egyptologist from the fifth generation of an Olyphant mining family, Evans was commissioned by the Lackawanna County Arts and Culture Office in 2014 to paint a four-panel mural depicting the history of Jessup Borough. Her choice of grayscale provided a fitting color scheme for the largely industrial subject matter. Two panels include anthracite imagery: one of a train and a breaker based on her memory of Olyphant Colliery,

Heather Evans, *Jessup Mural* (detail), grayscale, 2014. (Image: courtesy of the artist.)

Claude Harrington, Matt Leavens, Jeff Tweed, *When Coal Was King*, Shamokin, monochrome, 2016. (Photo: Cynthia A. Carmickle, 2021. Image: courtesy of Northumberland County Council for the Arts and Humanities.)

Ryan Hnat, *A Miner's Sunset*, Lansford, acrylic, 2019. (Photo: Cynthia A. Carmickle, 2021. Image: courtesy of the artist.)

the other of coal miners along with a sawmill and farm fields beside the Lackawanna River. Based on family photographs, the three miners she portrays are her great-grandfather and two other relatives. A third panel portrays Judge William Jessup, who opened the area to mining and railroading. A performative dimension also informed the creation of this mural; passers-by watched and commented as Evans worked and were encouraged to feel themselves a part of its production. Leaving space for alteration and addition, Evans aims to set a mood of historical reality combined with a full and immediate sensory experience. In 2016, in Shamokin, local artists Claude Harrington, Matt Leavens, and Jeff Tweed painted *When Coal Was King* in monochrome on the side of the Heritage Restaurant on Market Street downtown. The seventh of twelve murals in the town sponsored by the Northumberland County Council for the Arts and Humanities (NCCAH), it depicts two mining forefathers of the restaurant's owners, three child workers, the Glen Burn breaker, a railroad, a mule, a loaded coal car, and a scatter tag featuring a baseball-shaped logo inscribed with the Glen Burn name and the slogan "A Ball of Fire" associated with the colliery (formerly the Cameron) that closed in 1970 after 107 years of operation. This colliery gained notoriety for piling up the tallest culm bank in the world. In 2019, the Lansford Alive regeneration project commissioned Ryan Hnat, Coaldale native and founder of Scranton-based Northeast Art Project, to paint a commemorative mural, *A Miner's Sunset*, on the walls of an abandoned garage on US Highway 209, the town's main thoroughfare. Hnat's design is a likeness of the old LC&N No. 6 Breaker outlined in black and identified by its number on the painting along with the slogan "Welcome to Historic Lansford, PA." He chose a burnt orange color scheme that evokes an "industrial" Panther Valley sunset and cannot fail to catch the bystander's eye. That the artist worked on his piece using a digital projector hooked up to a laptop emphasizes the growing potential of computer technology to play a central part in the representation of anthracite history. In Carbondale, at the Lackawanna River Heritage trailhead, Hnat incorporates the head and shoulders of a helmeted miner into a 75-foot long, two-sided mural painted on a stone railroad abutment that also represents a train and Carbondale's "Pioneer City" nickname.

MIXED MEDIA

In the posthistorical period, artists influenced by technological advances and postmodern forms such as conceptual art, performance art, and environmental art have sought to represent anthracite history in unconventional ways. The grandson of a Lithuanian miner, Stashu Kybartas created *King Anthracite* (1990), a tri-gallery installation with a video on ethnic migration to the coal region. In this exhibition at the Everhart Museum in Scranton, Kybartas focuses on attempting to locate historically his grandfather, who died of "white lung" (asbestosis) in 1927 at the age of thirty-five. The exhibition space contains found objects and photographs (first gallery), slide and video projections (second gallery whose darkness "evokes the cave or coal mine—the mythic site of origin"), and twenty iron beds (third gallery evoking the orphanage/sanatorium). The epigraph to the exhibition brochure quotes Michel Foucault on power and knowledge: "It seems to me that the real political task in a society such as ours is to criticize the workings of institutions which appear to be both neutral and independent; to criticize them in such a manner that the political violence which has always exercised itself obscurely through them will be unmasked, so that one can fight them." Kybartas explains that "the difficulty of reconstructing the past is a primary theme of the installation, [which] looks at the nature of the codes . . . used to represent the past," including "the videotaped oral history of my great aunt who has difficulty remembering her brother." The video component juxtaposes the oral testimony of older coal region people with the upbeat expository mode of typical industrial films of the time. Kybartas summarizes his installation as "a palimpsest in which the harsh social and economic specifics of working-class life serve as a backdrop for personal issues of memory and loss."

As a radical and restorative extension of the Land art of the 1960s and 1970s, Reclamation art adopts an aesthetic approach to repairing and rehabilitating damaged structures and landscapes. The belief that art can play a part in reclamation efforts while imaginatively commemorating the anthracite industry and its abandoned sites spurred environmental artist and ecofeminist Harriet Feigenbaum to undertake several projects in the coal region in collaboration with local professionals and community members. In 1999, Sue Spaid and Amy Lipton coined "ecovention" (ecology + intervention) to describe the rise of such projects; Feigenbaum, who had first visited the region in 1965 and had grown to understand the regenerative potential of derelict mine sites both literally and as symbols of cultural heritage, was already actively intervening from the early 1980s. Her first two anthracite projects, in 1983 and 1984, took place on a strip-mined site at the former Storrs pit in Dickson City. In the first, *Land Waves: Valley of 8000 Pines*, she planted thousands of seedlings over a twenty-acre area asymmetrically. Hilary Anne Frost-Kumpf explains that Feigenbaum "used the trees as a sculptural element by planting them in a serpentine design to evoke a well-known local image of a coal train snaking its way down the mountain, as well as to suggest the gently rolling slopes that surrounded the valley before industrialization." Sadly, a combination of dirt-bike and ATV riders destroyed the plantation. In the second project, *Land Waves: Black Walnut Forest*, she planned to plant 2000 seedlings over a 1400- by 700-foot area in a spiral design inspired by ritual circles and rings, a concept invoking native American culture and one that overlaid a spiritual and pre-anthropocentric element onto the interpretation of the landscape. But the project lacked funding, and the site was subsequently developed for commercial and residential purposes. The moral of this and similar stories is that unless the community, especially landowners and local authorities, value such heritage/reclamation initiatives to the extent of recognizing, protecting, and nurturing them, the prospects for future projects of this kind look dim. "Local citizens' role as stakeholders," insists Spaid, "is of paramount importance to an ecovention's survivability, since citizens are the stewards who will protect and maintain the ecovention once it's built." (2) Feigenbaum returned in 1985 to plant over sixty trees plus shrubs at the site of the former Greenwood Colliery in Scranton. *Erosion and Sedimentation Control Plan for Red Ash and Coal Silt Area—Willow Rings* involved encircling a silt pond with two rows of trees as a barrier to erosion and in a manner again suggestive of spiritual ritual. The developers of the surrounding Montage Mountain office park neglected to care for the project, and many trees either died or were damaged. With the accent on time and memory, Feigenbaum had better fortune with her *Greenwood Colliery Sundial* project in 1988. In a more protected location within the same development, she created a steel, granite, and bronze sculpture on a concrete base surrounded by a ring of rocks and twelve lozenge-shaped plant beds in a clock-face pattern. The sundial is appropriately coal-black; its gnomon, resting diagonally on a perforated dial that brings to mind colliery head-frame machinery, is equally suggestive of a lengthy breaker conveyor belt. It is currently in need of repainting, and the site needs some general maintenance; it remains to be seen if and how it continues to be valued as a provocative meditation on the site's ravaged history.

In 2005, the Melberger Arts Center and Gallery in Scranton presented a mixed-media show, *Anthracite Incorporated: Contemporary Art and Local History*. It featured the work of three regional natives—David Klevinsky, Joseph Burinsky, and Michael Thomas—each with his own take on the representation of anthracite history and culture but sharing an interest in object-based art. The term "incorporated" in the exhibition's title invites viewers to think about the literal embodiment of the anthracite region in artworks of different kinds. Creator of large-scale neo-Expressionist paintings and installations that make use of nontraditional materials such as coal silt, tar, trees, mud and water from the Susquehanna River, rust, wood, and nails—a key strategy also in the work of Sue Hand and Denis Yanashot—Klevinsky invites us to reconsider what constitutes an authentic understanding and representation of anthracite history. Inspired by the "down and dirty" hands-on ethos of his teacher Salvatore Scarpitta, Klevinsky acknowledges the physical reality of the region and the importance of working unapologetically from an awareness of self and origins. According to Scarpitta, one of whose passions was racing stock cars, "there are racers who like the dirt, and there are those who run the high banks. The high banks are cleaner, but the dirt is more truthful, more exciting, more dangerous." Klevinsky runs the "low banks," too. For his part, Burinsky (1939-2015) reconsiders anthracite history mainly from the perspective of performance by staging field events documented in this exhibition by photographs. Believing the past to be indissociable from the present, these events reflect his shamanic practice in focusing on healing and regeneration of the scarred land. This kind of spirit work resembles that which we find in Feigenbaum's landscape interventions. With a background in architecture and photography—he was commissioned, for instance, to photograph the demolition of the Harry E Breaker in Swoyersville in 1995, made architectural drawings for HAER projects on the Huber Breaker, and modeled the Dorrance fan complex as part of an effort to save it from demolition—Michael Thomas here offers a social and ethnic approach to anthracite history. His Marcel Duchamp/Joseph Cornell-style box constructions contain various found objects that throw fresh light on regional patterns of immigrant, religious, and family life.

Formerly an airbrush artist, Denis A. Yanashot now concentrates on stone and mixed-media sculpture. His assemblage and relief sculptures use debris typical of the region, such as coal, culm ash, plywood, slate, and scrap metal. An example is *Channel Lands*, "a hanging wall relief

Denis Yanashot, *December 9, 1914* (detail), mixed-media, 2016. (Image: courtesy of the artist.)

of an abstraction of defunct coal fields." Having grown up within sight of the Marvine Colliery in Scranton, Yanashot harvested materials from that site for his 2017 exhibition *Anthra-Sight: A Sculptural Narrative of the Anthracite Industry of Northeastern Pennsylvania*. For instance, in *Marvine Sunset*, one of the twenty-six pieces on show, Yanashot uses multicolored oxide hues derived from burnt culm ash to create a brilliant mosaic pattern. In *December 9, 1914*, an eight-foot-tall wall relief, he offers a visual narrative of a cage accident in the Tripp shaft of the DL&W's Diamond mine in Scranton in which thirteen of fourteen miners plunged to their deaths.

SCULPTURE

In the section on purpose-built sites in Chapter Three, I have indicated the important function of various forms of sculpture in telling of the anthracite. Public art, as in statues and other monuments, is found throughout the coal region. The three-dimensionality of sculpture allows it to embody anthracite history in original ways. In a typical statue of a miner, for instance, the figure materializes within its setting and gives full shape to the human form, emphasizing the subject's physicality, whether it be rendered in action or repose. In the section on souvenirs in Chapter Three, I have also indicated the function of carved coal sculpture in the forms of jewelry, trinkets, and figurines. As mass-produced and largely unoriginal as these objects may be, they remain a part of the story insofar as they bring aspects of anthracite history, if often indirectly, to the mind of the browsing tourist and souvenir hunter. However, this type of sculpture exists on a more elevated aesthetic plane in the small but declining tradition of hand-carved anthracite art. Originating as a spare-time hobby among miners, the art resulting in these objects may possess an austere beauty. One example in the Smithsonian Institution is an engraved scene of a breaker at Coaldale carved in the 1930s by Constantine "Koste" Molotzak, who died in a mining accident in Tamaqua in 1942. Charles Harner, from the Trevorton area, was another accomplished artist of the form who carved over 1000 sculptures over 65 years. More recently, Frank Magdalinski owned a dedicated store, Anthracite

Coal Crafts in Wilkes-Barre, where he specialized in producing carved coal souvenirs. The outstanding name in this field is that of C. Edgar Patience (1906-72), the fourth of six sons of former breaker boy Harry B. Patience, from whom he learned the art. Like Magdalinski, Patience produced souvenirs for income but was primarily an artist of the form. Among his large-scale works are a 4200-lb. coal altar in the chapel of King's College, Wilkes-Barre, and a 3500-lb. piece in the Smithsonian Museum.

A native Tennessean, who came to the coal region to teach at Wilkes University, Herbert Simon has created several breaker sculptures from aluminum and rusted steel, plus a set of related etchings. Moving from the abstract to the representational, Simon explains that "since coming to this region in 1969, I had been struck by the stark, gritty quality of the area, but it was only after 1987 that it occurred to me this landscape might provide the raw material for art." He adds that he wished "to capture the stark, austere grandeur of these twentieth-century ruins." His interest in hexagonal shapes, like that of fellow artist Sue Hand, reminds us that the hexagon is also associated with skeleton formulas for *carbon* atoms in molecular chemistry. Simon's aquatint etchings bring out hidden tonal qualities in the postindustrial landscape. These prints include images of breakers and culm banks; several of the latter, such as *Culm II* depicting an area around Pittston, suggest a curiously figured space between realism and abstraction.

One of the more disturbing representations of the crushingly hard life of the coal fields is *The Miner* by Georgian American George Papashvily (1898-1978), who was also widely known for his humorous books; *Anything Can Happen* (1945), his immigrant memoir, sold over one million copies worldwide. Though *The Miner* is not a posthistorical work, having been sculpted in the 1940s, it has a prominent place in regional public art. Located in the forecourt of the Anthracite Heritage Museum in Scranton, this granite piece embodies the oppressiveness of a man forced to kneel beneath huge rocks in pursuit of his work and his subservience to an unfair system that dominated his every move. Its rudimentary, semi-abstract form reflects the joint influence on Papashvily of naïve and modernist art.

Herbert Simon, *Culm II*. Etching, 2007. (Image: courtesy of the artist.)

Another potent symbol of earlier anthracite history is the ubiquitous mule that hauled coal barges on canals, coal cars in mines, and agricultural equipment on the land until mechanization replaced it. To pay fitting tribute to this hardworking and dependable animal, the Delaware and Lehigh National Heritage Corridor launched an unusual public art project in 2003. *Miles of Mules: History with a Colorful Kick* involved the production of 175 painted fiberglass mules. Many artists participated and were paid an honorarium for decorating them in freestyle. The mules were auctioned off to sponsors and placed in public spaces across much of the anthracite region and beyond. Though the painted designs range widely in appearance and theme, each mule nonetheless implicitly carries a memory of the industrial and agricultural past. Several explicitly invoke anthracite mining: for instance, *Moxie the Miner's Mule,* located in front of the Luzerne County Courthouse in Wilkes-Barre, painted by members of the Wyoming Valley Art League, and sponsored by the Luzerne Foundation. Combining sculpture, painting, and environmental art, this successful project took its lead from similar initiatives elsewhere in the country, such as Chicago's *Cows on Parade*, Cincinnati's *Big Pig Gig*, and Santa Fe's *Trail of Painted Ponies*.

The assemblages of James "Jim" Popso (1922-98) belong to the folk-art tradition of these mules and of painters "Wyso," Savitsky, and McCormick. Furthermore, Popso is a mixed-media artist using various found materials—such as scrap wood, random objects, glue, household supplies, and bargain paints—to create his models of anthracite structures, machines, people, and places. A native of Hazleton and son of a coal miner, Popso at first sold his work informally in local circles. After the gift shop at Eckley Miners' Village began carrying his pieces in 1989, they became more widely known and popular among folk art dealers and collectors. Woodward S. Bousquet points to the thin line in Popso's work between folk art and souvenir merchandise as expressions of anthracite region culture: "Besides increasing the demand for the products of his labor, market forces . . . affected Jim's work in other ways. Shortly after [Eckley] accepted his paintings and models, Jim expanded his repertoire to include simple necklaces, key chains, painted pieces of coal, mine carts, and other items with 'Eckley' painted on them." A good example of this tension between historical accuracy and generalized nostalgia is "Lokie" (1994), a model of a typical short-line locomotive used in coal country in the first half of the twentieth century. On display in Eckley's museum along with other Popso works, it has "Eckley" printed on its side "probably," writes Kyle Weaver, "to give the sculpture souvenir value rather than indicating that this particular engine actually ran through the mining village."

The capacity of literature and the arts for telling of the past in imaginative and entertaining ways makes them especially effective forms to preserve an anthracite heritage. As long as the creative spirit lives on in the work of writers and artists, we may expect interesting and valuable contributions to the representation of anthracite history. Yet, as those artists committed to the subject grow fewer in number and the range of unexplored subject matter available to them narrows with time, we may also expect a diminishing output of all these representational forms.

For the time being, the stock of more than two centuries of anthracite history remains so rich in people, places, objects, and events that whenever literary or artistic talents manifest themselves, audiences may savor enlightening and pleasurable experiences that tell anew of the anthracite and its deep regional roots.

CHAPTER FIVE

MINE WITH A MOVIE CAMERA: ANTHRACITE ON FILM

In this chapter alone, my chronology differs partly from that in this book overall in that I go back to the earliest days of film as an art form to trace its entire representation of anthracite. As with photography earlier, the evolution of motion picture film may be compared to that of anthracite mining as an example of a modern industry based on and driven by advances in science and technology. The only films I omit here are those on the Knox and Centralia disasters; my discussion of them may be found in Chapter Two.

THE SILENT ERA

As with the invention of photography in the early nineteenth century, the arrival of the motion picture in the 1890s vastly broadened how we represent the reality of the world around us. The new medium soon became central to many cultures as a form of mass entertainment as well as an informational and educational tool. From its beginning, film thus developed two main forms: narrative fiction and documentary (originally called "actualities" in French). Likewise, companies and organizations quickly realized the huge potential of the medium. In the silent era lasting broadly up to 1930, companies began to commit substantial budgets to sponsor a form of documentary that became known as industrial film. These films, of which most were produced on commission by independent specialists in the field using the latest cinematic technology, had promotional and educational value as well as the capacity to reach large audiences in theaters and smaller ones in local workplaces and social settings.

Since the documentary as a recognized artistic genre did not emerge before the 1920s, most early coal mining documentaries were industrial films with clear instructional functions. In later years advertising agencies, many of which boasted extensive motion-picture departments, frequently supervised production for their clients. Industrially affiliated representative agencies often assumed this responsibility. After World War Two, for instance, the Anthracite Institute, founded in Wilkes-Barre in 1929, had its own public relations department handling advertising and public relations on behalf of the anthracite industry. On this agency's use list of channels of public information, motion pictures figured alongside newspapers, magazines, radio, television, trade press, consumer literature, merchandising aids, exhibits, and displays. Once made, these movies needed to be distributed to target audiences locally and further afield. This was problematic since the industrial sponsorship of these films severely limited their marketability. Made on limited means relative to Hollywood budgets, most industrial films were produced as advertising or training vehicles, goodwill films for customers and employees, or for general educational use in the classroom. They could not remotely rival either Hollywood's huge resources or, up to the late 1940s, its equally vast nationwide system of producing, distributing, and exhibiting its own entertainment product. They were distributed through special agencies or film libraries established by larger sponsors. In the case of coal mining and related industries, many films were produced free of direct advertising content and distributed free of rental charge by the Bureau of Mines of the US Department of the Interior. This represented unusual cooperation. The industries paid for the entire cost of production, while the governmental agency took care of film maintenance and circulation. The audiences for industrial films remained primarily non-theatrical, either intramural (employees and their families) or communal (schools, social and cultural organizations). Some limited theatrical exhibitions occurred, too, of short advertising films ("minute movies") and sponsored general interest films, but these required the production of more expensive 35-millimeter prints. Moreover, in the case of general interest films, great care was taken to avoid overt advertising of a particular company or its product so as not to alienate or offend the box-office patron.

The filmed story of anthracite coal began to be told via primitive footage of mining operations. As early as 1904, for instance, the Edison Company shot some obscure views of operations at Drifton in the eastern middle field. As the medium's creative potential evolved through advances in camerawork and editing, anthracite-related documentaries began to use narrative elements to portray the industry and tell its corresponding human tales. *The Story of the Preparation of D&H Anthracite* (1925) depicts an entire colliery operation, including coal cars, shakers, cone cleaners, railcar loading, and product inspection per Anthracite Conference standards. It utilizes pans, captions, graphics, high-angle shots, and other techniques showing how rapidly film form was evolving during this silent decade. Also made in 1925 by General Electric for the Anthracite Coal Service, *Anthracite: A Prepared and Serviced Product* already highlights the benefits to producer, retailer, and customer alike of efficient service in support of safe burning methods, of assistance to retailers from district offices, of servicing classes and training of retail representatives, and the publishing of a trade magazine, *The Anthracite Salesman*. Another film, *The Mining of Anthracite*, is one of four in a series sponsored by the Anthracite Institute. Though the film dates from around 1931, it is silent, as most industrial documentaries of this kind still lacked the new sound technology available to Hollywood and the additional funds required to implement it. Sound projection facilities were also not yet widespread.

The silent era marks the first thirty-five years of cinema. Many films of this period have been lost, including a good number dealing with mining all kinds of minerals and precious metals. Mine settings were particularly effective in narrative fiction films that introduced romantic or adventurous escapades in harsh or lonely places, perhaps the best known being *The Gold Rush* (1925), one of Charlie Chaplin's masterpieces. Among lesser films, *Buried Alive in a Coal Mine* (1913) was set in Scranton, while the saga of the Irish anthracite miners' renegade band of the 1860s received early treatment in *The Molly Maguires: Or, Labor Wars in the Coal Mines* (1908).

The Price of Carelessness is a fifteen-minute instructional film produced in 1915 by the powerful and influential Edison Company as part of a series for the Delaware, Lackawanna & Western Railroad Mining Division. Among the six major anthracite combines, the DL&W was at the forefront of training programs and, in 1914, began to supplement its course of illustrated lectures with motion pictures. According to Mary Ann Landis, former Director of the Anthracite Museum Complex, "the discovery of the film . . . was simply by a stroke of luck. The canister containing the film was found in a dark corner of the Lackawanna Railroad station [in Scranton] as renovation work began on that building. When the film was cleaned of its oily coating and copied onto safety film, it revealed a priceless glimpse of mining technology and mining town life . . . in the years before World War One." (2) Shot at the Truesdale Colliery in Nanticoke, at one time the largest anthracite-producing mine in the world, the film includes shots of town streets and of miners' homes in a purpose-built scheme known as Concrete City in the Hanover section of Nanticoke, which stands in a derelict state today and has become a destination of "dark" tourists. The film was made partly in response to the uproar over the deplorable safety record of the railroad industry. In films of this kind, write David E. James and Rick Berg, the Edison Company, a firm known for its anti-union policies, "portrayed employers as deeply concerned with the safety of their employees and shifted blame for workplace accidents to the carelessness and stubbornness of a few bad workers." (34) The rhetoric of this film suggests as much. Nonetheless, a caption at its beginning states that the film is not meant to be critical of miners but that its purpose rather is to instruct them in the value of temperance and the avoidance of accidents. For numerous immigrant workers from eastern and southern Europe, many of whom understood little English, the captions offered a simple language lesson, while the entire film offered a fully comprehensible visual lesson. *The Price of Carelessness* is distinctive for several reasons. It is structured mainly as a narrative to support an entertaining plot. The storyline traces the fortunes of a miner, John Blank (possibly played by a miner with amateur thespian talent), who is partial to the drink. Sleeping it off on the job results in the death of his assistant. Blank drowns his sorrows and falls asleep in a bar. After dreaming of his death in an accident and its terrible consequences for his wife and family (his fourteen-year-old son has to leave school and work as a breaker boy), Blank reforms and is later promoted to mine foreman. An appended sequence pictures various other common accidents caused by lighting matches, carrying tools improperly, and so forth. By incorporating systematic shots of mining procedures into the narrative, the film was able to instruct and entertain. Furthermore, the plot allowed the film to illustrate life in the mining community rather than simply showing the workplace, its machinery, and the production of coal. As a result, it evokes greater sympathy in the viewer for the general living conditions of the labor force. At the level of the film's exhibition, it is notable that it was intended partly for wired or battery-powered projection in miners' homes, thus prefiguring the impact of televised documentaries by forty years.

THE SOUND ERA

HEYDAY OF THE INDUSTRIAL FILM

The coming of sound around 1930 greatly expanded the documentary film, as scripted narration, dialogue, sound effects, and music could now be added to the mix. Several anthracite documentaries were made by Hazleton native Don Malkames (1904-86). An accomplished filmmaker, he had worked in Hollywood in the 1920s and early 1930s before establishing his own Malkames Educational Film Company with offices in Hazleton and later in New York City. Expanding his activities, his company became the Malkames Motion Picture Corporation in the 1950s. His first coal mining film is *The Story of Anthracite* (1925), made for the Lehigh Coal & Navigation Company at its Jeddo-Highland Colliery, and remade with sound as *The Wonders of Anthracite* (1929), shot at Coaldale and produced for Old Company's Lehigh Anthracite, a branch of the LC&N, by Philadelphia-based producer DeFrenes & Co.

Two of Malkames's sound films from 1934, *Digging Deep* and its counterpart *Buried Heat*, prove to be his best coal-related work. As were most industrial films, they were made primarily to promote the coal company's image, but their creative elements show that Malkames was aware of technical advances in Hollywood and sound documentaries as a budding international art form. This awareness is evident in the opening sequence of *Digging Deep*, where a shot of a train with superimposed titles is followed by a long shot of the Hazlebrook breaker, the "home of black sunshine" in the eastern middle field. This shot gives way to another long shot of a group of miners about to start their shift and to watch a film crew load a movie camera onto the car that will take them inside the mine. Malkames uses an Audio-Akeley, the first single-system 35-mm single-vision camera, a type used by Twentieth Century Fox in its *Movietone* newsreels. After a brief close-up of a miner attaching a lamp to his helmet, Malkames cuts first to a medium shot of himself adjusting the camera, then to a long shot from the same angle in which he signals his readiness to the driver of the cars, which duly begin their descent. To the speeded-up strains of the "Jupiter" section from Gustav Holst's orchestral suite *The Planets* (to which Malkames held the film rights), the viewer sees the daylight of the tunnel mouth recede in a striking reverse shot from the moving car. The entire sequence has an artistic quality that implicates the viewer kinetically in the illusion of an adrenaline-fueled experience, that of going down the slope of a mine. This reflexive element—drawing attention to itself as film, thus disrupting the illusionism of the medium—is another interesting aspect of the film. It is quite unusual in a promotional film of this kind and is highly reminiscent of the style of Dziga Vertov's classic 1929 documentary *Man with a Movie Camera*, a title I have adapted for this chapter of the book. Vertov, who had also filmed scenes inside a coal mine as part of his 1928 documentary *The Eleventh Year*, repeatedly mingles his images of daily life in the city with shots of the filmmaking process, such as camera operators installed on cars and bridges, or strips of film being processed in the editing room. Malkames's establishing shot of coal breaker and rail traffic, depicting the daily interaction of two large and interrelated industries, also resembles in style the school of British social documentarists led by John Grierson at that time. Equally, the final shot—of a cloudy, windy landscape with trees as "THE END" appears—recalls the work of Humphrey Jennings, the British movement's most lyrical documentarist, in its poignant evocation of the natural world as a timeless counterpoint to the industrial scene. Malkames's editing is also varied. We witness the use of pans (e.g., a fascinating shot from right to left across a lake of pumped-out water), of dissolves (during scenes of preparing the detonating charge and of transferring coal from colliery to railroad cars), and of a fade-out from those cars to a snowscape, evoking the typical regional winter and the cozy warmth provided by anthracite, in the film's penultimate shot.

In a manner made famous by the CBS series *The March of Time*, which grew out of a radio series and debuted on film in 1935, it was common practice in industrial films to recruit a narrator whose lines, delivered in mellifluous and occasionally stentorian tones, added an extra dimension to the often-mundane images associated with scientific, technological, and industrial subject matter. *Digging Deep* is no exception. Its voiceover is by Lowell Thomas, once a miner himself, a filmmaker and broadcaster with a growing reputation for eloquent and authoritative commentary. Thomas had been involved in documentary film since the silent era, and, during the 1930s and 1940s, became a household name through his commentaries for Fox's *Movietone News*, while in the 1950s, he took partial control of the innovative wide-screen Cinerama process. Thomas contributes a lively, witty, occasionally poetic narration to *Digging Deep*. Yet he also demonstrates the drawback of the voiceover technique, for when, writes the pioneering German film theorist Siegfried Kracauer, "all important communications are entrusted to the commentator from the outset . . . it is inevitable that the synchronized pictures should be cast in a subsidiary role." (119) The articulate and seamless flow of the narration thus determines to a great extent our perception of the images. We see repeated shots of miners at work in the pit and breaker, yet the narration tends to privilege mining technology over human toil. Thomas describes the activity of the subterranean pumps as "the ponderous iron arms in endless labor," while in the breaker, "human hands come into action at only one place in all this: where men drag out the larger chunks of stone and slate and fragments of timber—all sorts of refuse. The remainder of the process is sheer mechanism." In the 1930s, mineworkers may well have become breaker *men*, but their difficult and dangerous task was formerly one notoriously assigned to mere boys, of whose plight Lewis

Hine's celebrated 1911 photographs continue to bear eloquent witness. In *Digging Deep*, the machinery appears to be the "real" worker on which the industry depends, that which "toils on—the cold power of modern efficiency." Such comments correspond in spirit to the shot composition and editing of the film, whereby Malkames—somewhat in the manner of Fernand Léger's 1925 Cubist-influenced experimental film *Ballet Mécanique*—emphasizes the rhythmic and choreographic qualities of moving mechanical parts. And though Thomas refers to the "world of peril" inside the mine, his rhetorical tone—generating statements such as "the old dreadful story: miners trapped in a living tomb"—tends to mythologize rather than confront the deeper implications of the risk and hardship faced daily by those living and working beneath the surface of the earth.

A film of this kind, purporting to offer an accurate overview of an industry in action, depends upon a notion of truth that is strictly relative to its immediate goal. Unsurprisingly, the film represents the anthracite industry as productive, efficient, safety-conscious, and blessed with a cooperative and industrious workforce. Most importantly, it was a force *at* work. Yet, the film was made when the industry was already in decline and suffering from continuing labor unrest. In mid-January 1934, the United Anthracite Miners of Pennsylvania (UAMP), having broken away from the official United Mine Workers of America (UMW) under John L. Lewis, called a general strike of about 14,000 men in District One (Wyoming Valley, northern field), stopping or disrupting production at every colliery. Furthermore, in the spring of 1934, times were so hard in the coal region that the miners' unemployment councils found it necessary to organize a hunger march on the state capital, Harrisburg. *Digging Deep* is thus an excellent example of a persuasive response by a beleaguered industry to a bleak reality. In seeking to convince its audience that the industry remained viable and prosperous, the film succeeds in doing what its brief required of it: to conceal any evidence of economic or political troubles in the anthracite fields of the early- to mid-1930s.

The March of Time series covered the anthracite region in *Bootleg Coal* (1935). This typically short, pithy film of excellent visual quality and using dramatic reconstructions to enliven the narrative drew attention to one of the worst consequences of the Great Depression and the mass unemployment it brought: the illegal mining of coal by disadvantaged workers in the region. The narrator Westbrook Van Voorhis, the original "Voice of God," calls the practice "the most menacing industrial crisis in the United States today," yet the film is notable for its non-judgmental view of these activities and is generally sympathetic to those who engaged in what most considered to be wholly justifiable. Bootleg mines were, in Bill Conlogue's striking phrase, "manifestations of counternarratives" whose practitioners "challenged the political and economic system that had dominated the coalfields for decades. Returning mining to its earliest days, bootlegging reasserted the power of the miner to control his work." (142) In this respect, the film anticipates by three decades the liberal slant of many television documentaries of the 1960s. It points out that most bootlegging took place on abandoned properties, though the coal companies still tried to shut down these operations by dynamiting them, sending in police to raid them, and posting such areas as private property. It includes a segment on the Shamokin agreement whereby 350 men agreed to halt bootlegging in return for real jobs, so the film tries to move the topic toward negotiation and conciliation rather than open conflict.

The Mining and Preparation of Blue Coal (1938) was shot at the Huber Colliery in Ashley, where the last breaker in the old northern field escaped demolition until 2014. The Jam Handy Organization produced the film for the Glen Alden Coal Company, which owned and operated the colliery. Established after World War One in Detroit by Olympian swimmer Henry Jamison Handy, the Jam Handy Organization became a major player in educational and industrial films. Over almost seventy years, it produced 7,000 films shown in theaters, schools, and other communal venues. As the film begins with the accompaniment of breezy music, a caption attributes the presentation to the giant DL&W company. Though Glen Alden had been formed from an antitrust break-up of the DL&W in 1921, it seems that the larger company remained in a position to distribute films about its former subsidiaries. The film portrays the manufacture and distribution of a unique brand of coal whose blue color—"a positive trademark of identification"—symbolized its vaunted status as "America's finest anthracite." As expected of Jam Handy, this eleven-minute film displays a range of cinematic qualities. Albeit in the conventional "Voice of God" style that strikes modern audiences as quaintly formal and occasionally overbearing, the narration is clear and, as befits a vehicle for commercial promotion, relentlessly upbeat. The editing largely avoids the standard cut, opting instead for a smoother transition between shots afforded by dissolves, fade-outs/ins, irises, and wipes—the latter an old-fashioned type of edit that here is used vertically, horizontally, as a V-shape, and as a diamond. Compared to the primitive style of *The Price of Carelessness*, we notice a far more varied selection of shots and camera angles, while a lively montage of images corresponds to the pace and cadence of the soundtrack. As in the Malkames productions, the result is an effective industrial film that continues to evoke quality and efficiency in an anthracite industry that was already in some measure of economic difficulty.

We may underestimate how pervasive documentary film was (especially in the relatively cheap and portable 16-mm format) in the decades before the 1960s and the rise of television documentaries. Writing in 1949, Gloria Waldron declared that "the range of nonentertainment or nonfictional films is staggering. In terms of cost and quantity, probably the largest category is the industrial film . . . Many businesses have film budgets running into hundreds of thousands of dollars." (18) While many such films seem unsophisticated, stiff, and often patronizing in tone, the industrial films of the 1950s were conceptually and technically far in advance even of the creative efforts of Malkames and earlier filmmakers of his ilk.

In this regard, *Black Diamonds: The Story of Anthracite* (1954) offers a good example. The film was made by Paul Alley Productions of New York City to showcase the "Sterling" coal of the Hudson Coal Company, a subsidiary of the powerful Delaware & Hudson Canal Company. As in *Digging Deep* twenty years earlier, the film's positive tone and optimistic message mask the increasingly desperate attempt of a deeply troubled industry to restore consumer confidence in anthracite. Two years later, the failing Hudson company was sold to the Blue Coal Corporation of Maine, a Glen Alden subsidiary. Sponsoring the film was the Anthracite Industry Council, now the main representative agency of the coal companies and extant as the Pennsylvania Anthracite Council. In a set-up possibly influenced by a similar journalistic sub-plot in Orson Welles's fictional classic *Citizen Kane* (1941), Lowell Thomas reappears as a framing narrator who assigns a "filmmaker" (Jack Alexander) to investigate the anthracite industry: "See what's going on. Get the feel of the hard coal region. Find out what they're doing to streamline the industry." Alexander hits the road with a film crew in tow (reflexive shots of a camera fixed to the roof of a car also recalling a similar ploy at the beginning of *Digging Deep*) and assumes the narration until he reports back eventually to Thomas with the completed film in hand—the story within the one we're watching. This allows Thomas to make concluding and encouraging remarks in accordance with the remit of the film.

Plainly different from many earlier anthracite films, *Black Diamonds* shows little interest in depicting the hard graft of the underground mining process. We see shots of a manned cage descending a shaft and loaded coal cars emerging from the slope but little else. This may be explained by the reluctance or inability of the producers to shoot below ground, a difficult undertaking at best, but it may also reflect a preference on the part of the film's sponsors to emphasize the quality of the finished product and its commercial network. Along with the conventional use of graphics, a 3-D model of a colliery explains much, though we see location shots of a breaker as well as of a coal stripping operation, the latter suggesting an industry-wide shift already underway from deep to surface mining. In the company of the narrator, we travel beyond the confines of the colliery: to an idealized session of the Conciliation Board, to a social club in Lansford, to a family home in Pottsville, to a delivery point in New Jersey, to coal trains cutting through the mountains, and especially to places where scientific research reinforces the continuing viability of anthracite as a superior and marketable fuel. Shots of the Anthracite Institute in Wilkes-Barre, a laboratory of the US Bureau of Mines in Schuylkill Haven, and Lafayette College in Easton lead to Alexander visiting the College of Mineral Industries at Penn State University, where two professors lecture students on the history and composition of anthracite and the progress of its combustion technology. To demonstrate the versatility of "black diamonds," one professor displays several art objects fashioned from this extremely hard substance; his secretary even sports a pair of anthracite earrings. The film stresses the quality of the finished coal product, its efficient and comprehensive merchandising, and particularly the marketing of automated stoker stoves—a technology that had existed since the 1930s but one that the industry had been slow to promote—for both domestic and large-scale uses in places such as schools, churches, hospitals, and apartment buildings. Duly impressed, the narrator speaks of "streamlined equipment I never dreamed existed." Jet-age streamlining was central to the image of American consumer products of that time; compare, for instance, the sleek design of late-1950s automobiles. This focus on being up to date represents a last-ditch effort to persuade the public that anthracite remained competitive, clean, and easy to use and that its burning equipment was as advanced as any other form of heating. We tend to believe that the pollution and natural resource problems we urgently face today were given little attention in the booming and visionary postwar atmosphere of American life. Yet, in a startling foreshadowing of our current dilemmas, the film's conclusion warns of severely depleted raw materials—timber, oil, and gas—and dirty air caused by the burning of soft coal and other emissions. Smokeless anthracite is compared favorably to other fuel sources, while coal, representing eighty-seven percent of natural fuel resources, alone promises a 150-year supply.

Blue Coal (Golden Triangle), made in 1955 for the Glen Alden company by Depicto Productions, covers much of the same ground as *Black Diamonds* in stressing the value of automatic anthracite burners for domestic, industrial, and commercial uses. It offers another example of the effort by the industry to promote new combustion technology in an ultimately unsuccessful bid to counter the competition from other fuel sources. Glen Alden was working at this time with two companies based in the Pennsylvania Dutch region: Electric Furnace Man (Emmaus) and Motor Stokor (Mannheim). Where this film differs from *Black Diamonds* is in its use of color. As advances in color film technology lowered the cost of using 16-mm color stock, industrial films took advantage of the appeal of a vibrant and more contemporary-looking viewing experience. It enabled blue coal to be seen for what it was, likewise for the golden triangle signifying the cooperation among Blue Coal, its distributors, and the automatic equipment makers.

FICTION

A relentlessly pro-business stance was expected in commissioned industrial films, but it was disappointing if no less expected, in the products of the Hollywood studio system. Based on selling escapist fantasies of fame, fortune, and romance, the American film industry has never been particularly comfortable in dealing candidly with the lives of ordinary working people and especially workplace situations often fraught with danger and discord. Yet, even Hollywood was not immune to the growing radicalism of the 1920s and 1930s, nor would it have been unaware of G.W. Pabst's renowned German coal mining film *Kameradschaft* (1931); of the international development of socially conscious documentary, such as the Grierson-inspired British films, of which *Coal Face* (1935) is a prime example; and of the Soviet agitprop cinema of those decades. Some big studios and their smaller counterparts began to make occasional movies with class and labor themes, though they lacked the radicalism of corresponding silent-era films. Nonetheless, *Black Fury* (Warner Bros, 1935)—Hollywood's first attempt at a coal mining community film in the sound era—remains a considerable achievement in being quite daring by Hollywood standards. Set in the western Pennsylvania bituminous coalfields, it is tangential to this book, as is *Pittsburgh* (Universal, 1942), which portrays the worlds of both soft coal and steel. *The Miracle of the Bells* (1948), however, made by veteran producer Jesse Lasky for Republic Pictures, does concern us directly. It tells of a Slavic girl from the anthracite region, played by Italian actress Alida Valli, who becomes a film star but dies young leaving unreleased her last movie, in which she seeks to rally the natives of her depressed hometown. A miracle occurs, allowing this far-fetched Frank Capra-style melodrama to end positively.

POSTHISTORICAL FILM

FICTION

To continue with fiction film, the only other Hollywood studio product to portray the anthracite region, *The Molly Maguires* (1969), is more important than *The Miracle of the Bells*. Shot on location in and around Jim

Thorpe, Eckley, Llewellyn, Wilkes-Barre, and Bloomsburg, *The Molly Maguires* was produced by Paramount and directed by Martin Ritt, who later cemented a reputation for liberal films such as *The Front* (1976) and *Norma Rae* (1979). Based on Arthur H. Lewis's account of the saga, *The Molly Maguires* stars Sean Connery as renegade miners' leader Kehoe and Richard Harris as Pinkerton's detective McParlan (*aka* McKenna) sent to infiltrate the band. Ritt's political sympathies make themselves felt in a moral victory accorded to the Connery character, though the film suffers from Hollywood's chronic need to individualize the story around its two stars, thereby deflecting attention from the provocations of the coal company, from collective action, and from some important roles played by lesser figures in the community. As William Puette writes, the film "paints such a violent picture of union organizing that most Americans are more likely to see the Maguires as terrorists than to be aware of the theme of betrayal or the inhuman treatment of the miners." (24) Shot by noted cinematographer James Wong Howe, the film has a stark beauty but ultimately seems more of a detached exercise in social history than a fully developed story with a genuine power to move the audience.

Wanda (1970) occupies a curious place in hard-coal-related fiction. It is the only commercially produced feature film to engage with the nature of regional life in the early postindustrial phase. It won the International Critics Award at the 1970 Venice Film Festival and has become something of a cult favorite in some circles. It is the only film directed by Barbara Loden, who died in 1980 aged 48. Loden, an actress and wife of the film director Elia Kazan, also plays the young woman from the coal region who abandons her dysfunctional family for a drifting existence of bar rooms and brief sexual encounters before meeting a feckless, unpleasant small-time thief (played by Michael Higgins) and embarking with him on a *Bonnie and Clyde*-style adventure, though one less glamorous, that culminates in a botched bank heist and her persisting sense of emptiness and entrapment. Set beside the extravagance of *The Molly Maguires*, which barely predated it, *Wanda* has purposely low production values: a rough soundtrack and a grainy visual quality evoke a bleak scenario on both personal and public levels. Most of its exterior scenes were located around Scranton, Carbondale, Olyphant, and Forest

City in the northern field. Shot and edited in 16 mm (blown up to 35 mm for theatrical release) by Nick Proferes, the film at times resembles a late-1950s or 1960s observational documentary of the kind on which Proferes had cut his teeth. At any rate, it offers enough static long shots of the protagonist framed within a ravaged landscape to leave no doubt as to her state of disconnection as well as to that of the coal region at the dawn of the 1970s. The film's unvarnished mood of physical, emotional, and verbal numbness, captured particularly in Loden's performance, suggests an honest, if one-sided, view of a working-class life with which she was familiar from her own North Carolina upbringing. Yet, the film fails to deliver fully on its gritty promise; it deteriorates steadily into a mind-numbing, melodramatic agony of crime and abuse that risks self-parody the longer it lasts. Nonetheless, as a portrait of marginalized female underclass alienation, it is important in anticipating later, more accomplished films of its kind, such as Debra Granik's *Winter's Bone* (2011), starring Jennifer Lawrence, or Jean-Pierre and Luc Dardenne's *Rosetta* (1999), starring nonprofessional actress Emilie Dequenne. For instance, in equally dead-end situations, Lawrence's and Dequenne's characters display notably greater intelligence, initiative, and willpower than Loden's unhappy "Wand(a)rer."

Since the 1970s, documentary has held sway in portraying the anthracite region and its history. Fictions continue to be made occasionally in the area, but their subject matter, unless indirectly, is not anthracite coal and the culture it spawned. One exception is a short film, *From the Hard Coal* (2014), directed by James Nevada, in which a miner teaches his son some hard life lessons during the labor wars of the late nineteenth century.

TELEVISION DOCUMENTARY OF THE 1960s

In the early 1960s, a combination of television, rising liberalism, and new audiovisual technology bred a new type of labor-related documentary whose progressive form shifted attention to the workers themselves, their living and working conditions, and the state of their physical surroundings. As portable filming techniques allowed for a more intimate presentation style, television began to interest itself more in the documentary form. Made in the spirit of investigative journalism by independent producers and television companies, coal documentaries of this type were considerably more sympathetic to miners and unions than conventional industrial films. A more progressive social agenda emerged in network television documentaries on hardship in rust belt communities, epitomized by *Christmas in Appalachia*, a 1961 *CBS News* "Special Report" narrated by Charles Kuralt, which poignantly exposed the desperate poverty of the Eastern Kentucky soft coal fields.

In the anthracite region, the 1960s was a decade of growing uncertainty and anxiety over how once vibrant mining communities might face the future. *The Invisible Man* (c.1961) was produced as a public affairs documentary by the news department of WRCV-TV, an NBC affiliate station (later KYW), Channel 3, Philadelphia. Shot in wintry conditions in Minersville, its main theme is of a man who has lost his identity in the industry's decline and has "become invisible in a world he helped to create." Narrated in voiceover by legendary Philadelphia broadcaster Vince Leonard (real name: Homer Venske), the story follows fifty-year-old Burton Hiram Wythe, the last in his family of five generations of Welsh American miners, who has worked in the mines since 1936 but since 1957 has expected no more than three to four months of work per year. As in other Appalachian films of that time, such as *The Captive*, a 1960 NBC documentary on a West Virginia coal miner seeking work, the narration of *The Invisible Man* places great store on rehabilitation methods through retraining and relocation. Twenty-week courses in sewing machine repair and sheet metalwork are available to men, while the textile industry recruits their womenfolk. Men are encouraged to move their workplace if not their home; 8300 of them commute up to 100 miles per day to earn a living elsewhere. Another emphasis is on material support from state welfare programs. Yet, in scenes of Hiram buying what he can afford at the grocery store checkout and receiving a monthly package on the food line, "the recipient is bewildered," wondering "why he can no longer find an outlet for his fundamental skills." Ironically, the building housing the state office where men draw their dole money is also the center for the Area Redevelopment Administration Program. A semi-staged scene in the local firehouse presents a miner and a commuter holding a lively debate on the value of the coal industry. Communal pride and solidarity in the face of unemployment and deprivation remain evident, but the overriding mood of the film is bleak and discouraging. A poignant final shot shows Hiram, in semi-darkness, slowly climbing the stairs of his house.

A similar scenario unfolds in *The Miners' Story*, produced by WCAU-TV, Channel 10, Philadelphia, then a CBS-owned station. The film's setting ranges across the entire anthracite region from Wilkes-Barre to Hazleton to Lansford and Coaldale; it includes scenes of mine fires that may have been shot in several affected locations. The program aired on March 26, 1965, and features an onscreen narration by Jack Palance. The Hollywood star was a perfect choice for this role, as he had grown up as the son of a miner in Lattimer and had worked in the mines as a young man. His relaxed delivery, far from the stiff narration of traditional documentary, and his emotional commitment to the story are two strengths of the film. He also benefits from a good script by Glenn Bernard and some additional material by Arthur H. Lewis. The film won an Emmy for WCAU in the Station Award category. It also features uncredited musical compositions and vocal performances by 21-year-old Jim Croce, who was starting a career as a singer-songwriter that would bring him international fame in the 1970s before his accidental death in 1976. Croce was introduced to the project by fellow musician Joseph A. Salviuolo (*aka* Sal Joseph), the production associate responsible for the film's soundtrack. Closely involved in every facet of the production, Palance was impressed by Croce's demo tape and approved his hiring to work on the music with Joseph. The pair completed the soundtrack in two weeks and chose "Coal Tattoo" by country artist Billy Edd Wheeler as the theme song; it laments the short, oppressed lives of miners symbolized by the blue coal dust indelibly embedded in their bodily wounds. A nascent postmodern documentary style is evident in the use of still images for historical documentation, in the informality of Palance's narration, and in that he appears on screen as our guide in a set of interviews first with miners and their wives and then with a group of graduating college students from Wilkes-Barre. Watching and hearing these young people, it is notable how clean-cut and smartly dressed they are by today's easygoing standards and how an insistent theme is their anticipated need to leave the area for better career opportunities. However, many interviewees stated that they would consider returning to the area if things were to change. One sequence is given over to efforts in the Wilkes-Barre area to foster new commercial and industrial development in the region, a refrain that continues to sound loudly in the present day. As a document of terminal industrial decline, *The Miners' Story* emphasizes the human and environmental tolls on the region taken by the prolonged mining of coal. In structure and style, the film is far from the confident and boosterish tones of the period before the 1960s; as in *The Invisible Man*, the anthracite story has turned into one of loss, regret, and an unsure future.

POSTMODERN DOCUMENTARY

In *An Introduction to Television Documentary* (1997), Richard Kilborn and John Izod propose four basic modes (expository, observational, interactive, and reflexive) in the evolution of documentary film. Though the expository, like any other mode, allows for conscious aesthetic choices as part of its appeal, for several decades it formed the documentary standard with the interpretation of images in sound films tied mainly to an authoritative narration. The observational and interactive modes, characterized by "fly on the wall" or interview techniques, correspond to the emergence of direct cinema and its French equivalent *cinéma vérité* in the late 1950s. Since the 1970s, the reflexive mode has embraced a postmodern turn, write Izod and Kilborn elsewhere, by "refusing the visible or epistemological bases upon which certainty is founded" and accommodating "theoretical goals of the kind that [Bertolt] Brecht or [Jean-Luc] Godard might have advocated for documentary." (1998, 430) This mode is most amenable to different types of representation occurring within a single film text. The authors add more recent categories to these four basic modes, such as dramatized documentaries, "reality programming," and video diaries. In *The Art of Record: A Critical Introduction to Documentary* (1996), John Corner distinguishes further between "dramatized documentary" comprising a solid documentary base while employing dramatic strategies and fictive elements to enhance its vision of "truth," and "documentary drama" (or "docudrama"), basically a playful form based on "true" historical events and familiar to the viewer today from its televisual popularity. A revival of agitprop filmmaking and an emergent women's movement from the late 1960s to the mid-1970s brought innovative approaches to labor and gender issues facilitated by these shifts in documentary film modes. Postmodern documentaries have, by way of what Corner calls a "hybridization" effect, freely mixed various visual materials, performative elements (though the use of these, it should be noted, date from the earliest days of documentary), and interpretive strategies in a quest to engage dialectically with questions of truth, historical representation, and ideological positioning. At the same time, they seek to offer the viewer an experience that is informative, stimulating, and pleasurable. Postmodern documentary has set new standards of representation and reached new levels of aesthetic refinement. Most anthracite film since the 1970s reflects this evolved form, while several postmodern documentaries have been made about the Knox and Centralia disasters. I remind the reader of Chapter Two, where I discuss those particular films.

Though relatively conventional, *Coal and Water* (1977) evinces high production values and extensive detail. Made for the Pennsylvania Department of Environmental Resources (DER), it shows how effective a well-made documentary could be in promoting postindustrial reclamation initiatives during the 1970s. These projects centered on the $500-million-dollar "Operation Scarlift" launched by the Commonwealth of Pennsylvania in 1969. This scheme aimed to deal with mining pollution without obstructing industry, a difficult line to follow in the best circumstances, but one whereby the state sought to avoid politicizing the problem. The government was also keen to present itself as a progressive force, so the film describes its reclamation techniques as "setting a model for the entire nation." Its sweep is trans-Commonwealth, so it is not solely an anthracite film, though much of it portrays the region, as we learn about sulfurous air in the lower section of Throop, notorious culm bank fires at the Glen Burn colliery in Shamokin and the Marvine colliery in Scranton, the latter shown being extinguished live on camera in the presence of former Governor William Scranton; dangerous gasses on Cedar Avenue in Scranton; and a mining wastewater treatment plant in Wanamie.

Fire in the Hole! A Coal Miner's Tale (1997), produced and directed by Len Smith, is a dramatic monologue in which actor Rich Pawling, who specializes in "living history" projects, plays a coal miner telling his life story to his offscreen children. Pawling's performance offers an alternative to conventional third-person narration. What the film thereby may appear to lose in documentary rigor, it gains by creating a convincing illusion of a real miner's testimony, which invites broad audience identification with the character's personality, background, and experience of adversity. Though close to docudrama in form, selected archival materials intersperse the monologue, while each segment of the miner's account of his progress from breaker boy to miner "with papers" is followed by a musical interlude in which singers and musicians perform around a table. Again, this creates an intimate atmosphere to which the viewer may readily relate. While the story seeks to tell generally of a coal miner's life, it is clearly set in the anthracite fields since Pawling plays a character named Jack Kehoe, after the leader of the alleged Molly Maguires, and mentions their episode in history as well as the Lattimer Massacre, the growth of the United Mine Workers union, and the Great Anthracite Strike of 1902. An installment of Pawling's "History is PEOPLE!" series, *Fire in the Hole!* was shot at three sites: Eckley Miners' Village, the Anthracite Heritage Museum, and the Pioneer Tunnel. Perhaps because of its status as a mainstream television production (for Time Warner Cable), the film evokes the hardships of a miner's life without investigating his labor relations and conditions in depth. Nonetheless, by entertainingly conveying a welter of social and technical information, it succeeds as an educational documentary and a stimulating theatrical experience. *Stories from the Mines* (2000), written and directed by Greg Matkosky and produced by Thomas Currá in collaboration with numerous local and regional institutions and organizations, utilizes the now standard blend of archival footage, still photographs, talking heads, and dramatic reconstructions. The late Jason Miller's narration enhances the film's continuity, already assured by the judicious selection of archival material, while the various reenactments of private and public events feature a cross-section of regional theatrical talent. Following its theatrical premiere in Scranton in October 2000, *Stories from the Mines* quickly became local PBS affiliate WVIA-TV's most watched and most lucrative fund-raising program. After national syndication, it received a nomination for an Emmy award.

With a title reminiscent of the 1930s *March of Time* documentary on the subject, *Hard Coal: Last of the Bootleg Miners* (2007), directed by Mark Brodzik and produced by Seymour Levin, throws light on a relatively unheralded aspect of anthracite history: the survival into the twenty-first century of an artisanal tradition of mining coal. Though the term "bootleg" now denotes perfectly legal as opposed to illegal mining, it still refers to the practice of small independent mine operators. The film depicts how these operators struggle to survive under pressure from the government, big business, and unions. As with other anthracite documentaries, such as *The Town That Was* [on Centralia], it sets an ominous and valedictory mood yet strikes a proud and defiant note. Though *Hard Coal* was shot in and around Joliett, Pine Grove, and Hegins in the western part of the southern anthracite field, it includes references to similar operations in the relatively adjacent western middle field, as in Trevorton and beyond toward Sunbury in Northumberland County. Over the main credit sequence, in a narrational "framing" trope, archival footage from *Black Diamonds* shows the *Citizen Kane*-style scene of Lowell Thomas tasking a reporter to get the story of the anthracite industry onto film. As the contemporary narrative kicks in, we are introduced first to 67-year-old Bill Lucas, one of two miners running a mine, followed by handheld shots of its interior accompanied by voiceovers, one lamenting dependence on foreign oil, the other of a politician pushing a bill to support coal. A set of still photos of the Lucas family emphasizes generational continuity, kinship bonds, and a roster of employees consisting, if not entirely of family members, then usually friends and neighbors. Self-sufficiency is another theme. "Not only a job, a way of life": we hear of thirty-five family members on one 143-acre homestead, mining coal, growing their own vegetables, and, unlike farmers, happily receiving no federal aid. Unlike the massive mechanization of corporate mining in both underground and surface operations, the bootleggers continue to work mainly in a time-honored tradition of pick-and-shovel mining. Footage of vast mountaintop removal processes in bituminous fields such as West Virginia offers a striking contrast to the relatively benign environmental impact of artisanal mining. During a public screening of their film in 2009, Levin stated that he found these independent miners to be unfailingly helpful and courteous, adding that he and Brodzik had entered the mines and believed them to be safely and skillfully run. The official safety record confirms this impression.

State laws were designed to support the bootleggers, but federal laws binding both anthracite and bituminous mining failed to respect or recognize the special nature of the bootleggers' work. The miners believe the establishment has exploited these laws to put them out of business. Starting in 2001, district managers from bituminous fields were brought into the area with powers to seize properties that were defaulting on penalty payments, thus opening the door to corporate takeovers of those sites. At the level of individual officialdom, however, sympathy for the bootlegger exists, as shown in remarks made on camera by a disguised district inspector, who tells of being instructed to harass bootleggers and to issue citations. From the bootleggers' viewpoint, the federal Mine Safety and Health Administration (MSHA), the federal Bureau of Alcohol, Tobacco, Firearms, and Explosives (ATF), and the United Mineworkers of America (UMWA) pose a triple threat in this battle between small entrepreneur and "Big Brother." Words such as "vendetta," "vengeance," and "nitpicking" suggest a conspiracy to close down self-owned operations by applying unnecessary regulations, issuing numerous safety violation citations, and so forth. The miners, says one, are being "forced out of [a] business [that is] in their veins." In 1995 there were sixty such mines; by 2009, only four remained, among which more were due to close. In a telling sequence, a mine owner recites a litany of closed family firms. For its part, the Lucas family mine closed in 2007. We sense a lack of compassion by the authorities on hearing of one operation under closure orders at Christmas, an episode reminiscent of the eviction of unemployed Michigan automobile workers at that time of year in Michael Moore's celebrated documentary *Roger and Me* (1989). As expected of a feature-length documentary, *Hard Coal* offers a comprehensive analysis

Interviewing Huber Breaker Preservation Society president Bill Best on location. *Beyond the Breaker*, film, 2019. (Image: courtesy of John Welsh/Bill Best.)

of its subject presented engagingly. It mounts a strong defense of the right of these small businesses to play a viable role in the continuing production of anthracite coal.

One of more than 400 breakers in the northern field alone, the Huber, built in 1931 by the Glen Alden company in Ashley, stood 130 feet high and, at its peak, processed over seven thousand tons of coal daily. The most advanced breaker in the anthracite region at its inception, it survived years of disuse and dereliction to become the last regional breaker standing. After a long campaign to save it, led by the Huber Breaker Preservation Society, it was demolished in 2014. A Miners' Memorial Park now stands on part of its site. John Welsh's *Beyond the Breaker* (2019) begins with an epigraphic caption quoting author Stephen Crane on his 1894 visit to the northern field as a young reporter for *McClure's* magazine: "The breakers squatted upon the hillsides and in the valley like enormous preying monsters, eating of the sunshine, the grass, the green leaves." Mournful strings and percussive sounds accompany a series of descriptive captions over a shadowy shot of the breaker that becomes, in turn, a color image cueing a sequence of talking heads: Ray Clarke and William Best of the Preservation Society, historian Robert Wolensky, architect Andrew Hart, former Huber miner Phil Voystock, Robert

Hughes of EPCAMR, and artist Sue Hand. All bemoan the destruction of the breaker, which Wolensky views as another example of "a nation's, a state's value system regarding our past." While many local people choose to forget about this heritage, Voystock's memory of the colliery is primarily a valuable place of employment. "There was something good about it," he says. Hart speaks of the "aura" and "soul" of a building that was "a cultural icon of who we were, what we are, and what we can be." The film's elegiac tone, reinforced by sublime (in our aesthetic sense) interior and exterior shots, including aerial ones captured by a drone, mingles with a sense of frustration and anger at the loss. Shots of the site under snow during its final days heighten this tone. Some footage is intercut with still and moving archival images to accentuate the contrast between formerly furious activity and the quiet, empty present. Speaking at times emotionally of the "insensitive" demolition of a "part of the fabric that wove us together," Hand, to whom painting numerous images of breakers has become her way of preserving their history, is a key figure in the film's effectiveness. Its final scene, which shows an exhibition of her work giving new life to the memory of the vanished breakers, offsets what might otherwise have been an overwhelmingly bleak coda following scenes of the breaker's last day in which, as demolition proceeds, smoke and dust rise to fill the screen. Hand regrets a missed opportunity to repurpose the breaker: "It could have been an incredible educational tool, but it didn't happen, and now it's just a scar." Welsh wisely leavens his film's solemn elegy with informal scenes of jovial communality at the Ashley Memorial Day Parade, an event culminating in the unveiling of the Memorial Park and a plaque in tribute to the related efforts of Ray Clarke. *Beyond the Breaker* succeeds in placing the poignant Huber story in a broader context of the loss of both communal identity and physical evidence of the anthracite industry.

The short film—generally definable as any film with a running length of fewer than forty minutes—has played an important part in the history of cinema. In the earliest years, shorts set the film standard, later becoming a staple of theatrical programming until the rise of television rendered them superfluous to audience needs. Nowadays, they are useful to independent filmmakers working on small budgets and are effective as industry calling cards or teasers for bigger projects. They aim mainly at the film festival circuit with the ultimate goal of being purchased by television companies to fill suitable slots in program schedules. Documentary shorts may highlight and summarize subjects that receive more extensive coverage elsewhere. Such is the case with *Scorched: Mine Fires in Pennsylvania Coal Country* (2017), a six-and-a-half-minute film directed by John Welsh, written by Alana Mauger, and produced and narrated by Mark Clement. In the context of more than eighty mine fires still burning in urban and rural locations across the state, the film uses its brief duration to identify several of them: Centralia, Shamokin (culm bank), Laurel Run (burning since 1962), Olyphant (Dolph Colliery), and two in Carbondale. One of these two, the catastrophic West Side fire of the 1950s, has been contained and the land remediated, while the other, at the Powderly Creek site, aflame for twenty years, was finally extinguished in 2018. Accompanied by suitably ominous music by Sheila Hershey, the film opens with a caption stating that the state's "Operation Scarlift" was halted in the late 1970s. The main theme—emphasized by the presence as a talking head of Robert Hughes, executive director of EPCAMR—is that efforts at control and reclamation remain imperative across both hard and soft coal regions of the state.

For those particularly interested in the technological history of anthracite mining, documentaries focusing on that aspect occasionally appear. A recent example is *Anthracite Draglines and Shovels* (2019). Filmed by George Buck and produced in conjunction with the Anthracite 250th Anniversary celebrations, it offers two hours' worth of machines in action featuring many different "Monsters of the Pit" operated by various coal companies. Instrumental music accompanies a dizzy succession of images whose intertitles identify the objects. While appealing mainly to mechanical specialists, films of this kind are instrumental in tracing the history of strip-mining activity and its technology in the anthracite fields.

CONCLUSION

A HERITAGE TO SAVE

In *How Modernity Forgets*, his counterpart to *How Society Remembers*, Paul Connerton argues that in a highly technologized and mobile late-capitalist society that places relatively little value on the past, "place is no longer felt as the force of destiny . . . [and] the memories of local identity on the part of subaltern groups are more and more threatened." (89, 144) If this is the case, then the future of anthracite history is at stake. It may be kept alive only if rendered meaningful and attractive to a general public grown overly habituated to the new, the immediate, the superficial, and the disposable. It is disheartening that many people seem either unaware of, unengaged with, or blithely indifferent to their history. Particularly concerning is the case of the younger generations for whom no direct memory of the coal age exists. The survival of anthracite history depends on knowledge and memory, appreciating and understanding the past. A sound education remains the best solution to this problem since, ideally, it leads younger people to seek opportunities for historical experiences that are most visibly afforded by the heritage industry. Unfortunately, the signs are less than propitious.

One prominent local figure in the arts shared his conviction that if we wish our youth to take pride in their region, then a local history course of at least one semester in length should be a required part of the high school curriculum. Sadly, the teaching of local history, which in northeastern Pennsylvania must have anthracite at its heart, is conspicuously absent from its schools other than as a short-term option by a handful of committed teachers. We may explain this absence partly by the demands of a broad-based history curriculum designed to meet the priorities of positive institutional assessments and successful student test scores. We may explain it also by a chronic devaluation of the humanities and the arts in favor of scientific, technological, and business-centered subjects. The educational system now seems to place little value on history as a subject both worthy in itself of study and holding a promise of personal and intellectual reward. Moreover, the study of history has shifted much of its focus from that of the American melting pot, so crucial to anthracite's story, toward that of marginalized racial and sexual groups.

A commitment to regional history is equally scarce at the college level. One part of the mission of the Anthracite Heritage Foundation, via its association with King's College, is to "prepare and administer an ongoing program of events that will educate students and the public about the lives of our anthracite coal miners and their families." Occasional events take place, but this program has not yet translated into a solid commitment to introduce this vital aspect of regional heritage into the classroom, though Robert Wolensky and Thomas Mackaman focused on anthracite history in a 2021 Labor History class at King's and propose to repeat it. Luzerne County Community College has offered an Anthracite History course, while Penn State University has an American Studies course on its books entitled "Literature and Lore of Mining," though it appears to be offered rarely at regional campuses and, in any case, is not specific to the anthracite region. We have to go out of state to the University of Maryland, where in 2009, Paul Shackel and Donald Linebaugh established the Anthracite Heritage Project, which runs an annual field school on archaeology and preservation in the eastern middle coal field.

An informal canvass of a Penn State University, Scranton campus undergraduate history class revealed that twenty students in the room had relatives who had worked in the mines in some capacity or other. For instance, one had worked at the Knox mine, another as a union employee, another as a mine foreman, and several below ground. Five students described experiencing some form of tuition in local/coal history lasting between one semester and one year of high school. Two students reported taking school tours of the Lackawanna Coal Mine and the Anthracite Heritage Museum. The overall impression gained from the canvass was that anthracite history instruction in area schools is patchy at best and dependent almost entirely on the initiative of individual teachers, such as the Jessup bridge muralist Heather Evans. Having set Bartoletti's *A Coal Miner's Bride* as a text in her eighth-grade English class, Evans introduced elements of coal mining history by supplementing her teaching of the novel with visual presentations and a field trip to the Lackawanna Coal Mine.

In a partnership among the Lackawanna Historical Society (LHS), Scranton Public Library (SPL), and the Scranton School District (SSD), LHS Assistant Director Sarah Piccini published a short curricular guide, *The History of Scranton*, for projected use in grades 4-6 of the sixteen SSD institutions. Four SSD teachers were involved in aligning the content with state standards. Though the book is not exclusively concerned with anthracite history, it describes various aspects of the central role of coal mining in the development and identity of the city. One thousand copies of the book were presented to the SSD Board in 2016; unfortunately, the project fell afoul of an unsettled administrative situation occurring within the district at that time. Consequently, the guide has yet to be adopted district-wide, though the LHS continues to work with several enthusiastic history teachers within the district and in two other area schools. The slow response of the SSD to the instructional potential of this publication serves to reinforce an impression that local history, anthracite-related or not, is presently considered a low curricular priority by educational authorities.

Before anthracite history may be comfortably introduced into the secondary school classroom, the matter remains of teaching the prospective teachers. In 2006, according to Robert Wolensky, "a group of teachers, professors [one of two being Wolensky himself], and local history enthusiasts received permission from the Luzerne Intermediate Unit to plan and conduct two semester-long programs on anthracite history open to all Luzerne County teachers." Each program attracted fifteen to eighteen participants. The overall project was well received; most of these teachers proceeded to take anthracite history into their classrooms. "We do not know whether it had any lasting impact," adds Wolensky, "but it was a 'demonstration project' showing what could be done." Another adult educational opportunity, open to anyone, is an Industrial History

Tour to the United Kingdom, sponsored by the Anthracite Heritage Museum, on which participants may learn what the UK has done to preserve its industrial past and may then consider similar initiatives for the anthracite region, which currently lags behind British and European models in this respect.

Many older people in the region whose abiding memory is of a dirty environment, grinding toil, and economic struggle may prefer to forget the history of anthracite. As one regional historical society director put it, the problem now is to get local people not merely to acknowledge their heritage but actively to own it. Therefore, the greatest challenge is ensuring that younger people keep this heritage alive since most regard it as little more than something involving their families two or more generations ago and as largely irrelevant to their own lives. A cultural fixation on the present and the future at the expense of the past and what we may learn from and enjoy of it reinforces this viewpoint—the forgetfulness of modernity, again. The extraordinary speed and facility of information technology, matching the rapid pace at which our lives move, have normalized this ahistorical sensibility in ways that could not have been imagined even a quarter-century ago. It is crucial to involve younger people actively in historical pursuits, and one way is to embrace and expand online and interactive access to historical sites, exhibits, and projects. Nonetheless, we should be concerned that easy access to online information sources masks a faux-sophisticated process of knowledge acquisition, and may discourage, even inhibit, more traditional methods of deeper historical inquiry and rigorous critical thinking. That said, we should acknowledge that digital culture, especially in the reach and application of social media, has empowered the younger generations, in particular, to rethink their relationship to time and place and so to design and document their historical activity accordingly. We have noted the rise of groups of maverick adventurers, mainly Millennials, who enjoy exploring derelict and abandoned places in often physically daring ways, and whose respect or otherwise for these sites is founded upon a set of unconventional and often iconoclastic views. These historical thrill-seekers see spaces as habitable and transformable in their own subcultural image. In discussing the "performativity of reminiscence," John Urry empathizes with that viewpoint by rejecting the convention of passive spectatorship and reminding us that "sites are not uniformly read and passively accepted by visitors." (101) His assertion applies to the anthracite region, where the heritage of coal mining may be interpreted freely by different age, demographic, and political groups.

As the main promoter and purveyor of anthracite history to the general public, the heritage industry needs to acknowledge the changing appeal of history to the younger generations. The industry, public and private, offers many worthwhile and well-run attractions across the region, but in functioning within a fiercely competitive leisure economy, it relies for its success on a strategic commodification of the historical experience. A clear challenge facing it is adjusting to shifting public tastes, choices, and habits. In packaging anthracite history for consumption by a public eager to spend its time and money on heritage experiences, the industry needs to ensure that these experiences are as captivating as they are enlightening, that they are not solely spectacular or acquisitional, and that they are as open to multi-directional exchanges as to conventional transactions between purveyor and customer. In one sense, a victim of its own rapid expansion and success, the heritage industry has been subject since the 1990s to trenchant critiques of its inherent structure, method, and ideology. Pierre Nora laments the overwhelming effect of an "era of commemoration" in which "identity, memory, patrimony [are] the three key words of contemporary consciousness." (635) In pursuing his theme of forgetful modernity, Connerton argues that while "forgetting is built into the capitalist process of production itself," (125) commemorative culture functions to resist the threat of forgetting the past. It ends up, however, by rendering it safe, classified, and consumable so that the "threat of forgetting begets memorials and the construction of memorials begets forgetting." (29) A paradox thus prevails, in that "our world is hypermnesic in many of its cultural manifestations and post-mnemonic in the structures of the political economy." (147)

In a fierce polemic, Kevin Walsh dismisses much of museum and heritage culture, driven by the tourist industry, as disconnecting people from their histories by turning those histories into spectacles and commodities. Postindustrial capitalism exacerbates this tendency in its drive to negate cultural differences and identification with place by globalizing the economic system and its concomitant social structures. Walsh may be overly harsh in this criticism since museums and heritage centers can only function within those socioeconomic norms that facilitate their existence and survival. If they cannot provide the main avenue into historical understanding, we may contend that they are worthless. Yet is it not better that they offer the public a way to discover history, albeit commercialized and programmed, than for the public to have no heritage resources at all? A burning question remains how best to promote a historical experience that appeals to the non-specialist yet respects and protects the integrity of its subject matter. Walsh argues for a "new museology," such as in the form of ecomuseums, that "must concern itself with involving the public, not just during the visit to the museum through interactive displays, but also in the production of their own pasts." (161) He objects to a heritage industry that "has been concerned to market ephemeral images of the past" and has shown a lack of "concern with the discussion and consideration of the past and its contingency upon the present." (4)

Locating anthracite history within critical ecological and philosophical contexts produces fresh approaches for the heritage industry to adopt. One example of this trend is a 2021 exhibition, presented on-site and online, at the Library Company of Philadelphia, an institution specializing in printed materials from the nineteenth and early twentieth centuries. The online introduction to *Seeing Coal: Time/Material/Scale* states that "through its dynamic materiality, coal connects us to Deep Time and Nature. It reminds us of our own Earth origins and helps us to re-vision how to live on a fragile and finite planet." Featuring various early images and texts, the exhibition invites us to reflect on the geological history of anthracite coal and question "the significance of its visible and invisible presence in our world." The show includes several pieces by its curator Andrea Krupp whose acrylic/graphite/stenciled images, such as "Underland Coal Ripens Slowly in the Vein," incorporate anthracite soot in a manner comparable to the use of such materials in the work of David Klevinsky, Denis Yanashot, and Sue Hand. The online version of the exhibition demonstrates that virtual spectatorship, intensified by the global coronavirus pandemic, has now become an important means of experiencing history, one that the heritage industry cannot fail to exploit in the years ahead.

Anthracite history is a fundamental part of northeastern Pennsylvania's regional life and identity and deserves to be remembered in both its positive and negative aspects. It is also a history to which new approaches may help us to understand and address urgent and increasingly politicized concerns: threats to the environment; issues of discrimination, oppression, and social justice; health care and provision. In a world faced with a climatic emergency, an approach that investigates further the physical depredations of anthracite mining may enlighten us on the social and environmental consequences of extracting coal from the earth and burning it into the air. Another approach may reconsider the idea of mine workers in the anthracite region historically as the "slaves" of "King Coal" and prompt us to look deeper into the history of labor ownership, workplace oppression, economic dependency, and discrimination against different ethnic groups. As early as 1849, Robert Klotz, a Carbon County state legislator, saw parallels between the plight of anthracite miners and that of slaves in the South, many of whom, said Klotz in an address to fellow members of the General Assembly, "are better fed, better clad and have more of the comforts of life than these unfortunate laborers, who serve dishonest employers, and are swindled out of their hard earnings." We may also develop an approach to the history of health care and provision in the anthracite region: in hospitals and other institutions; in the home and by communal caregivers; in treatment of diseases and injuries suffered by mine workers; and in attitudes toward and treatment of psychiatric and sociopathic disorders brought on by the hardships of life in the coal fields.

Historians, artists, curators, guides, and droves of amateur enthusiasts continue to do sterling and exciting work in keeping this history alive and presenting it to the public in authentic and attractive ways. In a society ever more focused on instant gratifications and its hopes and fears for the future, in a culture alarmingly careless of or oblivious to the values and lessons of the past, how we move ahead in the "telling of the anthracite" will determine whether this precious heritage may be saved.

BIBLIOGRAPHY

Akren-Dickson, Melanie. *This, Their Friendship's Monument: How Finding an 1800s Autograph Album Led to a Quest for a Lost Town and Its People in the Anthracite Coal Fields of Pennsylvania*. Published independently, 2020.

Amato, Joseph A. *Rethinking Home: A Case for Writing Local History*. Berkeley: University of California Press, 2002.

Aurand, Harold W. *Population Change and Social Continuity: Ten Years in a Coal Town*. London: Associated University Presses, 1986.

———. *Coalcracker Culture: Work and Values in Pennsylvania Anthracite, 1835–1935*. Selinsgrove: Susquehanna University Press, 2003.

Aurand, Harold W. and William A. Gudelunas. "The Mythical Qualities of Molly Maguire." *Pennsylvania History* 49 (1982): 91-105.

Bachelard, Gaston. *The Poetics of Space*. Trans. by Maria Jolas. New York: Penguin Books, 2014.

Bakerman, Theodore. *Anthracite Coal: A Study in Advanced Industrial Decline*. New York: Arno Press, 1979 (orig. Ph.D. dissertation, University of Pennsylvania, 1956).

Barrett, Thomas, Jr. *The Mollies Were Men: The Final Chapter*. 1st Books, 2003. (Second edition of original work by Thomas Barrett, Sr.) New York: Vantage Press, 1969.

Bartoletti, Susan Campbell. *Growing Up in Coal Country*. Boston: Houghton Mifflin, 1996.

———. *A Coal Miner's Bride: The Diary of Anetka Kaminska, Lattimer, Pennsylvania, 1896*. New York: Scholastic Inc., 2000.

Becher, Bernd and Hilla. *Pennsylvania Coal Mine Tipples*. New York: Dia Center for the Arts, 1991.

Beiner, Guy. *Forgetful Remembrance: Social Forgetting and Vernacular Historiography of a Rebellion in Ulster*. Oxford: Oxford University Press, 2018.

Beniquez, Lorena. *Lost Coal Country of Northeastern Pennsylvania*. Arcadia, 2017.

Berger, Stefan and Christian Wicke. "Deindustrialization, Heritage, and Representations of Identity." *The Public Historian* 39 (2017): 10–20.

Blatz, Perry. *Democratic Miners: Work and Labor Relations in the Anthracite Coal Industry, 1875-1925.* Albany: State University of New York Press, 1994.
Bloch, Marc. *The Historian's Craft.* Trans. by Peter Putnam. New York: Knopf, 1953.
Blomain, Karen, ed. *Coalseam: Poems from the Anthracite Region.* Scranton: University of Scranton Press, 1996.
Bloomsburg Theatre Ensemble. *Hard Coal: Life in the Region.* In *Ensemble Works.* Ed. by Ferdinand Lewis. New York: Theatre Communications Group, 2005.
Bodnar, John. *Anthracite People: Families, Unions and Work, 1900–1940.* Harrisburg: Pennsylvania Historical and Museum Commission, 1983.
Bousquet, Woodward S. "Jim Popso and His Coal Country Folk Art." *Pennsylvania Folklife* (Spring, 1995). www.folkartisans.com/sup/popso1.html
Broehl, Wayne G., Jr. *The Molly Maguires.* Cambridge: Harvard University Press, 1964.
Bronner, Simon J. "Folklore and Folklife." In Randall M. Miller and William Pencak, eds. *Pennsylvania: A History of the Commonwealth.* University Park/Harrisburg: The Pennsylvania State University Press/Pennsylvania Historical and Museum Commission, 2002.
Bryson, Bill. *A Walk in the Woods.* London: Black Swan, 1998.
Buchanan, R.A. *Industrial Archaeology in Britain.* London: Allen Lane, 1974.
Burtynski, Edward. Quoted in Derrick Price, *Coal Cultures: Picturing Mining Landscapes and Communities.* London: Bloomsbury Visual Arts, 2019.
Campbell, Patrick. *A Molly Maguire Story.* Jersey City, NJ: Templecrone Press, 1992.
Conlogue, Bill. *Undermined in Coal Country: On the Measures in a Working Land.* Baltimore: Johns Hopkins University Press, 2017.
Connerton, Paul. *How Societies Remember.* Cambridge: Cambridge University Press, 1989.
———. *How Modernity Forgets.* New York: Cambridge University Press, 2009.
Cubitt, Geoffrey. *History and Memory.* Manchester: Manchester University Press, 2007.
Currá, Thomas M. and Gregory Matkoski. *Stories from the Mines.* Scranton: University of Scranton Press, 2006.
Dailey, Lucia. *Mine Seed.* Bloomington, IN: 1st Books, 2002.
Davies, Edward J. *Anthracite Aristocracy: Leadership and Social Change in the Hard Coal Regions of Northeastern Pennsylvania, 1800-1930.* DeKalb: Northern Illinois University Press, 1985.
Deasy, George F. and Phyllis R. Griess. "Tourism for the Anthracite Region—An Alternative for Unemployment." *Mineral Industries* 30 (1961): 1-8.
Degnen, Cathrine. "Commemorating Coal Mining in the Home: Material Culture and Domestic Space in Dodworth, South Yorkshire." In *Materializing Sheffield: Place/Culture/Identity,* 2016. www.dhi.ac.uk/matshef/degnen/MSdegnenp.htm
DeKok, David. *Unseen Danger: A Tragedy of People, Government, and the Centralia Mine Fire.* San Jose: toExcel, 2000. (orig. Philadelphia: University of Pennsylvania Press, 1986.)
———. *Fire Underground: The Ongoing Tragedy of the Centralia Mine Fire.* Guilford, CT: Globe Pequot Press, 2009.

Dellosso, Mike. *Centralia*. Carol Stream, IL: Tyndale House, 2015.
Devers, John. *The Coal Cracker*. Laytonsville, MD: Layton Publishers, 1997.
Dinteman, Walter. *Anthracite Ghosts*. Scranton: University of Scranton Press, 1995.
Doak, Melissa and Thomas Dublin. "Miner's Son, Miners' Photographer: The Life and Work of George Harvan." *Journal of MultiMedia History*, 2000–01. www.albany.edu/jmmh/vol3/harvan/index.html
Dougert, Ed. *The Black Land: Remnants of the Once & Great Anthracite Coal Industry*. Pottsville: Schuylkill Living Magazine, 2003.
Dublin, Thomas. *When the Mines Closed: Stories of Struggles in Hard Times*. Ithaca/London: Cornell University Press, 1998.
Dublin, Thomas and Walter Licht. *The Face of Decline: The Pennsylvania Anthracite Region in the Twentieth Century*. Ithaca/London: Cornell University Press, 2005.
Filipelli, Ronald L. "Colonial Work, Colonial Workers." In Howard Harris and Perry Blatz, eds. *Keystone of Democracy: A History of Pennsylvania Workers*. Harrisburg: Pennsylvania Historical and Museum Commission, 1999.
Folsom, Burton W. *Urban Capitalists: Entrepreneurs and City Growth in Pennsylvania's Lackawanna and Lehigh Regions, 1800-1920*. Scranton: University of Scranton Press, 2001 (orig. Johns Hopkins University Press, 1981).
Fox, Travis. *Remains to Be Seen*. Daylight Books, 2020.
Frost-Kumpf, Hilary Anne. "Reclamation Art: Restoring and Commemorating Blighted Landscapes." 1995. https://nmr.collinsandgoto.com/weblinks/frost/FrostTop.html
Furek, Maxim W. *Sheppton: The Myth, Miracle and Music*. CreateSpace, 2015.
———. *Somebody Else's Dream: Dakota, The Buoys, and "Timothy."* Mechanicsburg: Sunbury Press, 2021.
Gillespie, Angus. *Folklorist of the Coal Fields: George Korson's Life and Work*. University Park: The Pennsylvania State University Press, 1980.
Glodek, Geraldine. *Nine Bells at the Breaker: An Immigrant's Story*. Iowa City: Barn Peg Press, 1998.
Goin, Peter and Elizabeth Raymond. "Living in Anthracite: Mining Landscape and Sense of Place in Wyoming Valley, Pennsylvania." *The Public Historian* 23 (2001): 29-45.
Goldbeck, Christine. *A Tribute to O'Hara and Other Stories*. Lutherville, MD: McKeever Publications, 2000.
Goodman, James A. *Two Weeks Under: The Sheppton Mine Disaster/Miracle*. Bloomsburg: Coal Hole Productions, 2003.
Gourley, Catherine. *The Courtship of Joanna*. St. Paul: Graywolf Press, 1988.
The "Great Strike": Perspectives on the 1902 Anthracite Coal Strike. Easton: Canal History and Technology Press, 2002.
Green, Archie. *Only a Miner: Studies in Recorded Coal-Mining Songs*. Urbana: University of Illinois Press, 1972.
Greene, Victor. *The Slavic Community on Strike: Immigrant Labor in Pennsylvania Anthracite*. Notre Dame, IN: University of Notre Dame Press, 1968.

Greenfield, Briana and Patrick Malone. "'Things' That Work: The Artifacts of Industrialization." *Magazine of History* (Bloomington) 15 (2000): 14–18.

Gudelunas, William A. and William G. Shade. *Before the Molly Maguires: The Emergence of the Ethno-Religious Factor in the Politics of the Lower Anthracite Region, 1844–72*. New York: Arno Press, 1976.

Haldeman, James. *Panther Valley Tales*. Baltimore: Eric McKeever, 1997.

Hall, Stuart, ed. *Representation: Cultural Representation and Signifying Practices*. London: Sage, 1997.

Harnett, Natalie S. *The Hollow Ground*. New York: Thomas Dunne Books/St. Martin's Press, 2014.

Harvan, George. *The Coal Miners of Panther Valley*. Easton: Canal History and Technology Press, 1998.

Healey, R.G. *The Pennsylvania Anthracite Coal Industry, 1860-1902: Economic Cycles, Business Decision-making and Regional Dynamics*. Scranton: University of Scranton Press, 2007.

Hiss, Tony. *The Experience of Place*. New York: Vintage, 1990.

Hoover, Stephanie. *The Kelayres Massacre: Politics and Murder in Pennsylvania's Anthracite Country*. The History Press (Arcadia), 2014.

Howard, Walter T. *Anthracite Reds: A Documentary History of Communists in Northeastern Pennsylvania during the 1920s*. 2 vols. iUniverse, 2004.

———. *Forgotten Radicals: Communists in the Pennsylvania Anthracite, 1919–1950*. Lanham, MD: University Press of America, 2005.

Humes, Harry. *Robbing the Pillars*. Easthampton, MA: Adastra Press, 1984.

———. *Pennsylvania Coal Town: The Girardville Poems*. Kutztown, PA: Moonpenny Press, 2004.

Hydro, Vince. *History of the Lehigh Coal & Navigation Company's Room Run Gravity Railroad*. Jim Thorpe, PA: Vince Hydro Publications, 2019.

Izod, John and Richard Kilborn. "The Documentary." In John Hill and Pamela Church Gibson, eds. *The Oxford Guide to Film Studies*. Oxford: Oxford University Press, 1998.

Jacobs, Renée. *Slow Burn: A Photodocument of Centralia, Pennsylvania*. Philadelphia: University of Pennsylvania Press, 1986.

James, David E. and Rick Berg, eds. *The Hidden Foundation: Cinema and the Question of Class*. Minneapolis/London: University of Minnesota Press, 1996.

Jenkins, Philip. "Mis-Remembering America's Industrial Heritage: The Molly Maguires." American Historical Association: The Pacific Coast Branch, Vancouver, Canada, August 2001. Unpublished paper.

Kammen, Carol. *On Doing Local History*. Lanham, MD: Rowman and Littlefield, 2014.

Karig, Martin Robert, III. *Hard Coal and Coal Cars: Hauling Anthracite on the New York, Ontario & Western Railway*. Scranton: University of Scranton Press, 2006.

Keil, Thomas J. and Jacqueline M. *Anthracite's Demise and the Post-Coal Economy of Northeastern Pennsylvania*. Bethlehem: Lehigh University Press, 2015.

Kelley, Paul. *Anthracite*. Vancouver: Black Stone Press, 1981.

Kenny, Kevin. *Making Sense of the Molly Maguires*. New York/Oxford: Oxford University Press, 1998.

Kilborn, Richard and John Izod. *An Introduction to Television Documentary: Confronting Reality*. Manchester: Manchester University Press, 1997.

Klimek, Ray. *Black Deserts/Welsh Tips*. Sordoni Art Gallery, Wilkes-Barre, 2007. Exhibition catalog.

———. "Ray Klimek." May 12, 2016. www.loosenart.com/blogs/magazine/116350 021-ray-klimek

———. "Black Desert: Nineteen Remnants." *Raritan* 40 (2020): 52–67.

———. *Carbon*. Sordoni Art Gallery, Wilkes-Barre, 2021. Exhibition catalog.

Kline, Michael and Carrie Nobel Kline. "Report." In Cory R. Kegerise, ed. *Come to the Old Country: A Handbook for Preserving and Shaping Schuylkill County's Cultural Heritage*. Pottstown, PA: Schuylkill River National and State Heritage Area, 2005.

Klopfer, Tom. *The Anthracite Idiom*. 1995. Author's publication.

Klotz, Robert. Quoted in Georgie Pauff, "Coal Miners Were Like Slaves." *The Morning Call* (Allentown), February 3, 2000. www.mccall.com/news/mc-xpm-2000-02-03-3296191-story.html

Knies, Michael. *Coal on the Lehigh, 1790-1827: Beginnings and Growth of the Anthracite Industry in Carbon County, Pennsylvania*. Easton: Canal History and Technology Press, 2001.

Koontz, Dean. *Strange Highways*. New York: Warner Books, 1995.

Korson, George. *Minstrels of the Mine Patch: Songs and Stories of the Anthracite Industry*. Philadelphia: University of Pennsylvania Press, 1938.

Kracauer, Siegfried. *Theory of Film: The Redemption of Physical Reality*. New York: Oxford University Press, 1960.

Kroll-Smith, Stephen J. and Stephen Robert Couch. *The Real Tragedy Is Above Ground: A Mine Fire and Social Conflict*. Lexington: University Press of Kentucky, 1990.

Kubicki, Jan. *Breaker Boys*. Boston/New York: Atlantic Monthly Press, 1986.

Landis, Mary Ann. "The Anthracite Museum Complex of Northeastern Pennsylvania and Film *The Price of Carelessness*." In *Proceedings of the First Annual Conference on the History of Northeastern Pennsylvania: The Last 100 Years*. Luzerne County Community College, Nanticoke, 1989.

Le Goff, Jacques. *History and Memory*. Trans. by Steven Rendall and Elizabeth Claman. New York: Columbia University Press, 1992.

Leonard, Joseph W., III. *Anthracite Roots: Generations of Coal Mining in Schuylkill County, Pennsylvania*. The History Press (Arcadia), 2005.

Lewis, Arthur H. *Lament for the Molly Maguires*. New York: Pocket Books, 1969 (orig. 1964).

Lindermuth, John R. *Schlussel's Woman*. iUniverse, 2003.

———. *Digging Dusty Diamonds: A History of the Pennsylvania Coal Region*. Mechanicsburg, PA: Sunbury Press, 2013.

Long, Andrew. "The Afterlife of Extraction in the Coal Region: An Exploration into the 'Land of the Living Dead'." *Anthropocenes—Human, Inhuman, Posthuman* 1: 1, 7 (2020). https://doi.org/10.16997/ahip.8

MacGaffey, Janet. *Coal Dust on Your Feet: The Rise, Decline, and Restoration of an Anthracite Mining Town.* Lewisburg: Bucknell University Press, 2013.

Magda, Matthew S. *Oral History in Pennsylvania: Summary Guide to the Oral History Collections of the Pennsylvania Historical and Museum Commission.* Harrisburg: Pennsylvania Historical and Museum Commission, 1981.

McCarthy, Charles A. *The Great Molly Maguire Hoax.* Wyoming, PA: Cro Woods, 1962.

McCormick, Robert J. *Almost Touching: Shades of a Coal Town Childhood.* Ashland: Bob McCormick Art, 2016.

McDonough, Jack. *The Fire Down Below: The Great Anthracite Strike of 1902 and the People Who Made the Decisions.* Scranton: Avocado Productions, 2002.

McGuigan, John E. *Part of a Geography.* Kingston, PA: Paper Kite Press, 2003.

McKeever, Eric. *Tales of the Mine Country.* Lutherville, MD: Eric McKeever, 1995.

McKerns, Gerald L. *The Black Rock That Built America: A Tribute to the Anthracite Coal Miners.* Xlibris, 2007.

Meade, Melissa R. "In the Shadow of the Coal Breaker: Cultural Extraction and Participatory Communication in the Anthracite Mining Region." *Cultural Studies* 31 (2017): 376–399.

Miller, Donald L. and Richard E. Sharpless. *The Kingdom of Coal: Work, Enterprise, and Ethnic Communities in the Mine Fields.* Philadelphia: University of Pennsylvania Press, 1985.

Mosley, Philip, ed. *Anthracite! An Anthology of Pennsylvania Coal Region Plays.* Scranton: University of Scranton Press, 2006.

———. "Mine with a Movie Camera: Early Anthracite Documentaries." *Proceedings of the Fifth Annual Conference on the History of Northeastern Pennsylvania* (1993): 1–12.

Munley, Kathleen P. *The West Side Carbondale, Pennsylvania Mine Fire.* Scranton: University of Scranton Press, 2011.

Nora, Pierre. *Realms of Memory: Rethinking the French Past.* Vol. 3, "Symbols." Trans. By Arthur Goldhammer. Ed. by Lawrence D. Kritzman. New York: Columbia University Press, 1998.

Novak, Michael. *The Guns of Lattimer: The True Story of a Massacre and a Trial, August 1897-March 1898.* New York: Basic Books, 1978.

Nunes, Jadviga M. da Costa. "From Monuments to Memory Sites: Representing Pennsylvania's Anthracite Industry in Public Sculpture, 1855–2010." *Journal of the Society for Industrial Archeology* 34 (2008): 101-116.

Nye, David E. *American Technological Sublime.* Cambridge, MA: MIT Press, 1994.

O'Boyle, Shaun. *Modern Ruins: Portraits of Place in the Mid-Atlantic Region.* University Park: The Pennsylvania State University Press, 2010.

Palladino, Grace. *Another Civil War: Labor, Capital, and the State in the Anthracite Regions of Pennsylvania, 1840-1868*. Urbana/Chicago: University of Illinois Press, 1990.
Parini, Jay. *Anthracite Country*. New York: Random House, 1982.
———. *The Patch Boys*. New York: Henry Holt, 1986.
Park, John R. *Scranton Area Mining Heritage Guide*. South Miami, FL: Stonerose Publishing, 2005.
Parton, Julian. *The Death of a Great Company: Reflections on the Decline and Fall of the Lehigh Coal and Navigation Company*. Easton: Center for Canal History and Technology, 1986.
Pasternak, Stephanie. *A New Vision of Local History Narrative: Writing History in Cummington, Massachusetts*. MA Thesis, University of Massachusetts-Amherst, 2009. https://scholarworks.umass.edu/theses/359/
Percival, Gwendolyn E. and Chester J. Kulesa. *Illustrating an Anthracite Era: The Photographic Legacy of John Horgan, Jr.* Harrisburg: Pennsylvania Historical and Museum Commission, 1995.
Perez, N.A. *Breaker: A Boy's Story of the 1902 Pennsylvania Coal Miners' Strike*. Boston: Houghton Mifflin, 1988.
Petrosky, Anton. *Jurgis Petraskas*. Baton Rouge/London: Louisiana State University Press, 1983.
Piccini, Sarah. *The Story of Scranton*. Scranton: Lackawanna Historical Society, 2016.
The Poems of Anton Piotrowski. Compiled by Jule Znaniecki. Ed. by Harold E. Cox. Wilkes-Barre: Wilkes University Press, 1998.
Poliniak, Louis. *When Coal Was King: Mining Pennsylvania's Anthracite in Picture and Story*. Lebanon, PA: Applied Arts Publishers, 1970.
Prown, Jules David. "Mind in Matter: An Introduction to Material Culture and Method." *Winterthur Portfolio* 17 (1982): 1–19.
Puette, William. *Through Jaundiced Eyes: How the Media View Organized Labor*. Ithaca: ILR Press, 1992.
Rafferty, Virginia. *The Road to Lattimer*. Mechanicsburg, PA: Milford House Press, 2019.
Reilly, Robert T. *Rebels in the Shadows*. Milwaukee: Bruce Publishing, 1962.
Remes, Jacob A.C. and Andy Horowitz, eds. *Critical Disaster Studies*. Philadelphia: University of Pennsylvania Press, 2021.
Richards, John Stuart. *Early Coal Mining in the Anthracite Region*. Charleston, SC: Arcadia, 2002.
Roberts, Ellis W. *The Breaker Whistle Blows*. Scranton: Anthracite Museum Press, 1984.
———. *Flames and Embers of Coal*. Washington, D.C.: National Welsh American Foundation, 1990.
Roller, Michael. "'Excavating Labor History': Exploring Class Struggle through Archaeology and Material Culture." *Labor: Studies in Working-Class History* 17 (2020): 25–43.
Roselle, Jody. "A Town Honors Its Past." *Scranton Times*, June 18, 2007.

Rushton, Michael G. *Relics of Anthracite in Northeastern Pennsylvania*. Arcadia, 2018.
Sabol, John G. *Centralia PA: The Fiction That Fuels the Fire*. CreateSpace, 2013.
———. *The Absence Above, A Presence Below: Re-envisioning Centralia, Pennsylvania*. CreateSpace, 2013.
———. *Centralia: A Vision of Ruin*. CreateSpace, 2014.
———. *Anthracite Heritage: A Still "Unmined" Landscape*. CreateSpace, 2014.
———. *The Afterlife of Centralia: Presences in a Landscape of Destruction*. CreateSpace, 2015.
Salay, David L., ed. *Hard Coal, Hard Times: Ethnicity and Labor in the Anthracite Region*. Scranton: Anthracite Museum Press, 1984.
Salay, David L. and Adrienne Horger. *The Anthracite Miner: The Photographs of George Harvan*. Scranton: Anthracite Museum Press (Catalog Series—No. 1), 1986.
Schlereth, Thomas J. Quoted by Carroll W. Pursell, Jr. in "The History of Technology and the Study of Material Culture." *American Quarterly* 35 (1983): 305–315.
Schnable, Rebecca. "A View from Pittston: The End of Anthracite in the Wyoming Valley." Local History Projects, Misericordia University, Dallas, PA, 2015. https://mulocalhistoryprojects.org/oral-histories/schnable/
Shackel, Paul. "Immigration Heritage in the Anthracite Coal Region of Northeastern Pennsylvania." *Journal of Community Archaeology and Heritage* (2017): 1–13.
———. *Remembering Lattimer: Labor, Migration, and Race in Pennsylvania Anthracite Country*. Urbana: University of Illinois Press, 2018.
Shecktor, Andrew. *Centralia PA: Devil's Fire*. CreateSpace, 2014.
Silliman, Stephen W. "Struggling with Labor, Working with Identities." In Martin Hall and Stephen W. Silliman, eds. *Historical Archaeology*. Malden, MA: Blackwell, 2006.
Spaid, Sue. *Ecovention: Current Art to Transform Ecologies*. Cincinnati: The Contemporary Arts Center/ecoartspace/greenmuseum, 2002.
Stanford, Michael. *A Companion to the Study of History*. Oxford: Blackwell, 1994.
Stanislaus, Richard and Darlene Miller-Lanning. "John Willard Raught: Scranton's Beloved Artist." In *John Willard Raught*, vol. 1. Exhibition catalog, Hope Horn Gallery, University of Scranton, 2019.
Stevens, James. *Coal Cracker Blues*. Baltimore: PublishAmerica, 2003.
Sturken, Marita. *Tourists of History: Memory, Kitsch, and Consumerism from Oklahoma City to Ground Zero*. Durham, NC: Duke University Press, 2007.
Thornbrook, Bill. "The Art of Anthracite Coal Carving." *Journal of Antiques and Collectibles*. July 28, 2015. https://journalofantiques.com/features/the-art-of-anthracite-coal-carving
Troutman, Mitch. *The Bootleg Coal Rebellion: The Pennsylvania Miners Who Seized an Industry, 1925-1942*. Oakland: PM Press, 2022.
Urry, John. *The Tourist Gaze*. London: Sage, 2002.
Varonka, Steve. *Molly Justice: A Story of Molly Maguires and Modocs in the Mahanoy Valley of Pennsylvania*. Bloomsburg, PA: Coal Hole Productions, 2001.
Waldron, Gloria. *The Information Film*. New York: Columbia University Press, 1949.

Wallace, Anthony F. C. *St. Clair: A Nineteenth-Century Coal Town's Experience with a Disaster-Prone Industry*. Ithaca: Cornell University Press, 1981.

Walsh, Kevin. *The Representation of the Past: Museums and Heritage in the Post-modern World*. London/New York: Routledge, 1992.

Weaver, Karol K. *Medical Caregiving and Identity in Pennsylvania's Anthracite Region, 1880-2000*. University Park: The Pennsylvania State University Press, 2011.

Weaver, Kyle R. "Jim Popso's Lokie." *Pennsylvania Heritage* (Spring, 2016). https://paheritage.wpengine.com/article/jim-popsos-lokie-eckley-miners-village/

Wellington, David. *Vampire Zero*. New York: Three Rivers Press, 2008.

Williams, William G. *The Coal King's Slaves: A Coal Miner's Story*. Shippensburg, PA: White Mane Publishing, 2002.

Wolensky, Kenneth C., Nicole H., and Robert P. *Fighting for the Union Label: The Women's Garment Industry and the ILGWU in Pennsylvania*. University Park: The Pennsylvania State University Press, 2002.

Wolensky, Robert P., Kenneth C., and Nicole H. *The Knox Mine Disaster: January 22, 1959. The Final Years of the Northern Anthracite Industry and the Effort to Rebuild a Regional Economy*. Harrisburg: Pennsylvania Historical and Museum Commission, 1999.

———. *Voices of the Knox Mine Disaster: Stories, Remembrances, and Reflections on the Anthracite Industry's Last Major Catastrophe, January 22, 1959*. Harrisburg: Pennsylvania Historical and Museum Commission, 2005.

Wolensky, Robert P., ed. *Sewn in Coal Country: An Oral History of the Ladies' Garment Industry in Northeastern Pennsylvania, 1945-1995*. University Park: The Pennsylvania State University Press, 2020.

Wolensky, Robert P. and Joseph Keating. *Tragedy at Avondale*. Easton: Canal History and Technology Press, 2008.

Wolensky, Robert P. and William A. Hastie. *Anthracite Labor Wars: Tenancy, Italians, and Organized Crime in the Northern Coalfield of Northeastern Pennsylvania, 1897–1959*. Easton: Canal History and Technology Press, 2013.

FILMOGRAPHY

DOCUMENTARIES

The Price of Carelessness, 1915, produced Edison Co. for the DL&W Co.
Anthracite: A Prepared and Serviced Product, 1925, p. General Electric Co. for Anthracite Coal Service.
The Story of the Preparation of D&H Anthracite, 1925. Production details unknown.
The Wonders of Anthracite, 1929, directed by Don Malkames, p. DeFrenes Co. for Old Co. Lehigh Anthracite.
The Mining of Anthracite, c. 1931, p. Anthracite Institute.
Digging Deep/Buried Heat, 1934, d. Don Malkames.
Bootleg Coal, 1935, p. CBS (*March of Time*).
The Mining and Preparation of Blue Coal, 1938, p. Jam Handy Organization for DL&W Co.
Black Diamonds: The Story of Anthracite, 1954, p. Paul Alley for Anthracite Industry Council.
Blue Coal (Golden Triangle), 1955, d. William Alley, p. Depicto Productions for Glen Alden Co.
The Invisible Man, c. 1961, p. Bob Shafer for WRCV-TV (NBC), Philadelphia.
The Miners' Story, 1965, p. WCAU-TV (CBS), Philadelphia.
Coal and Water, 1977, d/p. Ted Thompson/Concept IIIII Cinema for Commonwealth of Pa. DER.
The Knox Mine Disaster: A Photographic History of Hard Coal Mining in Northeastern Pennsylvania, 1981, p. WYOU-TV (CBS), Scranton/Wilkes-Barre.
Centralia Fire, 1982, d/p. Tony Mussari, Stan Leven, Bob Achs/MLA Productions.
Baptism by Fire, 1983, p. Marcia Henning/The Press & Public Project for PBS (*Inside Story*).
Knox: A Disaster, 1984, d. Ray Pernot for WVIA-TV, Scranton/Wilkes-Barre/Hazleton.
Fire in the Hole! A Coal Miner's Tale, 1997, d/p. Len Smith for Time Warner Cable.
Centralia, 1999, d. David Grabias, p. Sinema Productions.

Stories from the Mines, 2000, d. Gregory Matkoski, p. Thom Currá/United Studios of America.
Hard Coal: Last of the Bootleg Miners, 2007, d. Marc Brodzik, p. Seymour Levin/Woodshop Films.
The Town That Was, 2007, d. Chris Perkel/Georgie Roland, p. Dog Player Films.
Centralia to Remember, 2010, p. Yuri Gorokhovich (YouTube).
Centralia: Pennsylvania's Lost Town, 2017, d. Joseph Sapienza II, p. Allyson Kircher/Centone Pictures.
Scorched: Mine Fires in Pennsylvania Coal Country, 2017, d. John Welsh, p. Mark Clement
Knox Mine Disaster: The End of Anthracite, 2019, d. David Brocca, p. pitch films.
Beyond the Breaker, 2019, d/p. John Welsh.
Anthracite Draglines and Shovels, 2019, d. George Buck, p. G&D Productions in association with Anthracite 250th Anniversary.

FICTION

The Molly Maguires: Or, Labor Wars in the Coal Mines, 1908 (no further information).
Buried Alive in a Coal Mine, 1913, p. International Feature Films.
The Miracle of the Bells, 1948, d. Irving Pichel, p. Jesse Lasky/Republic Pictures.
The Molly Maguires, 1969, d. Martin Ritt, p. Paramount/TAMM.
Wanda, 1970, d. Barbara Loden, p. Foundation for Filmmakers.
Made in USA, 1987, d. Ken Friedman, p. De Laurentis Entertainment Group/Hemdale Film Corporation.
Nothing but Trouble, 1991, d. Dan Ackroyd, p. Robert K. Weiss/Applied Action.
Silent Hill, 2006, d. Christophe Gans, p. Davis Films/Konami/Silent Hill DCP, Inc.
From the Hard Coal, 2014, d. James Nevada, p. Teaberry Entertainment Company.

DISCOGRAPHY

Library of Congress, Archive of Folk Culture, *Songs and Ballads of the Anthracite Miners*. Recorded by George Korson, 1947 (78), 1958 (LP), Rounder CD 1502, 1997 (CD).
Irish Balladeers, *The Molly Maguires*. Avoca Record Co. 33-ST 162, 1968 (LP); Drops of Brandy Records, n.d. (cassette).
Donegal Weavers, *Last Day of the Northern Field: Memories of Pennsylvania's Coal Mines*. Donegal Weavers DW 9201T, 1992 (cassette).
Tom Flannery, *The Anthracite Shuffle*. Kikomusic KM 102, 2000 (CD).
Lex Romane, *Diggin' Dusty Diamonds: Songs from the Coal Mines*. Lucky Duck Records LD 2003, 2004 (CD).
Where the Coal Trains Load: World Music of Eastern Pennsylvania. Recorded by Michael and Carrie Kline. CD Baby, 2007 (CD).
Jay Smar, *Heritage & Coal Mining Songs of Northeast Pennsylvania*. Fuzzy Bugger Records, 2009 (CD).
Van Wagner, *Coal Dust, Rust & Saw Dust*. Lulu.com, 2009 (book + double CD).
Julia Wolfe, *Anthracite Fields*. Cantaloupe Music, CA 21111, 2015 (CD).

GAZETTEER OF ANTHRACITE REGION PLACE NAMES

followed by county and coalfield,
found in the text and in image captions

N=northern; EM=eastern middle; WM=western middle; S=southern

Archbald, Lackawanna, N
Ashland, Schuylkill, WM
Ashley, Luzerne, N
Blakely, Lackawanna, N
Buck Run, Schuylkill, S
Carbondale, Lackawanna, N
Centralia, Columbia, WM
Coaldale, Schuylkill, S
Dickson City, Lackawanna, N
Drifton, Luzerne, EM
Drums, Luzerne, EM
Dunmore, Lackawanna, N
Dupont, Luzerne, N
Duryea, Luzerne, N
Eckley, Luzerne, EM
Exeter, Luzerne, N
Frackville, Schuylkill, WM
Freeland, Luzerne, EM
Forest City, Susquehanna, N
Georgetown, Luzerne, N
Girardville, Schuylkill, S
Glen Lyon, Luzerne, N
Harwood, Luzerne, EM
Hazleton, Luzerne, EM
Hegins, Schuylkill, S

Hughestown, Luzerne, N
Jeansville, Luzerne, EM
Jermyn, Lackawanna, N
Jessup, Lackawanna, N
Jim Thorpe (old Mauch Chunk), Carbon, S
Joliett, Schuylkill, S
Kelayres, Schuylkill, S
Kingston, Luzerne, N
Lansford, Carbon, S
Lattimer, Luzerne, EM
Laurel Run, Luzerne, N
Llewellyn, Schuylkill, S
Mahanoy City, Schuylkill, WM
Mauch Chunk (new Jim Thorpe), Carbon, S
McAdoo, Schuylkill, S
Minersville, Schuylkill, S
Mount Carmel, Northumberland, WM
Nanticoke, Luzerne, N
Nesquehoning, Carbon, S
Old Forge, Lackawanna, N
Olyphant, Lackawanna, N
Pardeesville, Luzerne, EM

Pine Grove, Schuylkill, S
Pittston, Luzerne, N
Plymouth, Luzerne, N
Port Carbon, Schuylkill, S
Port Griffith, Luzerne, N
Pottsville, Schuylkill, S
Shamokin, Northumberland, WM
Schuylkill Haven, Schuylkill, S
Scranton, Lackawanna, N
Shenandoah, Schuylkill, WM
Sheppton, Schuylkill, EM
St. Clair, Schuylkill, S

Sugar Notch, Luzerne, N
Summit Hill, Carbon, S
Swoyersville, Luzerne, N
Tamaqua, Schuylkill, S
Taylor, Lackawanna, N
Throop, Lackawanna, N
Tower City, Schuylkill, S
Tremont, Schuylkill, S
Trevorton, Northumberland, WM
Wadesville, Schuylkill, S
Wanamie, Luzerne, N
Wilkes-Barre, Luzerne, N

ABOUT THE AUTHOR

Philip Mosley is Distinguished Professor Emeritus of English and Comparative Literature at Penn State University. He has been an Associate Editor of *Comparative Literature Studies* and has served on the board of the Pennsylvania Humanities Council.

He has written a number of books on literature and on cinema including *Anthracite!* (2006), an anthology of Pennsylvania coal region plays. Other book publications include a translation of François Jacqmin's *Book of the Snow* (2010), shortlisted for the international Griffin Poetry Prize; *The Cinema of the Dardenne Brothers: Responsible Realism* (2013); and *Resuming Maurice and Other Essays on Writers and Celebrity* (2019). He was awarded the 2008 Literary Translation Prize by the French Community of Belgium in recognition of his contribution to the dissemination of Belgian francophone literature.

A native of England, who immigrated to the USA in 1988, he attended Norwich School from 1957 to 1965, holds a BA (Honors) in English from the University of Leeds (1968), an MA in European Literature (1970) and a PhD in Comparative Literature (1976), both from the University of East Anglia. In 2000 he was Visiting Professor at the University of Toulouse, France; in 2003-04 was Fulbright Visiting Professor at the Université Libre de Bruxelles, Belgium; and in 2013 was Visiting Professor at the University College of Sint-Lukas, Brussels, Belgium.

www.ingramcontent.com/pod-product-compliance
Lightning Source LLC
Chambersburg PA
CBHW031600110426
42742CB00036B/339